good read.
Love
Antony, Christine
and Katie
xxx
1995.

COTSWOLD TALES

COTSWOLD TALES

Selected by

ALAN SUTTON

ALAN SUTTON

First published in 1991 by Alan Sutton Publishing Ltd

First published in this paperback edition in the United Kingdom in 1992 by
Alan Sutton Publishing Ltd · Phoenix Mill · Stroud · Gloucestershire

First published in this paperback edition in the United States of America in
1992 by
Alan Sutton Publishing Inc · Wolfeboro Falls · NH 03896–0848

John Darke's Sojourn in the Cotteswolds and Elsewhere
first published 1890
Willum Wurkman's Wit and Wisdom first published 1915
Cotswold Characters first published 1921

British Library Cataloguing in Publication Data

Cotswold Tales.
I. Sutton, Alan *1949–*
942.417

ISBN 0 7509 0164 0

Library in Congress Cataloging in Publication Data applied for

Typeset in 11/14 Bembo.
Typesetting and origination by
Alan Sutton Publishing Limited.
Printed in Great Britain by
WBC Print Ltd, Bridgend, Wales.

CONTENTS

Introduction   vii
JOHN DARKE'S SOJOURN IN THE COTTESWOLDS AND ELSEWHERE
A Preliminary Canter   3
The Farmer   5
At the Public   11
The Verdict   17
The Ram Fair   22
The Old Shepherd   30
The Wood Sale   36
The Harvest Home   40
The Wedding   52
Two Hundred Pound Apiece for 'Em   65
Cottage Interior   71
Past Work   76
'Taters   82
A Dead Sheep   85
The Election   87
A Simple Picture   91
In a Public-house Kitchen   94
A Dead Child   103
Where the Missus is Master   107
Drink   110
A Drunken Wife   114
Autumn   118
The Closing Scene   123

COTSWOLD CHARACTERS
Thesiger Crowne, the Mason   127
Simon Rodd, the Fisherman   130
Rufus Clay, the Foreigner   134
Pony, the Footballer   138
Joe Pentifer and Son   143

WILLUM WURKMAN'S WIT AND WISDOM
Willum Introduces Himself   149
Reminiscences of Pig-keeping   152
Election Stories   155
Willum and His Family   159
Willum's Grandchildren   162
The Christmas Ghost   165
Cures for Rheumatism   171
A Miraculous Cure   174
Letter Writing   178
The 'Earl o' Siplas'   181
Shepherds and Sheep   185
Springtime   189
Curious effects of Weather Changes   192
Good Friday Potato Planting   195
A Village Romance   199
Biblical Matters   203
A Hidden Fortune   206
A Tragedy   210
The Golden Valley   215

A NATRAL 'ISTORY TALE   221

ROGER PLOWMAN'S JOURNEY TO LONDON   226

Notes and Glossary   231

Acknowledgements   241

INTRODUCTION

Over the last one hundred years the Gloucestershire dialects have been greatly watered down into mere accents. The influence of universal education, the radio, cinema and then television, has brought a standardization to our language that has resulted in the loss of a direct linguistic link back to Saxon times. It is true that very strong accents remain, and the use of provincial words may still be demonstrated to exist in use among the elder generation in quiet rural areas, but the depth and antiquity of the language in everyday use during the nineteenth century and before, sadly, has gone forever.

This diverse selection of Cotswold tales is the work of five writers: S.S. Buckman; G. Edmund Hall; John Drinkwater; James Nicholls; and J. Arthur Gibbs. The primary intention of Buckman and Hall was to reproduce the dialect with humour and poignancy. Drinkwater's contribution is literary rather than linguistic; Gibbs reproduces a piece commonly used at village Christmas tea-parties as a monologue; and, finally, Nicholls simply wrote a dialect treatise on 'dimestic hanimals' for the *Gloucester Journal*.

The majority of tales come from two books, *John Darke's Sojourn in the Cotteswolds and Elsewhere* by Sydney Savory Buckman, and *Willum Wurkman's Wit and Wisdom* by George Edmund Hall.

Buckman was born in 1860 at Cirencester, where his father, James Buckman was Professor of Geology and Botany at the Agricultural College and curator of the Corinium Museum. He inherited his father's interest in geology and published his first paper on the subject at the age of eighteen, and from then on devoted his life's work to it, becoming an internationally recognized expert.

His father had moved to Dorset in 1863 to take up farming, and unfortunately little is known of Sydney's early life and career. In his early twenties he came to live in Cheltenham, and this was a time when he was actively studying the dating of inferior oolite, the main Cotswold stone, through the study of ammonites and brachiopods (mollusc-like animals). It was during this period that he gathered together the anecdotes that he later used under the name of John Darke. This was obviously a pseudonym that amused him. Being intellectual, and interested in the history of dialect, he would have been aware of the ancient use of 'dark' meaning to listen privily, or with insidious attention.

A keen early cyclist, he explored much of the Cotswolds for his work and must have come across many rustics with whom to engage in conversation. His health was poor and troubled him greatly throughout his life. If John Darke is a pseudonym, then it was Buckman whom the doctor ordered to rest, and it was Buckman who had the chance of re-acquainting himself with his father's neighbours of twenty years before. Some evidence for this being primarily autobiographical is contained in chapters 19 and 23. In chapter 19, 'Where the Missus is Master', John Darke is in conversation with a public house landlady and enquires about the best way to an old hill-fort camp; he gets this reply: '. . . Well, well, I've a-yeard tell as there was a summat up there, an' I've a-yeard as the townsfolk do come a-prying around to look at un; but Lor' bless 'ee, I've never troubled my yead about such things as that thereimy. There's enow for we sort o' folk to do about our own housen, wi'out caddling about what other folks may a-done as is djed an' buried this long while.' The evidence is more obvious in chapter 23, 'The Closing Scene', for here, right at the end of the book, he says: 'The last day of my walking tour I fell in with a friend also on holiday, and on the tramp like myself; but combining these with the pursuit of geology . . .'.

John Darke's Sojourn was published in 1890 when Buckman was still in his late twenties, and the book has the style and flavour of a young man's writing. Although he was obviously from a reasonably privileged background, Buckman demonstrates an empathy for the Cotswold labouring man and no doubt managed to communicate in an easy manner, gaining the confidence of his correspondents, be it in the field with shepherds among their sheep or in a public house. The style has a certain echo of Thomas Hughes's book *The Scouring of the White Horse*, published in 1857, and this may well have been the model, if not for the whole book, at least for the opening chapters. In turn, Buckman's book must have been known to J. Arthur Gibbs, who, writing just seven years later, was to adopt some of the style in his classic book *A Cotswold Village*.

Sydney Savory Buckman published many other works, and although of great importance in the academic geological world, it will be his modest volume *John Darke* that will surely prove to be his longest-lasting epitaph yet. Buckman died in 1929 when his obituaries related his academic career in great length, while *John Darke* was not mentioned once.

George Edmund Hall was of a similar age to Buckman when he wrote his 'Willum Wurkman' pieces for the *Stroud News*. Hall was born in Gloucestershire in 1875 and received his early education in Cirencester. He first decided upon a career in teaching, but due to defective sight in one eye he was barred from entrance to the teaching college. He went to London and studied shorthand, and soon became one of the fastest and most accurate writers of the day, achieving proficiency in speeds of up to 210 words a minute. This ability resulted in him being asked to go to America to represent England at the world shorthand speed championship, but the state of his health prevented him from accepting the honour. He eventually became head of a firm of shorthand writers, with clientele among prominent men in law and politics.

Sydney Buckman was beset with health problems throughout his life, and it was undoubtedly during a period of convalescence that he worked on *John Darke*. George Hall had a much worse illness – tuberculosis. He spent long periods at a sanatorium, but eventually the illness became so severe that in 1908 he retired to France Lynch near

Stroud to battle for his life. It was during these last two years of his life that he wrote his dialect studies – *Willum Wurkman's Wit and Wisdom.* Willum is an invention, a vehicle to carry the tales, tales Hall constructed from the information garnered from the many contacts and friends he made in France Lynch and Chalford Hill. Day by day he would sit out in a shelter, taking the air in the hope of a cure. Here in his shelter he would converse with passers-by, and the ease of his manner assured him of constant company. In one obituary it was said that he was intensely religious but did not push religion down any man's throat. His faith gave him an inner strength and, always being cheerful, interested, interesting and sympathetic, he drew men to him like a magnet, and never failed to help them.

George Edmund Hall died in February 1910 at the age of thirty-four, just two years after moving to the area in what proved to be an unsuccessful attempt to restore his health. In those two years he left a wealth of dialect tales, of which those reproduced here are just a few. These constitute his own selection, which he made at the request of the editor of the *Stroud News* for publication in book form. Many more tales lie among the archive copies of the *Stroud News*. George Edmund Hall lies buried in Bussage churchyard, the spot that he made Willum say commands the fairest view in all the Cotswolds, a place where he often walked during his last few months; with his imaginary friend and raconteur, Willum Wurkman.

A third book has been used in this omnibus collection: *Cotswold Characters* by John Drinkwater. This very rare, slim volume does not seem to have had a very wide circulation in England. For some unknown reason it was published by Yale University Press in the United States in 1921. Possibly because of its overseas publication, it has escaped the attention of lists of Drinkwater's publications listed in the *Dictionary of National Bibliography*, and the more extensive list of publications given in *Who Was Who*.

Drinkwater was born in Leytonstone, Essex, in 1882. After a schooling in Oxford, his father, an actor, placed him in what he considered a secure employment, the Northern Assurance Company at Nottingham. After twelve years of insurance drudgery, Drinkwater

escaped and followed his father's profession. In 1907 he became
co-founder of the Pilgrim Players, and in 1909, with the help of Barry
Jackson, he created a professional company – the Birmingham Reper-
tory Company. During these early professional days Drinkwater
developed his writing skills, and in 1918 had a stage success with his
play *Abraham Lincoln*. He wrote several other plays among a varied
literary career, but none of the follow-up publications achieved the
success of the first. *Mary Stuart* was published in 1921, *Oliver Cromwell*
the same year, and *Robert E. Lee* in 1923. Between these we have
Cotswold Characters. Not a play, but short studies in prose.

His connection with the Cotswolds is unknown, but presumably he
had friends in the area. He says in his introduction to the original
edition that he was a tenant of a small cottage in the Stroud area. He
may also have read *Willum Wurkman*, for although the style is totally
different, there is, nevertheless, a similarity in approach, as Drinkwater
uses his character Thesiger Crowne to hang some of his tales around.

In his introduction he says: 'The Cotswold yeoman is as unoriginal
and as new and vital as an oak tree or a starry night. In a moment a little
outside the usual habit of my work, it came to me to set down in prose
a few of his characteristics, and here is the result with a due sense of its
incompleteness.'

Drinkwater tries to disguise the location of his cottage, but there is
little doubt that the hamlet of Thesiger Crowne and Rufus Clay was
Oakridge, four miles to the south-east of Stroud. Other disguises are a
smokescreen. In the chapter 'Rufus Clay' he makes out that Painswick
is seventeen miles away, but in reality it is just five. In 'Pony the
Footballer' he says the opposition is Edge Albion. Edge is a hamlet six
miles to the north-west; in reality he was referring not to Edge, but
Edgeworth, which *is* 'just across the valley'. But there are two
powerful clues which give the true location as Oakridge. The first is the
reference in 'Thesiger Crowne, the Mason' to the pest house. This
event is not fiction, for there was exactly such an event in Oakridge in
1895. Due to an outbreak of smallpox in Stroud, the health authorities
attempted to move some patients to the isolation hospital in Oakridge,
and this attempt was thwarted by a gang of locals burning the building

down. The second clue comes at the end of the chapter 'Rufus Clay'. Drinkwater refers to a canal, which could be reached through a gate at the village end with a footpath three-quarters of a mile long. This has to be the path running from Oakridge, past the Taut, down to Upper and Lower Locks on the Thames and Severn Canal.

There seems every likelihood that Drinkwater's tales are fact, or based quite closely on fact. The same cannot be guaranteed for either *John Darke* or *Willum Wurkman*, and yet in both collections there are tales which have a ring of truth. Surely both these latter must contain true happenings, no doubt dressed up and otherwise embellished by the teller and assiduously recorded by Buckman or Hall. The same cannot be said for the tale 'Roger Plowman'. The version given here was recorded by J. Arthur Gibbs and published in his book *A Cotswold Village* in 1898. Several other versions are known, and all are very similar. The tale is intended as a monologue, and was hugely successful as an entertainment at harvest homes, smoking concerts and village entertainments.

Finally, we have one other chapter which makes up this collection. This is a strange, rambling dialect tract from the *Gloucester Journal* of March 1851. The contributor gives himself as 'Jeems Nicks' and says he keeps a beer house at Kingsholm. In the Hunt & Co.'s *Directory* of 1849 under the heading 'beer retailers' there is an entry for James Nicholls, Kingsholm, and so it is reasonably safe to assume this is the same person.

Nicholls and Buckman refer to the Cotteswold Naturalists' Field Club in their tales. The club was founded in 1846 and reports of activities were regularly reported in the *Gloucester Journal*. Part of the joke in Nicholls's piece is that he, or rather his character, Jeems Nicks, is offering his 'Natral 'istory hannigotes' for the benefit of the editor, or members of the 'Cotswuld Club' in the hope that they might be interested in the tale of his domestic animals. It is almost possible to hear the humour mixed with derision in the taproom in Nicholls's beer house as one of the locals reads out loud a report in the *Gloucester Journal* of the Cotteswold Club. To these artisan city dwellers the antics of the dilettante gentlemen who searched for rare butterflies or went digging up ruins must have been a hoot. The 'hannigotes' of Jeems Nicks were not without some slight degree of sarcasm.

The geographical locations of the tales are worthy of some detective work. John Drinkwater was writing from Oakridge, or possibly Far Oakridge, as there are local recollections of him living at Frith House, near Tunley. George Edmund Hall was writing from France Lynch, and later from the adjoining parish of Chalford. With Oakridge being just two miles or so further up the valley, the characters described by Hall and Drinkwater came from virtually the same community. Hall quite cleverly tries to obscure the exact village that is the home of Willum Wurkman, and some of the clues are contradictory, no doubt intentionally. If anywhere is the true Willum Wurkman heartland it has to be Bussage.

The *John Darke* stories are more difficult to locate. The full title of the book is *John Darke's Sojourn in the Cotteswolds and Elsewhere*. The Cotswold bit is close to Cirencester, and instinct says Ewen, a few miles to the south, although this is conjecture built out of half-clues. Perhaps this was where his father lived when he taught at the college. This would fit, and no doubt further detective work would provide the answer. Chapters 1 to 8, built around Farmer Bates, are from this area, but chapters 9 to 17 are the 'elsewhere' element, and further clues indicate somewhere close to Cheltenham, at the foot of the Cotswolds, in the Vale of Gloucester facing towards the Forest of Dean. Somewhere in this area lay the farm of Mr Hillyard with his students, Willis and Short. This may, perhaps, have been at Churchdown or Up Hatherley, between Gloucester and Cheltenham, for in chapter 10 we have the village being described as split in two by the railway lines.

Determining the locations behind these tales does nothing at all to add to the enjoyment of the pictures they paint of the Cotswolders a century ago. But it is a detective challenge to seek the locations from the odd clues thrown out, and once found, interesting to visit and see the villages so depicted as they are today. The reader who is not familiar with the Cotswolds will get particular enjoyment from visiting the villages portrayed by Hall and Drinkwater, for the area known as the Golden Valley, including Oakridge, Chalford, France Lynch and

Sapperton, are, to my mind, the most beautiful in the Cotswolds. The beauty is not so chocolate-box as Broadway and is not without blemishes, but over all, the great natural beauty of the valley more than makes up for minor blights. To drive from Bisley through Waterlane and Tunley to Sapperton never fails to lift my spirits; especially if it is a sunny day.

The tales themselves are a varied bunch, some very funny and some extremely poignant or even sad. I would find it difficult to believe that any reader could not be touched by chapter 18, 'A Dead Child', or even more so, the touching end to chapter 37, 'Letter Writing', where Willum Wurkman comes across a lock of hair from his long-dead son, lovingly kept by his wife. It is beyond my description, but Hall narrates it with a skill that is enviable, and I find it difficult to believe that this particular piece is fiction.

Read on, be amused, but be warned, you may also be saddened.

Alan Sutton
Hydefield,
Uley,
Gloucestershire

JOHN DARKE'S
SOJOURN
IN THE COTTESWOLDS
AND ELSEWHERE

CHAPTER 1

A PRELIMINARY CANTER

My doctor having decided that I ought to give up work for some time, and take a complete change – by preference in some quiet country spot where I could enjoy plenty of fresh air and rural delights – I at once determined to write to an old farmer friend – one whom I had known well in my younger days before my father had retired from farming, and I myself had left the country for the town – and ask him and his good wife to take me in awhile as a boarder. The answer I received was characteristic, and though in the wife's handwriting, was unmistakably the husband's composition; it ran as follows:

'Dear Master John,

'Receive you as a boarder, of course we will; but this house aint turned into a public yet, I can tell you. Times is bad, as you know, but they aint drove Joe Bates to that yet. You come, and welcome; right glad we'll be to see you, and we'll try and make you comfortable-like, but not a copper of your money will I touch. Now, Master John, just you mind what I say, as you did when you was about half as high as you are now. You be to come here and visit us, and I won't take no denial, there now. Send word at once, and I will meet you with the mare,

'Yours Truly,
'Joe Bates.

'John Darke, Esq.'

Such a message was too genuine not to be meant, and I lost no time in acting upon so hearty an invitation. On arrival at my destination I was met by Farmer Bates, with the mare and dog-cart, and a right warm welcome.

The experiences of my country sojourn here and elsewhere I now proceed to relate.

CHAPTER 2

THE FARMER

Joseph Bates, more often called Old Joe, was one of those who are generally designated old-fashioned farmers, and whose calling cannot by any possibility be mistaken. His wife was just the woman one would expect to find the partner of such a husband, and it was generally said in the neighbourhood, although perhaps without much truth, that if Farmer Bates managed the farm, the missus managed the farmer. However, both united in according me a very hearty welcome, and they did everything that lay in their power to make my visit thoroughly pleasant and enjoyable.

It so happened that the funeral of their landlord, the squire, who had been suddenly taken ill while journeying from town, and had expired before he could reach home, had been fixed to take place the day after my arrival. He had been a good and indulgent landlord, between whom and his tenants there had been a mutual, and nowadays unfortunately rare, feeling of thorough confidence, a man whose word they could trust, and who would willingly stretch a point in order to benefit his tenants. Naturally Farmer Bates had to attend the funeral, and consequently I was left to my own devices until dinner-time, after which the farmer had promised to drive me to attend a small sale in the neighbourhood. I passed the morning in looking about me, and as one o'clock drew near I encountered the farmer returning from the funeral. His wife came to the door as we entered the house.

'Well, Joe, an' how did the funeral go off?' she cried.

'Oh, well enow,' rejoins the farmer.

'Well enow I don't doubt,' says his spouse, 'but,' with sudden energy, 'drabbut thee, jest thee look at the boots as thee's a-bringing into th' 'ouse. Git thee out along and wipe 'em agin the bissom, do. Here's the place but jest a-bin med tidy-like and a bit clean, an' thee must com a-spiling it a'. A body med slev arl day fur such as thee.'

'Whoa! old 'ooman! Who-ho!' says the farmer with a sly look, making towards the door. 'Thee's fur arl the world like Sam Mileses' clock, thee bist, as when 'ers[1] a-wound up goes on striking contineral. Thy tongue do clack wuss nor Maister Brown's mill wheel. Thee know'st as thee were main ager to year arl about et, an' cudn'st wait for I to screap 'um.'

'Thee see to thy boots an' ne'er min' 'bout my tongue. I war'n thee wast more main set to tell, nor I to year,' responded the good dame. 'When thee's tidy thee come an' tell's arl the news.'

The farmer finished wiping his boots, and got comfortably settled in his arm-chair, when Mrs Bates begins:

'Who was thur, Joe?'

'Oh, bless 'ee! a sight o' volk. Thur wur arl we tenants, ivery one on us; leastways, 'cepting ould Farmer Garrett as is led up wi' the rumatiz arl down 'is back and can't muv' out o' dure no ways. Thay do say as th'owld genelman ain't a-bin able to git round ers farm for some wicks, an' young John, thee know'st 'ee, has to look arter the bizness hisself. Well, young John, 'ee wur to the fun'rel to-day in's father's place, and then thur wur very nigh arl the volk o' the village, and the gentry in thur kerridges from iver so fur roun', and tradesvolk fro the townd. Lor, thur wur quite a passel o' volk altogither. I war'n as th' owld squire must a' felt quite proud o' hisself to think as thur wur so many a-come to pay thur respex-like to un.'

'Oh, fur sure er did,' said Mrs Bates; 'but la! la! 'twur a sad an' suddint end for un, an' we've lost a good lan'lord, I'll be boun'.'

'Ay, ay, that's jest what I said to owld Peter Bassut — thee mind'st owld Peter, don't 'ee, him as I bought thic ches'nut mur from two yere ago come Candlemus. He wur thur, an' I met un today, an' I tould un how well thic mur 'ad a turned out, and er said, says 'ee, "I knowd 'er 'ood," er said, "I allus telled 'ee so; an' if I 'adn't a-bin dooced empty o'pocket yer 'ouldn't 'a 'ad 'er not at no price, I tell 'ee," er said; an' as I wur a-saying I met un, an' says to un, "Good marning, Mr Bassut," I says, "an' how's yerself today?" an' er says, "Marning." An' I says, "Poor sad job this, yent it?" I says, an' er says, "Ay, you be right thur, Mr Bates," er says, "'tis a poor sad job. When a man's owld and a-weered out, and begins to 'a a summat the matter 'ere and a summat the matter thur, and can't git abroad as er'd used to, then, yer know," er says, "if er do drop off quiet in 's bed like, 'tain't so much the matter, nor to be grumbled at, yer know, 'cause us 'a arl got to come to et," er says; "but when a man's hearty an' well, when er goes away from home, an's djed when er comes back agin, it do sim unnateral-like, an' a sorrer to them as belongs to un."

'"It do that, Mr Bassut," I says. But dost thee know ef the bouoy have a-shifted thay ca'ves into Little Close as I telled un?' says the farmer, suddenly addressing his wife.

'Yes, er 'ave,' answers his wife, 'for I seed un myself, and I telled un to min' as they didn't break away from un, else 'ee'd be skorting arl over the pleace for 'um.'

'Eh! dang ers buttons! they'd warm ers shirt for un, they 'ood, if they was a bit mischerful. But as I wur a-sayin', owld Peter Bassut says to I, er says, "This be a poor sad job for 'em arl; but then, yer know, as the passon says to I," says Peter, "when I met un a-coming down the road — er'd jest come from Missus Trotses." Mrs Trot, yer know, 'ave a-got 'er thirteenth cheild,' says the farmer, turning to me, 'an' poor Davvid, 'ee's a-running around the parish a-axing volks to vind a neame for un; er says as t'other dozen sim to a-got atween 'um arl as iver 'ee knowd. Er wanted at fust to call un Holy Cross, arter 's uncle. Owld Holy, yer know, as we'd used to call un,' explained the farmer, 'runned 'way to 'Meriky, an' left ers wife and childer to git along o' thurselves as best 'um could, an' the last as we've a-yeard on un is as 'ee got 'nother wife thur, owld Holy 'ave, an' another sich a vamily, so I reckons as ers wife 'ere won't see un back no more, for which I dare say as 'er yent sorry, fur volk do say as 'eed used to sard 'er shemful sometimes when 'ee'd a drap o' summat in to un. Howsomedever, th' passon wouldn't allow un to call un that thur; and when the passon came one day to ax un hows ers missus wur a-doing, Davvid says to un, "We guv' 'ee tithe o' the fust half-score on 'em, sur, an' it sims like as if we be most a-gwine fur to have another sich a passel for 'ee to teake tithe o'."'

'And very good it wur o' the parson to take to the child,' says Mrs Bates, addressing me. 'When 'ee arrove, as soon as iver the wimmin-volk 'ud let un, Davvid tuk the young un across to the parson's 'ouse, an' when er seed the parson, er says to un, says 'ee, "Ere lookee, sur, I've a-got to pay 'ee the tenth part o' arl my prodooce, an' so I've a-brought 'ee this 'ere child as 'ee's the tenth o' my vamily. I never paid 'ee no tithes cheerful-like 'et, but I can do et thease time."

"'Dear me! dear me!" says the parson, "is this your tenth child? Well I really do pity you."

"'Ay, this 'ere be the tenth," says Davvid, "an' thur's nine more on 'em at 'ome, arl a-cryin' out for thur breckfustes; but 'ere, sur, I'm a-gwine to leave this 'ere one along o' you, 'ee's the tenth, and 'ee belongs to the parson," and Davvid places un down on one o' the cheers.'

"'Oh, my good man, don't leave it thur," says the parson; "it's all nonsence, yer know, I can't take it like that"; but Davvid 'ee wouldn't take not no denial at all. He sed as how 'ee couldn't see why if 'ee paid the tenth part o' his other craps, he shouldn't pay the tenth child over to the parson. Well, then they argued for iver so long, and I 'spects the parson thought 'ee never would get rid o' Davvid; and the poor babby — poor little twoad — a-cryin' fit to bust his little self, thur upon the cheer. Th' end wur as the parson's wife, 'er come down a-yearing the nise to see what arl the caddle wur about, and when 'er comed into the room and seed the child, 'er picked up the babby as nat'ral-like as possible and began to quiet un. An then Davvid, he began for to tell 'er all about it, as 'ow it wur 'is tithe to the parson, and the good leddy 'er thought it a proper thing to do and sed it wur quite right o' Davvid, and as ers missus must certainly have plenty to do wi' nine on 'em.' ('I dunno what 'er thenks o' erself now wi' thirteen'), said Mrs Bates, in parenthesis.

'"Well," says the parson, "but we can't kip the child." "Kip un, no!" says ers missus, 'on course we can't, the mother can bring un up much the best." Oh, 'er allus do bring 'ers babbies on most oonderful, 'er do; while they've a-got she to nuss 'um the poor little dears does do well,' commented Mrs Bates.

'"'Er can 'ave un," said the parson's missus, "but we can pay summat to'rds ers clothes and schooling and the like." And so the parson 'ave; he've found un near arl ers clothes, and pays for un to go to school, and does quite 'ansome by un, I says. But what did the parson say to Peter Bassut, Joe?'

'Lor! I a'most forgot, now. Why, er said to un as 'ow it wur a poor sinfu' warld, an' as we'd never ought for to mourn for no one who'd a-gone, 'cos 'ee's got to a much better un. "Oh, I quite agrees wi' 'ee, sur!" Peter says, "I quite agrees with 'ee." And then I knowed,' said the farmer, 'as owld Peter wur off, an' I should get a sarmint a-tellin' I arl about wur I'd a-got to go to, and about the vire, and th' owld genelman wi' 'ers huffs an' 'ers harns and 'ers tael an' arl on't as nat'ral-like as if 'ee'd a-seed um arl hisself, so I jest slipped away, and thenks I to myself, Lor' bless 'ee, Peter! when thee's got jest a drap o' drink in to thee it's a very different style o' praching as thee doos; for Peter, yer know, arter arl, is a 'nation[2] sad feller for the drink, and when er's as

drunk as a genelman — that's what er calls et when er's a-talking o' any one else being that way, but 'ee hisself's never drunk, oh, no! 'ee's only in puffic 'ealth, 'e'll tell 'ee, not nothink else if er's very nigh blind-drunk — but, leastways, when 'ee've got more'n ers share in to him, why, it's blessing o' the wrong side o' ers mouth as er doos most on then.'

'Thur, howld thee tongue, do,' exclaimed Mrs Bates. 'I'm sur thee's caddled enow 'bout Peter Bassut and the fun'ral. Git an' finish thee dinner, do.'

'Phew!' whistled the farmer; and he buried his face in his tankard.

CHAPTER 3

AT THE PUBLIC

Very soon after the finish of dinner, I was sitting in the dog-cart beside the farmer, who was driving to a small local sale, which he wished to attend. His business thereat was very soon settled, and the next thing was to adjourn to the inn, so that we might partake of a 'puff of 'bacca, and a drop o' summat,' and where Mr Bates might meet his neighbours to discuss the general state of affairs and make future plans.

In a long, low room, distinguished by the suggestive title, 'Smoke Room,' sit some half-dozen countrymen, all busily engaged in consuming tobacco. Above their heads, about at a level with the eyes of any one entering, float thick wreaths of smoke, almost motionless. The further end of the room communicates by a door with a small bar from which, at intervals, beer, spirits, and the like, are supplied to moisten the palates of the smokers. Most of the men belong to what is commonly called the lower class – a term which we must not employ in the present levelling days; and yet, with all the Radical tendencies of the age, it is curious to find that none are more particular about matters of social position than these same lower classes. Mrs Blank is the wife of a struggling village shoemaker, who earns, in a week, far less money than a good shepherd; yet he is a tradesman, and she is the wife of a tradesman, and they both consider themselves as distinctly above the ordinary labouring classes — agricultural farm servants. These, in their turn, have social grades. The carter, shepherd, etc. — 'the cattle folk,' in fact — consider themselves certainly superior to the ordinary 'day-men'. Nor have we reached the lowest stratum when we come to these day-men. The fact is that we should have much difficulty in reaching the lowest stratum of society, for each one still considers that there are others yet lower. Beneath the day-men come the tramps, loafers, and riff-raff of the towns, and paupers of all kinds — in reality, too long a list to enumerate. If he have eyes to see, and ears to hear, the dweller in cities would be surprised to find that etiquette — a strong, unwritten law sanctioned by inveterate custom — was not by any means confined to the drawing-rooms of Belgravia. The laws that govern the use of 'thee' and 'thou' among agricultural workers, are not to be violated. They accord almost strictly with the modern German usage of the same person singular, and are doubtless a relic of Saxon ancestors. On no account must 'thou' be used to a superior; a co-mate, or inferior, is to be so addressed; but when they quarrel the 'thou' and 'thee' should not be dropped since that would be an admission of the adversary's superiority.

The use of titles, too, is governed by similarly strict rules. The above-mentioned shoemaker would be addressed as Master, or rather, 'Maister' Blank. Below him the Christian name of each individual is, in use, coupled with the pronouns 'our' or 'thy,' as 'our Bill,' and 'thy James,' or some other distinctive appellation, when there happen to be more than one of the same Christian name. Above Master Blank come the squire's head-gardener, and butler — both great men in their way in the village — who receive the title of Mister, and perhaps that of a slightly higher grade, Mister Dash. Mister with the surname is somewhat above plain Mister, and the two are in use for a very extensive series of people. The former is applied to the shopkeepers of the country-town with whom the agricultural labourers deal, while 'sir,' which is higher still, is especially kept for their employers and gentlemen generally. Beyond this the use of titles undergoes no change. 'Yes, sir,' 'No, sir,' extends to the squire.

Such had been my thoughts during the time that Farmer Bates had been exchanging some remarks with a neighbour; but now my attention was somewhat suddenly called to other things. Seated in a high-backed armchair is a big, burly man, who is a large farmer in his way, but like many another feels the pressure of hard times severely enough. He was vehemently giving forth his opinion of farming to Mr

Bates and the assembled audience. 'My advice as I now gies t' any one,' he said, 'is "never buy nothink!" If the varm doan't give 'ee arl 'ee warnts, do wi'out et; bit never buy nothink! That's th' on'y waay to meak thaay treadesvolk in the townds veel th' 'aard times s'well's we, and thin thaay 'oodn't want so much o' thease 'ere Vree Tread. Sell, say I, sell everythink as yer can ketch hoult on! but doan't 'ee buy' (delivered as a pathetic entreatly). 'Ef yer've got an owld coat an' yer thenks er's a'most done wi', doan't 'ee git another in's pleace, git the missus to do un up a bit vur 'ee, an' gie 'un a good sheak, an' wear un till er very nigh draps aff 'ee. Look a' this 'ere owld 'at,' taking off an antiquated headgear; 'how long d'ye think I've had that un now, and thur's a sight o' wear in un' it?' This hat was a piece of furniture well worth observation. At first it had been white, but now was inclining to a dirty green colour, the combined result of exposure to sun, wind, and rain; and it seemed as if some vegetation had elected to pursue a struggling existence upon it.

'Twelve year,' suggested one of his audience in answer to the last question.

'Twelve year? I doan't thenk twelve year will set it, look 'ee. Wall, yer know,' holding the hat out at arm's length, and carefully turning it round so as to survey it from all sides, while he pointed to it with the end of the churchwarden which he had been smoking, 'wall, it be a leetle damaged in the crownd, 'cos when et do rain I do vind o' the warter zoaking in thur a bit,' and as he spoke he raised a piece in the crown, which was broken away on the sides, by inserting the mouth-piece of the churchwarden and gently lifting it up. 'Also I knows thut et doan't do to wark agin a rough wind so as the wind can raiise thease 'ere bit up. It do bloaw cowld then, so I turns 'un hind-a-fore. Wall,' withdrawing the pipe-stem, 'the brim's broke abroad in a please or two, look'ee,' pushing the pipe-stem into the holes; 'but what I says is, Never buy no new un! wear th' owld un till the crownd draps out on un; wear un till the zides vall abroad; wear un, I says, till thur yent no more nor the brim a-leaved to putt around thy yead.'

A roar of laughter greeted the old farmer's speech; and it had scarcely subsided when two young men entered, one of whom was carrying a gun, and looked as if he had been drinking. We will call him Job, and his companion, George. Job walked up to the further door, and, putting down his gun, cried out to the landlady, 'I say, missus, I've a-bin out all day an' got nought an' I seed your owld gander as I come by; I do wish you'd let I have a shot at un.'

'No, I'll be danged if I do,' was the answer.

'Oh, yer might as well. I'll give 'ee summat to let I blaze at un.'

'No, I won't, so there now.'

'Well then, let's have two glasses o' whisky,' and Job retired to sit himself down at the table, and bury his head in his arms as if sleepy. Hereupon George got up quietly, went to the door, took up the gun, and began talking to the landlady. The result was that George inserted the ramrod, and, having withdrawn the charge of shot, replaced the gun in the corner. He then comes back and shows the charge of shot in his hand to the assembled company, winking all the time, and making faces, while he points with his thumb over his shoulder to Job.

'Missus, when's the grog a-comin'?' says Job, raising his head. 'Yer might let I have a shot at the gander.'

'What'll 'ee give me if I do,' says the landlady – 'a crownd?'

'No, I wun't, I'll give 'ee half one.'

'Well, look'ee 'ere then, you mustn't git no nigher to un than forty yards, and these genelmen shall see fair play.'

'All right, missus, let's have the grog. Here's for the grog, and here's the half-crownd,' says Job, offering the money.

The landlady took it with a beaming face, and Job, having drunk the grog, called on the assembled company to come and see the sport.

Accordingly we all adjourned to a meadow behind the house where the gander was to be found; and when he had been separated from the rest of the flock, 'Now then, Job,' was cried. Job put up his gun, took good aim, and fired. The gander turned a summersault and lay, evidently mortally wounded, upon the ground.

'Darze thy back, thee cussnation twoad,' screams the landlady, 'thee's bin an' shot my bird.'

'Well, I got summat to teak whoam now,' exclaims Job.

'Take home, indeed! take home I know thee sharn't,' cried the landlady, and then appealing to us, she said, 'Thur never was no word said about taking home, was thur now?'

We had to affirm that nothing had been said upon the point, when some one cried out: 'I tell thee what, Job, thee'd'st best teak thysel' whoam, yere's the landlord a-cummin'.'

Now the landlord was a big, burly man, so that Job and George required no second bidding, but made off without delay.

The rage of the landlord was something to behold. He threatened Job with a horse-whipping, with the County Court, with any and every punishment and infliction which he could imagine or devise. Nothing was to be too much to satisfy his vengeance.

'I fear 'tis a case o' the biter bit,' remarks Farmer Bates. 'Thy missus thought to best un entirely, but 'ee's a 'nation 'cute un is Job. I war'n as he'd two charges o' shot in's gun.'

Some time after I had left Farmer Bates' hospitable roof, I happened to meet the worthy old man, and, in course of conversation, he told me the sequel to the tragedy of the gander. It seems that the landlord did not carry out his vengeance against Job, but put the best face he could upon the matter. His wife took the gander indoors, and having hung the old bird a reasonable time, proceeded to cook it. First she baked it; but as it was then too tough to eat, she proceeded to boil it, and as it still remained refractory she, as a last resource, divided it into joints and fried it.

'Bost 'is kearcass vur a tough owld customer,' says the landlord. ''Tain't offen as we 'as a bit o' mate in this 'ere house beseps a jint o' a casalty ship; but when us does 'ave a bit I'm most ways sorry to see th' end o' it. Howsomedever, I can't say as I be thease time. It a bin a sad plaguy bird to get shut on, but we've a-stuck to un, and we've a-rossled wi' un, and I be summat glad as thur's no moor on un. It 'ave a-tried ivery tooth in me yead, and a'loosed some on 'em, I'm sure. Thay bean't so main plentiful as I can't 'ford to lose nurrun.'

CHAPTER 4

THE VERDICT

'Talking if liyers and coorts, and the like,' observed Farmer Bates to me
one evening, referring to a portion of our previous conversation, as we
were sitting round the fire with pipes in our mouths, and glasses of
whisky at our elbows, 'I s'pose I 'arn't tell'd 'ee o' the way we got a
verdick last time as I went on jury. 'Twur a bit hard I've thought since,
yer know, to make the chap gie in 's 'pinion to a verdick in that way;
but 'ee did et yer see, and I didn't 'a no 'ands wi'ut. I worr mortal tired
o' the job, an' I can't say as I disproved o' ers doing ut at the time.'

As all this was Greek to me, I begged the worthy man to commence
somewhere at the beginning, and let me have the story right through,
because I had never heard it, I was sure.

'Wall, yer know,' he said, 'I went down to that thur jury-job — sad
caddlin' piece o' work that thur gwine on jury be, teakes 'ee 'way just
when yer's busy, and don't gie yer not a varden vor't, and yer got to
pay rileroad and arl, and lose yer time inter the bargain. I calls it a
durned sheame, I doos, and I can't thenk why us goes on so long wi' et
as 'tis, and why thay don't git and alter that thur 'stead o' altering arl
thease 'ere t'other things as nobody don't care a button 'bout being
altered, an' as wur well enow fur we afore. Wall, as I told 'ee, I went
down to X——, and into coort. Twelve on us wur a-sweared for a
jury. Thur wur Willum Blarner, the butcher, yer knows 'ee?' I shook
my head. 'Noa! well 'ees veyther wur a queer sort o' 'twoad, 'ee wur
the son o'——'

Here followed the names of several of the jurymen, with personal
reminiscences of them and their parents, even to the penultimate

generation, together with a sketch of their chief actions during the last few years. These details I am reluctantly obliged to omit, since they were of merely local interest.

'Arter we'd a-got through several cases, yer know, thur wur a feller brought afore we, along wi' a 'ooman, for stjeling Missus Dash's pus, at the railway stashun in the crowd, as she wur a-comin' whoam from the shaow.'

Reminiscences of the show, and a short account of Mrs Dash which I omit.

'Thay also sed as the 'ooman 'ad a-salted the perleece when thay ketched 'er. Wall, the man says as 'ee never did it, and th' 'ooman 'er didn't denige a having o' the pus, but sed as 'er'd a-found un on the platform a-dropped, an' 'er wur a-gwine to teak un to the perleece. Well, the perleece sed as 'er'd just a had un giv' to 'er by the man, and as 'er wurn't a-gwine to'rds the perleece, but away from 'm fast as 'er could. Missus Dash sed as the feller pushed 'er, and 'er 'mediately found 'ers pus gone. 'Er swore 'er 'ad un just afore, an' so 'er went and telled the perleece as the man 'ad a-took it. The perleece, thay laid 'old on the man and th' 'ooman, and foun' the pus on the 'ooman 'stead o' on the man. I war'n they knowed sommat 'bout both that thur man and 'ooman afore this, look'ee, or they'd never a-gone an' laid 'old on both on 'em so neat, to my thinkin'. I don't justly mind arl as wur sed in coort, but I knows 'ow a sort o' a liyer-feller as worked for 'um, got up and talked 'way a rum-un. 'Er sed, sezs 'ee, as the man wurn't a-seed to teak the pus, not by nobody; as piple did get pushed about in a crowd a-bit; and as the wimmin-volk did lose their puses sometimes. As to the 'ooman, 'ee axed we jurymen to think what we'd a-done ourselves ef so be we'd a-picked a pus up on a platform and had bin a-gwine to teak un to the perleece, when thay started on we for stjeling of un. Wouldn't we a-got in a fury and let thay perleece 'ave it when we was innercent, just as this 'ere 'ooman had a-done? We was to think o' ourselves in 'er pleace, an' to be sure's we didn't take 'way a innercent 'ooman's kerecter for life. When that thur feller had a-left off, I'm dalled if I knowed whether ar' a one on 'em had a-took the pus or no. It 'ad a sort o' arl slipped out o' my yead. Howsomedever, I waits to year what the judge got to say for 'isself, an' when I yeard 'ee tell we to look at fax, an' not to be misguided by that ther feller's speech, then I knowed as them thur two had a-took the pus in his 'pinion, and that thur wur good enow for I. Then er very nigh upset I agin by saying as if we'd any doubt 't'all in the matter we mun let the pris'ners aff; but I thenks to myself as that thur wur on'y summat as 'ee'd got t'say fur the look o' the theng-like.

'Well, yer know, we was arl turned out o' coort, and shet up in a small room to think over our verdick. Some on us sed as both on 'em 'ad a-bin consarned in teakin' the pus, some as the man 'ad a-took it and dropped it, and some as neither on 'em 'ad a-touched it, but the 'ooman 'erself, Missus Dash, yer know, had a-dropped it 'erself unbeknownst. So some say one thing and some t'other thing, and we arl talk's fast and loud as us can; but 'taint a mossel o' use. Then Willum Blarner says to we, "Genelmen," er says, "look'ee yere, some on 'ee be for convicting neither, some for convicting the man 'lone, and some for convicting both. Now, ef they as be fur neither will convict the man to please thay as be fur both, and if they as be fur both 'ull lev' the 'ooman alone to please they as be fur neither, then that'll be 'bout vair doos a both ways, and we can arl convict the man." But that thur don't suit neither one nor t'other on us, because us arl thought we was right, yer know, and we weren't a-gwine to give in our 'pinions in that thur way, yer know, not nurn on's if we was right. Wall, some on 'em says 'tain't no use to talk 'bout 'pinions; if we be to bring in a verdick at all, some on 'ee 'ull have to give way somewhur, and 'tain't likely as one's gwine to gie way more'n t'other. "Look'ee yere," says Willum Blarner, "I wants thease 'ere job a-yended, so's I can git whoam. I don't kere a brass button which way 'tis so long's yer gi'es in some verdick. I never 'ad no yead fur these-yerimy thengs. Thur's moor on 'ee fur convicting both on 'em than there be fur convicting neither, so I an' Garge" — his friend, yer know — "be a-gwine to join along o' thay. Now then!" er says, says 'ee to they as be for neither, "we'll 'ase yer conshunses by bringin' in only the man guilty if you'll 'gree to 't." Noa, thay 'oodn't 'gree to 't, not they. "Ye be dalled hard in the mouth," seys Willum. "Thenks we wants to bide yere arl night. Ef we don't 'gree to a verdick, we'll be mead to stop down 'ere at this 'ere d——d coort arl to-morror, and thay'll lock we up arl night, yer know." But they 'oodn't gie in, not a mossel; they said as they cud stand being locked up 's well as we. "Yere look," says Willum, "this yere's the very last I'll do fur 'ee; if ye'll 'gree to bring the man in guilty, we'll rec'mend un to mussy, 'cause th' evidence aint quite cler, yer thinks." Well, they 'gins to git a bit duberus about the matter, an' at last thay 'grees to't. "Wall, what's yer verdick?" says the formun to we. "Convict the man, but rec'mend un to mussy 'cause th' evidence ain't cler, and we've some doubts about it?" But I seys to 'im as that thur won't do, yer know; if yer've any doubts 'bout it you must let 'im aff. "Wall, rec'mend un to mussy and say nothing further," says one on 'em. "What d'yer want t' rec'mend 'im t' mussy 'tall fur; say er's guilty an' a done wi' it," seys another. "Noa yer shan't," says a little cobbler — I don't know ers neame — a-jumping up, "I won't 'gree ter yer bringing un in guilty at all." I do b'leeve a'most as 'ee bin 'sleep, I do; nurn on us seemed to a yeard of 'im afore. Willum Blarner's in a fine waay wi' un, 'cos we'd all but 'greed, an' yere was 'ee a-upsettin' o' us arl. "What the devil sort o' a vool bist thee," er says, "to set thyself agin the tother 'leven on us?" "I bean't no mur vool nor thee, mister," er says; "I med be right an' arl you med be wrong, now." "'Tain't likely as we 'leven be going to change our 'pinions fur sich a little twoad as thee, if us was wrong," says Willum. "Yere, I'll hould un down while yer delivers yer verdick," says Garge. "But er'll holler, Garge." "Darze ers back, I'll zit on un." "Noa yer karn't, Garge, not in thur." Wall, us begins to arge it arl over agin, an' that thur little cobbler putts up a questing as we can't none on us satisfy, so ther's nort to do but to send to the judge. We goes back inter coort, and er says, "Yer ain't 'greed on yer verdick?" "Noa, us yain't, thur's 'leven on us; it's on'y 'ee," says Garge, a-pinting un out. But the judge won't yere nothing o' this; he on'y tells we what us wanted to know. Then us got to go back to settle et. "Wall then," Willum Blarner says, says 'ee, to the cobbler, "yere, thee cussed little twoad, just thee 'gree to our verdick a' once." "Noa, I wun't," er says, "my conshuns won't 'low me." "D—n yer conshuns!" say Willum, "ef yer wun't 'gree I'll bump yer yead 'gin that thur warl till thur yent no

conshuns in yer," an' er ketches 'ould on un as if er ment to do't. But
the little man gies in then, an' says 'ee'll 'gree if we'd rec'mend un to
mussy. Wall, 'tain't no use to be too hard on the poor feller, neither 'ee
nor the chap as took the pus, so we says as we'll rec'mend un to mussy.
So us goos inter coort, an vinds the man guilty, but rec'mends un to
mussy, an' we lets that thur 'ooman off altogither. The judge can't 'tall
meak out why we rec'mended un to mussy, an' says thur yaint nothing
'tall in's case to call for 't; but o' coorse, er says, the jury 'ave a-given
this 'ere case a long considering, an' like honest men, 'ave come to the
verdick as they thenks best.

'Wall, yer know, as I comed back in train that thur night the
perleece-super told some on us as they'd a fine laugh 'bout we an' our
verdick. Thay sed as th' 'ooman was well-know'd as a 'complice o' the
man's, an' that thur man an' 'ooman 'ed a-bin convicted afore ever so
offen for stjelin', an' what ever he'd a-done to meak we rec'mend un to
mussy, not one on 'em could tell. I didn't tell un as it very nigh comed
to a fight afore we could git even that thur verdick.'

CHAPTER 5

THE RAM FAIR

Farmer Bates had proposed that I should accompany him to the Ram Fair held in the neighbouring town of Y——. However, the morning brought with it business, which necessitated his staying at home, but he ordered out the mare and trap, so that I could drive myself over there, and refresh my memory concerning old times. The morning was fine and bright, a contrast to the miserably cold, unsummerlike state of things which had so greatly interfered with the success of the hay harvest. As the mare rattled me along the road, I could not help thinking that on such a morning as this a farmer is about one of the luckiest mortals alive, to be engaged, as he is, in a business which takes him so much into the open air. All very fine, I reply to myself, being in one of those moods when one is apt to argue out questions with oneself with commendable intensity, but how about the last few weeks of wet, with the hay all rotting on the ground? How about the wind and storms and cold on a winter's night? How is it when he has to drive miles through a pitiless, howling storm of rain? or coming from market at Christmas time, has to get out and walk a few miles in the snow, beside his dog-cart, because the horse can scarcely draw the empty trap through the drifts?

'Go along!' the other side makes reply, 'go along! we know it ain't all beer and skittles, that there's some rough with the smooth. He's a poor chap who can't stand some rough weather. Go along, you won't convince me such a morning as this that a farmer's life isn't a happy one; you'll have to catch me in one of your snow storms.'

'Well, then, just look how he has to pay for the luxury of the enjoyment you make so much fuss over.'

'Well, certainly, at present he has to pay through the nose for the luxury of being a farmer; and I reckon he does not think there's much luxury belonging to it. Certainly there should be some pay attached to the business, better than there is now, to make it go down as sweet as it ought to.'

'Gee up, 'ole 'ooman.'

I duly arrive at the 'King's Arms,' where the mare and trap are known, if its occupant is not. However, the ostler generously allows the mare and trap to be sufficient introduction, and tells me that Mr Bates is a proper sort of genelman; and when I give some orders he further observes as if I've no objection, he'll treat the 'oss same as he allus used to when Mr Bates do come if only I'll let him; and how is the old genelman this morning — nothink wrong, he hopes?

Having reassured him upon this point, I wend my way to the market. Drawn up outside are numerous wagons with hurdles tied along their rathes, and on these wagons the names of celebrated breeders of the county round. Many a lonely, far-away farm was early astir this morning to start the rams — the objects of some eighteen months' diligent care and attention — fairly upon their way. The respective shepherds and carters have indulged in many speculations as to the prices which sundry favourites will bring, and whether this year they will be able to boast of having obtained higher prices than the sheep of Mr So and So, their rival.

Outside the yard are strings of horses belonging to dealers who are attempting to ply their noisy and vociferous trade; and who, when they have no customer to attend to, delight to pass their time in abusing one another. Evidently there's not much business in the horse line; and the specimens on show are of an inferior and rather weedy class. A few hardy Welsh cobs are the only leaven to the lump.

Entering the sale-yard I scarcely notice the rams, but make my way to where business is in full swing, that is, for the mutton, and the cull ewes, and the lambs. How fast that auctioneer can talk! Where in the world does he find breath to keep up such an extraordinary continuous flow? Never stopping a moment, but talking as he walks from one pen to the other, he keeps up the same quick string of words continuously.

'Now, then, what shall we say for the next pen? Same farm as the last! 47, 48, 48 and 6, 49, 49 and 6. Grand mutton! All the way, 50, 50 and 6. Against you, James. Won't yer? Ah, 51. You'll never repent it, 51 and 6. Thank you. Now, then, my old friend, 52. Any one any more? Stands at 52. Gone to Mr X———. What shall we say for the next pen? Hullo, Mr Dash,' greeting an old acquaintance who'd been absent for some time, 'I scarce thought to see your face again,' 'Belike you didn't want to,' is the quick reply, 'there's a small balance owing this way.' 'Ah, 'twas safer in my keeping; 'twould only 'a burned a hole in thy pocket. How much for the next pen?' So the tide goes on in a seemingly never-ending stream of winged words. Hollo, though, that was a sudden pull up! What, did no one bid the 42, 43, 44, that came so glibly? Ah, ha! you were beyond the mark, and there was no greenhorn to put his nod in and help you out. Back we must go, for no one responds to the queries:— Who is it? whose are they? Oh, dear! some one bids 40, 40 and 6, 41. 'Stands at 41; must I give 'em away? Gone at 41!' There's a slight laugh only. 'What shall we say for the next pen?'

Suppose, however, we leave the pushing, struggling, hot, perspiring crowd of butchers, dealers, and the like, and take a look round the yard. The rows of iron hurdles in the pavement of bricks are neat and handy, saving a lot of labour and trouble; but it is a pity that the weeds are not got out from between the bricks. There are the great, white-faced, long-wooled rams, with their ochre-coloured coats tightly clipped in one place, left long in another, to give them an appearance of squareness and symmetry — to make up, in fact, for any defects of nature. But the hands of the critics are testing them all over, so that their merits and demerits are quickly noticed and discussed. Here are the neat little, black-faced Downs, with their close wool stained with ruddle. By their respective charges, or within reach somewhere, are the shepherds. One does not see many smock-frocks nowadays — only one or two of the very old men sport such articles; nor does one see the crooks. Corduroy breeches, leather gaiters, a shabby black coat, a soft, squash hat with a large brim, and a long straight 'ashen' stick grasped with the thumb uppermost, complete the rig-out of the modern shepherd.

Have those who make physiognomy a special study, noticed the similarity in face which many of these shepherds bear to their sheep? It is a common saying that husband and wife grow alike as they get older. Can shepherds grow like their sheep from continual contemplation of the features of their charges? One frequently sees likenesses in the faces of animals to those of people. I remember a cow which was for many years called 'Harry' because of its fancied resemblance to a man of that ilk; and naturally, therefore, the man resembled the cow, although in this case I am not aware that he had anything to do therewith. I can vouch for the fact that shepherds often come to resemble sheep. What is the reason? How do we account for the strong, coarse features of butchers — of those butchers who 'kill themselves,' I mean, and of the men they employ? What gives the peculiar horsey character to those who have to do with equine race?

Even a sale-yard may suggest some intricate problems. Is the human face an outward index of its owner's character? Can you tell the man who is likely to be successful in his calling merely by looking at his face? I fancy so. Just observe those who we know have been fairly successful men, those who have the reputation of being good men of business in farming, cattle-dealing, and cognate industries where much hard-headed determination is required, and I fancy you will generally observe a width and squareness of jaw-bone, lips not too thick, the mouth generally closed, lower jaw somewhat underhung. I do not say the rule is invariable; that can scarcely be expected. Now look at some of these coarse, thick-lipped, large-mouthed men — veritable chaw-bacons you will say; but you would expect nothing refined in their minds. Loud-voiced, blustering, swaggering, and self-assertive, you will think; and probably you will be pretty correct in your judgment. Some assert that such qualities are hereditary, and not to be wholly credited to the individual; others, that the kind of food habitually consumed has a potent effect upon the mind and features, and hence 'chaw-bacon' is not an inappropriate term; while those again who advocate temperance will ascribe it to the unlimited consumption of inferior drink.

What is the influence that one mind can assert over another? If the reader in the course of his experiences has had much to do in the matter of driving a bargain, has he not found that with some men he cannot do it to his satisfaction — that they will assuredly get the better of him — while he himself in his turn can do just the same with others? Is it a mere question of stronger will? Has the will of one individual absolute power over that of another individual? Ere two words concerning a bargain have been spoken, does not one recognise the presence of a man of stronger or of weaker will? Possibly; but at the same time this is largely a matter of habit and of training, of judgment, but above all of self-confidence and self-reliance. Some men can take care of themselves from the very first; others require considerable training, require to have confidence in their own judgment and ability ere they are able to hold their own among their fellows.

It has been asserted that dress is characteristic of the individual, and surely there must be something in the hats which adorn the heads of some of the present company. Here is one which can be seen all over the yard. It is a top hat — sometimes called a silk hat — of the shape dear to City men and mashers. Nothing wonderful in that, you will say. Perhaps not, but this is not a common and ordinary black-topper. It is white — not a white, dull-looking felt hat, but a beautiful, sleek, glossy-white, shining in the sun as if of burnished silver, and set off by a black ribbon. Here is another tall hat of a hard, dull felt; it narrows towards the top, being somewhat conical in shape, and has a very small brim, while the whole rests but just on the top of a somewhat large head, and looks too small for its owner. Here's another hat something like that worn by bishops — a top hat which looks as if it had been cut down just one-half, and the crown replaced after that operation. Here is another which resembles that of a dean or other Church dignitary — a kind of 'bowler' hat with a very broad, flat brim. These hats stand out conspicuously among the sea of black and occasional brown 'bowlers' or 'billycocks'. Who are the men who possess these roofs? Why, well-known prominent men, celebrated ram-breeders all of them. The hats might almost serve as an advertisement; but at any rate the plan — for a man who is likely to be much sought after to wear a distinctive hat — is a good one. Have you any business with any one of these gentlemen, and wish to find him in a crowd, all you have to do is to mount some eminence overlooking the sea of hats, and having easily spotted the correct hat, if it be present, to make for it. The man whom you want you will find under that hat without doubt. I have known some of these hats for years, and the style never changes. You may know the man anywhere if only you remember which hat to look for. How do they manage to always obtain the same hat, while an ordinary mortal must perforce be content with the common domestic 'bowler' or 'billycock,' which changes shape every month or so; and he, poor fellow, can never obtain another hat quite the same style and shape as his old one? These worthy men must evidently make a study of the matter; at any rate, however they manage it, they always contrive to appear in public each beneath his own peculiar hat. Perhaps their friends and acquaintances would be in some doubt about recognising them did they appear in any other. Carlyle tried to prove that it was the clothes which made all the difference among men, but he did not get as far as the hats. Here is an interesting field of observation for some one to enter.

Let us, however, return to our sheep again. And, by-the-bye, what wonderfully expressive faces sheep have; but they should be observed in the quiet of their home pastures to be seen at their best — not here in the sale-yard, where they are somewhat frightened and bewildered. A cockney thinks that all sheep are alike, and is unable to see any difference in their faces. He knows them only as so much mutton; but what say the shepherds or those who have much to do with them? A shepherd can recognise the individuals of a flock by their faces as we recognise our fellow human beings; and he can tell you the history of this or that sheep almost from the time when they were lambs. He knows their dispositions and tempers; he knows, too, those that are sedate and sober-minded, and those that are unquiet and restless. What a fund of information he possesses concerning his charges! They know him, too, and they know his dog. They know that old, grey, weather-stained jacket or slop of his perfectly well. They know his voice; and if, perchance, they have broken bounds, are aware of their trespasses, and show that they have done wrong, by making a guilty, precipitate retreat, long ere he approaches. But it is the coat chiefly by which they recognise him. They look with distrust upon him if he dons a different coat, while they will tolerate a stranger who has a similar dirty-grey one; and the shepherd, profiting by this when he wants to catch one for any purpose, is careful to wear the old coat to which they have been accustomed. Then, if he be in the habit of always using them quietly, he may almost stumble over them, for they will not move at his approach. But let him only catch one, and the rest are on the alert. They resent such liberties, and are for a time somewhat wary until confidence be restored. Kindness and gentle usage go a long way in the management of a flock.

The ram-selling is about to commence, as we are informed by the lusty ringing of a bell and the auctioneer's shout: 'Now then, gentlemen, this way, please, for the rams.' There's a ring of hurdles around which the company assemble, while the auctioneer takes his stand upon a small raised platform facing the entrance by which the sheep are brought in. The head-shepherd stands in the ring with the ram which he leads with a halter, while his mates are outside bringing the sheep up one by one in succession from the pens. Now is the time to which the shepherd has been looking forward all these months. Now is seen the result of years of careful work and judgment on the part of his master and himself; and as he hears the guineas mount up, and listens to the approval of the spectators on any choice individuals, he cannot, if he is at all worth his salt — and he would hardly be shepherd over a good ram-breeding flock if he were not above the average — he cannot, I say, help feeling a certain amount of pride and satisfaction both on his own and his master's account.

What a load of flesh these rams bear! At one time there was a great idea among stock-breeders to try and produce the greatest weight of meat upon the smallest amount of bone. The pictures of stock so much in favour with breeders of a bygone age unintentionally caricature this trait to an amazing degree. One sees depicted upon the canvas a perfect parallelogram of meat supported on four legs as thin as straws, and no longer than castors, and the whole adorned by a head less than half the natural size. Such was the ideal standard; little wonder that an animal approaching it failed in constitution. Instead of allowing the bone to increase for the support of such an extra quantity of flesh, the chief object was to reduce the bone to a minimum. Scientific agriculture has done a great deal; but it is very apt to ride its hobbies to death.

'This flock is renowned for early maturity,' cries the auctioneer. Early maturity! Everything must be abnormally forced nowadays to an immature maturity. We must bring out our steers as beef at twenty months old, and our lambs as mutton at eight. Vegetables must not only come in extremely early, but must grow to an enormous and dropsical size. Peas and beans are awarded prizes, not for flavour or

nutriment, but for length of pod and size of berry. When we begin to tamper with Nature's laws, the result is not unfrequently akin to that of a tinker mending a worn-out kettle — for every leak that he stops two more are started.

CHAPTER 6

THE OLD
SHEPHERD

'Shall I give you a lift?' I asked a shepherd with whom I was acquainted, as I overtook him on my return from the fair. 'Well, zur, 'twill be a zet vorrud on the road whoam,' he replied, as he got up beside me into the trap. He had evidently been enjoying himself at the fair — not to any objectionable extent, but just sufficiently to cause his tongue to wag somewhat faster than usual, and to bring out his broad dialect in stronger relief. I knew him as a thoroughly respectable man — a rough diamond very probably, but full of honest intrinsic merit; and I liked his company none the worse because he was able and willing to talk. 'When the liquor's in, the truth's out,' says an old proverb; but as far as the liquor was concerned on this occasion, the amount that had been imbibed could not have been objected to by any but the most prudish. The excitement of meeting old friends, of seeing fresh scenes, the difference between a day off and a day at work, had probably had far more effect in exhilarating his spirits.

'Well, shepherd, so you had business at the fair today, I suppose?'

'Noa, zur. I can't zay as I'd a gurt zight o' bizness, look 'ee. I wint thur with just a feaow ship o' the gaffer's, and they were a-send more out of kuriosty-like, an' to zee 'ow thengs wur a-gwine. As I wur a-lookin' around 'm, I zeed owld Dan'l Iles, as I 'adn't a-zeed vur a 'mazin' long time, an' us 'ad about half a toothful of summat seeing as how we'd a-met together; an' I axd un 'ow er wur, and what er 'd bin doing o', an's got a-toarkin' o' the times when's wur but bits o' chaps.

Ay, I bin 'bout zum time, zur,' the shepherd replied to a question of mine. 'Vive-an'-vorty year, man an' bouoy, hev I bin at work yere-abouts. My veyther 'e'd mead a bit o' mony a keattle-djelin', an' 'ee set isself up in a pooblic on the road about twelve mile yerevrom. He'd a smartish vamily o' we bouoys, an' so us 'ad to scrobble along's best 's could like. A' sex yere owld I wur a-ledding vormust a-harvesting, and then wur soon put to drev plough. Ah, thur wurn't no skools o' any 'count 'bout i' them days. I wur niver larned nought of that thur — nether reedy, writy, nar zummy — the kearter larned I most as iver I wur wurth. I wur to do my wurk wi'out no nise and skulking, and I wurn't to knock the keattle about. Ah! he wur a sad maggoty cust'mer a' times, 'ee wur, if aught upzet 'im. One daay er caught hold of I an' whipped off 's belt an' leathered I a rum un. I hollered all I knowed. Up come th' varmer. "Hullo, Zamu'l, what's thee's got thee's 'ool up now fur? thee bist in a main teakin'." "This 'ere spiteful little twoad," zed the kearter, a-drowin' I vrom 'un yed fust into th' vur–r–r, "wur a-knockin' thaay 'osses as I leaved un to mind, while I 'ad 'm a bit o' bread, 'ee wur a-knockin' 'um about most skeandalous. I thowt vur all the wurld's they'd get away an' break the tackle all to pieces." "'Od rot ers little kearkiss," sed the varmer, "pick un up, kearter, and give un another cut or two." Wall, you kneaow, zur, 'twere a good lesson vur I, vur I didn't misuse hosses nor nothink else no more; but 'ow'd it be now? Yer dussn't lay a vinger on a bouoy now if er's iver zo, or er'll 'ave 'ee up vur 'salting ov un; and then they goes out into the ground to plough and knocks the keattle 'bout just as thaay be a-minded. This 'ere eddicashun's a fine thing fur 'um. It meaks 'um too proud vur the varm, and thaay must be off on a hol'day iver so offen, and no wurk o' Zundays. The Varmer he've hed to paay fur this 'ere eddicashun, and th' on'y good as it's a-done un is as er've got o paay more fur gurt, lubbering bouoys as ain't half nor quarter so handy as we little chaps wur. Ay! but times was different then, yer knaow; thur wurn't noan o' thease 'ere railroads about thease parts, and bread wur 'bout a shilling a loaf.'

'You found it rather hard to get on then, I suppose?'

'Well, 'twere sommat o' a scrobbling job then sometimes, I 'low; but

Lord bless 'ee, zur, we 'adn't used to look fur thease 'ere white bread then. Most offen 'twur brown bread, sometimes wi' barley among et, or 'twur oat keakes, or barly keakes and the like; and a man's missus could beake 'um 'erself then. Nowadays, look 'ee, zur, there's a fine caddle among the wimen-volk ef the beaker don't a-bring 'um the bread's white 's a millard's 'at; and nearn o' they wimin can beake not no 'count. Then, you kneow, yer cud git a cheese about dreppence a pound, a score or more o' yeggs vur a shelling, an' a pound o' butter belike didn't cost 'ee but tinpence. Mate us didn't used to git a sight on, but what us did git was about dreppence ya'penny or vourpence, and beacon, look 'ee, nigh for th' asking. Sugar wur dear then — skeandalous dear — but all us did was to do wi'out. Tay wur dear; th'owld wimin couldn't git arf so much o' thuc thur in to 'um as thay do now, and, to my mind, they'd be all the better if 'um 'adn't the chance at ut now so offen; but then we cud git cider fur most nuthin'. Measters ud giv' it to 'ee then arl the year round, without so much as a word, an' yer could take it whoam for dinner. Who'd do et now? Some doan't gie et 't all, some gies et only in the zummer, and they watches ivery mouthful on't an' they grudges the volk ivery drap on't as they gits inzide 'um. Oh, times wurn't so shemful bad then; I reckon a poor man, ef 'ee wur a-minded to wurk, got on's well then, or maybe better, nur er do naow; vur, look 'ee 'ere, ef thengs be chipper naow and a man's wages be more, yer see 'ow mony be out o' wurk arf thur time. What's the durned use of zaying to a man as is out o' wurk and arn't got a bit nor a zup in's belly, as thengs be chipper and wages be riz? He'd be better orf if wages was jest arf so low, ef 'ee wur allus in wuurk. 'Twud be sommat vor 'um to do, an' not meake un so restless an' onyeasy. Then thur wur piecework, look 'ee, arl zummer-time, when a man could yarn a hatful of mony ef er wur a-minded, and 'es wife and childer an' arl yelp un. Now the 'cheenery 'a took 'way most arl ers piecework, an' ers childer mun go to skeoole, an' thur yent 'nuff work fur to be ony call fur wimen-volk — y'earnt nuff work vur arl the men — an' et dursn't do vur the wimen to come a-teakin' the men's jobs; thay'd soon be shewed better nor that. Yer zee ef the wimen kip away, the varmer mun pay more money fur the zame wurk to the men, else thaay 'oodn't a' no 'ands wi't. I allus zays, yer kneaow, as the times be about the best fur the working-volk when the bread's 'bout sixpence or sixpence-yapenny a loafe, an' whate a-zelling about vorty or vive-an'-vorty shellin's a quaarter; the varmer's a-gittin' sommat then fur ers trouble, tho' 'tain't a zight; 'ee grows more whate and more carn, an' yef er grows more carn, yer kneaow, thur's more wuurk vur the volk, an' so that's more volk in imploy, an' wages be more reg'lar; an' if so be as a man's wages be reg'lar, an' ee's got work in the winter 'stead o' being idle, why, look'ee, 'nother tuppence a loave yain't much to yurt un, yer knaow. Arl I knaows is as when the bread yan't so skeandalous chip as thur yan't volk out 'o wuurk as thur be when 'tis chip; and zo, yer knaow, I can't zee as this yere chip loafe's a-doing a zight of good to ony on us.

'Wall, yer knaow, zur, I wur a-zaying to 'ee as 'ow I went to drev plough, when one winter the measter come to I and towld I to go aff and yelp the shapperd 'mong the yeaows. Thur I bid arl that thur winter a-kearrin' th'ay to them thur ship, and pecking the turmits, and a-doing a bit o' hurdle-zetting. I liked that there job a 'mazing zight better nor being 'mong thaay 'osses; it giv' 'ee zummat more to thenk on, yer knaow; and shapperd, er zaid 's 'ow I wur a good bouoy and minded my wuurk, and didn't git a-messing and a-keaddlin' and a-'oondermenting 'bout like zum on 'um. But then I wurn't long o' the ship much in the zummer. I had to go back among the 'osses and sich; but when next Michelmus comed round, the measter, er zed to I as I wur to go 'long as keind o' under-shapperd and help un wi' the ship, if I wur a-minded to be'ave myself. Well, so I wur, and I bide along wi' un vur some time, and er kipt a-razing o' my weages vur a time; but th' end o' it wur as I wur a-getting too owld for sich a job as that, and so I telled un one Michelmus as I wur wurth more money. Well, er said er didn't know as I wur, but I wur vree to try, er sed; er couldn't 'ford me no more, er sed. Wall, I went off to Mop and I got a pleaze along o' zum keattle a' two shillin' a wick more money, a'most directly. That thur measter 'ee wur a maggoty twoad, and 'twere arl 's iver I could do to sard my time out wi' un. Yer couldn't please un, not no waays, so aff I zlips next Michelmus. "What, yean't yer a-gwine to stop 'long of I another year?" er says; "you and I yean't fell out zo skeandalous bad. I wur quite a-minded," er says, "to putt up wi' ee." "So yer med, zur," I says, "but I tells 'ee as I bean't a-minded to putt up yeny longer o' you." Wall, he got hisself into a vine waay, and jumped all aroun' the pleace quite mad-like; and er called I all the neames as iver cud thenk on, swearing as er wudden't gie I no kerecter to go to Mop wi'. Wall, I let un have ers say out and walked off, and afore iver I'd 'casion to go to Mop my owld gaffer as I'd a-zard afore, I met un and er axed I what I wur a-gwine to do thease Michelmus, and when I zed as I wurn't a-gwine to stop, er warnted I to come back wi' un to his please to zard un agin, and zo I did; and thur I bid a zight of years, and was shapperd vor un till th' owld genelman died and 's things wur arl a-zelled, and the missus and the vamily went right away thure-from.

'Wall, yer kneaow, thur wur two or dree on 'em arter I then, a-wanting I to be shapperd vor 'um, an' I'd 'bout as lief go to 'arn on 'um; but th' owld squire 'ee steps in an' offers I more money nor the tothern, an' so I went along o' 'ee to look after ers ship vor un. An' thur I bid iver so many year as you do kneaow, a-getting vamous wages. Ah! but 'ee wur a sad 'oondermenting sort o' a customer, 'ee wur, and dooced prood o' the ship. 'Ee let I 'a just bout what I wur a-minded vor 'um. Us used to zend to sheaow then, yer kneaow, an' us went in for Rom brading. Ah! look'ee, thay wur a vamous lot o' ship; after I'd a-bin thur a year a two dalled if thur wur a better vlock o' ship to be voun' in th' wull keounty! Ah! an' thay thur rom-zale dinners as he'd a-used to gie, thaay wur sommat 'nation vine, thaay wur, the weind wur a-sard out to the volk like warter, it do meake I dry to thenk on't; an' the varmers, thaay'd a plenty o' money in them daays, an' thaay'd git that thur weind into 'em in 'mazing style, and 'ud come out, yer kneaow, an' gie vamous gurt prizes for thaay thur ship. Ah! but 'twur good to see thaay volks a-comin' down the lather. Thease 'ere rom-zale dinner wur a-gie'd up in a sort o' gurt tallet pleace as wur above the keart'us, an' thaay a got to clim' into un up a lather. Up thaay went, sprack enow afore dinner, but ofttimes 'twur a main queer job for some on 'em to find thair waay down arterwards. Lord! I've a-laffed thur afore now to zee how zum on 'em did boggle at 't. Them thur

rom-zales wur a smartish expense; thur ain't the sales an' dinners
a-gie'd now about the country as thur'd used to, only just one or two
old-fashioned uns bides about. Moast on 'em do zend thair ship now to
the fairs, and then they be zelled out in the market. 'Tis a different
dinner as the folks as buys do get then. Thaay must git thur own, an'
'tis most in general a plate o' hot meat an' some taters an' sich for a
shilling, an' on'y water to drink. Ah! thaay don't bid quite so wild arter
that, I war'n. As to the grog and such, thaay kips that thur till arter the
business be a-done; thur's mony on 'em as can't see the gig steps when
thaay wants to git int'un at night. But thur, things be quieter every year
now. There's plenty of ship an' plenty of volks do come, but 'tis all
done 'nation solemn-like. Thur yean't nonc o' the 'oondermenting
about now as there'd used to be. The townsfolks be got so 'nation
finnicking, thaay can't abear a bit o' nize.'

CHAPTER 7

THE WOOD SALE

'Holloa, Daniel!' I said to a labourer, a few mornings after the events last narrated, 'how did the wood sale go off yesterday?'

'Oh! 'twere a puffec' sale, sir, a puffec' sale! Thur wur just as much drink a-gwine as a chap wur a minded to he'. 'Twurn't no nasty stuff nether, but good, honest drink as 'ad a-got summat in't, yer knaow, an' made a man knaow soonish as he wur a-getting nicely forrud. Willum an' I, us went up thur together, an' when's got thur, thur wur th' owld squire a-stood outside a-telling on 'um to bring this 'ere drink up, an' to let the folks get it into 'um fast as iver they wur a-minded. "'Twun't hurt 'ee," er said, "'twun't hurt 'ee, 'tis some good wholesome tack," er said; "'tis some reubub weind as I've a-had by me this ten year, an' it's only gone off a mossel; it's good stuff for 'ee," er says, a-tossing off a glass as keind like as cud be. Wall, they brings up this 'ere licker in great warter cans, an' one on 'em says to I, "Will 'ee drenk?" "Sure as life I 'ull," I says. "Yer won't git such tack as this yere agen," er says, "thur's a bit of a querish taste to't," er says, 'but yer'll soon git used to that. It's a rare powerful drink," er says, "an' will warm 'ee up a rum un," er says, a-handing we a third lot on't. Wall, 'ee wur right enow about it. 'Twer querish tack, sommat like beer an reubub weind an' bacca-juice a-mixed, but I knowed we could git forrud on't, an' 'twur stuff as warmed a body right down to ers toes. Owld Job Smith got as drunk as a genelman on't, an' as blind as a 'oont, er couldn't see whur er wur a-gwine, an' vell yead furst into a faggit-pile.

"'Does 'ee zell th' owld genelman 'long o' this lot?" says one.

"'Twoud spile it if yer did," says another. "'Twoud cost too much in vind the skeandalous owld twoad wi' licker;" and he as sed it wur on's back afore we'd got much further.

'All the way as us went the folks kept a-drapping off one by one. Some on 'em had a-bought their bit most skeandalous dear; but then that wur wot thic tack wur a-sard out fur. 'Twoodn't never a-payed 'em else to perwide it. Owld Willum wur luckier nor I, somehow. He got a skinful afore I cud. Time was when Willum and I cud set down together with the mug atween us, and we was so ekal as none cud tell the one on us as wur forruder nor t'other. But this 'ere time I'd a 'ad to leave Willum a-hind, and, yer knaow, when us comed to the last lot the licker had a-knocked the company all abroad, so as thur wurn't nun on us beseps th' auctioneer, an's clerk, and mysel' around un. True as I be 'ere, that thur's true, measter. I'll teak my sollum Davy on't.[1] Yer cud look back and see all along and atween and atwixt the lots the volks a-lying and a-sprawlin' about the ground wur they'd a-bin auvercum wi' that thur tack of the squire's. Ah,' he said, smacking his lips, 'it wur proper powerful tack, thur's no doubt on't.

'"Wall," the auctioneer says, says 'ee, "who's a-gwine to bid fur this 'ere lot?"

'"Seems to I, sur," I sed, "as thur ain't much choice fur 'ee. Thur ain't a gurt sight of comp'ny around 'ee. You've a-bin a bit too quick-like for 'ee. Thur ain't a gurt sight of comp'ny around 'ee. You've a-bin a bit too quick-like for 'em thease time. Them volk o' the squire's had ought to a-bin a bit mussiful on 'em till you'd a-finished."

'"Strikes me, Dan'l," er said, "we've a-done some business to-day. I've a-knocked down all the folks as well as all the lots."

'I thowt about as how I best be a-getting whoam, so I goes and finds Willum a-leaning agin the faggit-stack; and putting my earm into hissen we makes our way — and a middlingish crukked way 'twere, I tell 'ee — into the road. Soon's ever we'd a-got upon 't, "Dan'l," er said, "this 'ere road's a-running away from under I like a mad thing," and down er went on ers back arl a-mullock in the middle on't. "Dan'l," er sed, a-setting up, "wi'm nought else to do but to sot down yere-right, and let this 'ere road take we straight whoam, ers muving hard thuc way." "No er ain't, Willum," I seys, "er ain't a-muving, thee'lt nivir git whoam to-night ef thee doesn't muv theeself." "Muv meself, Dan'l!" er said, "d'ye think I'm sich a fule as to walk when I can ride whoam free and fur nowt? I'se gwine whoam just like a genelman. Set down, Dan'l, do."

"'Wall, sum'ow I comed down just beside un, and dratted if I didn't seem to see the road a-running away wi' us, only it sim to I as if er wur a-gwine round and round 'stead of strait vorruds. So there us two sot in the middle of the road, wi' our fit stuck out in front on's, and let that thur road take us whur er was a minded.

"'Howld fast, Dan'l," seys Willum, "Lord, how the thing to go! Look 'ow the trees do vly by we, Dan'l."

"'Willum," I says to un, quiet like, "Willum," I seys, "how d'ye think ye'll stop the plaguey thing when yer comes anent the door?"

"'Why, I'll cry whoa, in course, Dan'l," er says.

"'Cry whoa! will 'ee? D'ye thenk as this 'ere road's a-gwine to stop for you a-crying whoa? If er should we'd best cry whoa! now, fur seems to I as er's a-gwine round and round, and us ain't a mossel nigher."

"'Lord, Dan'l, if er 'oon't stop we'll be carred right into the tound. I'll cry whoa!" says 'ee, and then er set to and hollered — but the theng

'ouldn't stop. "Darze your little back on 'ee, yer plaguey twoad! Whoa! can't 'ee."

"'Willum," I says, "strikes me we'ed best holloa whoa! together. 'Tis but nat'ral as a road is summat hard o' yerring."

"'Right you be, Dan'l," er says, "so look 'ee 'ere; when I says dree we'll holler whoa together. One! two! dree!" And wi' that we hollered whoa! loud enow to stop a dozen teams o' 'osses; but it hadn't no effec' on that thur road, er went off harder nor iver. Just then a young feller cum up to we.

"'What the deuce," er says, "be you two vules a-setting thur side by side in the middle o' the road fur?"

"'Why, thease 'ere road," says Willum, "have a-run'd away o' we, and us can't stop un nohow. We've a-hollered all we knowed."

"'Runned away with 'ee! it's the drink as 'ave runned away wi' yer heads, and as fur hollering," er said, "yer've hollered wuss nor a pair of bulls. I cudn't thenk wot the world had a-auvertook 'ee. But git up aff thease here road or you'll be run'd auver."

"'Wall, stop un, first," says Willum.

"'Stop un, you drunken vule!" er says, "stop un! why, er ain't a-muving. Git up with 'ee."

'Wall, I puts my hand on Willum's showlder to see if I cowd git up arra ways, but just as I wur half-ways, Willum, he catched hoult of my leg to try and pull hisself up, and down we two come agin in the road; and thur we was a-trying, fust one and then t'other on us, to git up by a-leaning one on t'other, and all we did was to vall about in the road while thic chap stood by and laffed fit to bust hisself. Bimeby Willum says, says 'ee, "Dan'l," er says, "tain't nere a mossel o' use a-trying to wark on a road as is a-running away from under 'ee arl the time; let's crawl quietly on to the sward at the zide."

'And so us did; us set to and crawled on our hands 'cross the road till us got on to the grass, true as I be here; but us couldn't neither on us stan' then, so us had to lie down theer-right and bide.'

CHAPTER 8

THE HARVEST HOME

Times have sadly changed in the matter of harvest homes; and I am afraid that such institutions must now be practically numbered with the past. I will not pretend to judge whether it were better, or whether it were worse, for the agricultural labourer that things should be thus altered; but at present one can scarcely help regretting that the opportunity of meeting together at a common board, once a year, entirely on pleasure bent, should be altogether lost. It was a custom which, I believe, exerted a beneficial influence both upon masters and upon men. Hard times have, however, told disastrously upon the former; while a spirit of greater independence, too often giving rise to a false pride, has manifested itself in the latter. Too often, again, master and man pull in opposite directions, the one trying how to get the most work for the least wage, the other how to obtain the highest wage for the least work.

All too soon my pleasant stay at Farmer Bates' came to an end; and taking my leave of him and his good wife, I set out to visit a friend in a different part of the country. Here I was due to assist at a harvest home to which, in fact, I had been specially invited. Mr Hillyard was a substantial, well-to-do farmer, who kept a good house for himself and two or three pupils. He had got on fairly well with his men, and it so happened that he determined to once again revive his old custom of harvest home, at which it was my good fortune to be present. The corn had all been 'kearted,' even the rakings had been picked up, and the last load had been hauled home; the last rick had been topped up therewith; the thatching was all but finished;[1] the strappers[2] had been dismissed, but with the invitation to come to the harvest home on such and such a day, and there was little now to look forward to except the wheat planting, the caving[3] of the few mangolds, and the winter ploughing.

Mrs Hillyard, her daughters, and some lady visitors had been busy decorating the barn. It was a large building consisting of four high walls and a roof; the floor was all of stone flags; the end wall was pierced for a large pitch-hole; in the middle of one side were two sliding doors running right up to the roof, wide enough and high enough to admit a large wagon loaded with sheaves; alongside these again ordinary doors admitting to either end, and in the opposite wall was a door opening into the back of the cow stalls. The building itself was of noble proportions, capable of allowing four loaded wagons to stand side by side with plenty of room at the end for other things.

The floor had been brushed up and made tidy; and down the middle stood a long table with another across its end, forming a T. Around the top table were arranged chairs; alongside the other, forms. The winnowing machine, the 'Booby,' the sack carts, and all the other implements had been moved to the two ends and hidden from view, at the one end by a large rick-cloth suspended from side to side, at the other end by an arrangement of rugs, backed by some large blankets, to keep out the draughts from the pitch-hole which, high above every one's head, was open to admit the necessary light. The sliding doors, too, were open for the same purpose to a certain extent, and the draught from the lower half-dozen feet prevented by a small tarpaulin nailed across the opening. Along the side were arranged evergreens, flowers, choice sheaves of corn, large vegetable marrows, and all kinds of ornamental devices local talent had suggested. The eventful day arrived in due course; two o'clock was fixed for the time of commencement, and the carter boys had gone without their 'muncheon,' so as to leave a larger vacuum. As Mr Hillyard and his party enter the building, they are greeted with a pleasant cheer, while they make their way to the cross table at the end. The men are standing in groups, neat and tidy in their Sunday-go-to-meeting clothes, and with their best hats on. Each one has been required to bring his own eating utensils, and these they carry with them, done up in large coloured pocket-handkerchiefs of various hues; one or two plates, according to circumstances, a knife, fork, spoon, and a glass or mug from the outfit. The cross table is set ready for Mr Hillyard's party, which consists of those staying in the house and two invited friends in addition, one of the latter being Mr J——, a wine merchant in the neighbouring town. On the cross table is everything ready for dinner, with some sherry for the honour of the guests; on the long table is nothing but the table-cloth, some prettily arranged flowers, and occasional salt-cellars and cruet-stands. We had observed the scene for a few minutes, when the women who had helped in the harvest-field, and who had been up till now engaged in assisting at the cooking, entered the barn.

'Are we all here?' inquired Mr Hillyard.

'Yes, sir,' is the general response.

'Then get to your places, and let's see about making a start.'

Off go the hats, to be placed under the seat which each one quickly finds — the three or four women being careful to huddle together towards one corner of the table. The yellow and red handkerchiefs are untied, and the various articles produced; the joints are brought in; before Mr Hillyard is set a huge joint of roast beef; before James Spencer, the head man, who occupies the end of the long table, the fore part of a sheep with baked potatoes; before Willis and Short — Mr Hillyard's pupils, who occupy places about half-way down the long table for the purpose of carving — other joints of mutton; a boiled leg of mutton is put before myself at the end of the cross table. Then ensues a rapping of Mr Hillyard's knife-handle, commanding silence as he rises to say grace. 'And now, my lads, fall to,' he concludes; 'if you only work amongst the vittles as well as you did among the wheat it will soon tell on it all.' Now's the time for the carvers to show dexterity and skill! In come enormous dishes of potatoes, of cabbages, of turnips, and of carrots, with which the plates are soon piled up till you would wonder where the meat would lie. Then, in large water-cans, the beer arrives, drawn from the barrels temporarily pitched in the cow-stalls behind. The constant rattle of knife and fork, and the general hum of voices, attest that work has begun in earnest. Two helpings, ay, and sometimes three! The proverbial hungriness of the hunter is nothing to the capabilities of the harvestmen; but at last the meat course is finished, the most voracious ploughboy has taken the edge off his appetite, and the time for the plum pudding has arrived. In they come! I should not like to say how many, but it seems to me about one to every four persons, and the remnants that go out make but a sorry show. Then follows bread and cheese, and salads; but nature is pretty well satisfied by this time, and declares herself unable to do much more.

Now the things are being cleared away; the knives, forks, etc., are wrapped up again in the red and yellow handkerchiefs, while the mug or glass alone remains out. Long church-warden pipes are distributed, and jars of tobacco are put upon the tables. Very soon a general out-pouring of smoke takes place; but there is plenty of ventilation and a lofty roof, so there is no fear of distress on the part of the ladies. Meanwhile the beer-cans circulate at the long table, and the sherry decanter goes round at the cross one.

Then uprises Mr Hillyard, and gives forth the customary loyal toast of the occasion, 'The Queen, God bless her! and the rest of the Royal Family.' To their honour the glasses are duly drained, amid much stamping of feet, knocking of tables, and cries of 'hear! hear!' Mr Hillyard proceeds: 'The next thing I mean to do is to drink to the health of James Spencer and all my good folks, men, women, and boys. Here's good health and long life to all of you.'

'Thanky, sir, thanky.'

'Yes, and I mean it too. We've gone through another year together, and reached the end of harvest, and reached it happily, I am glad to say. We've had our trials with the weather, and we've had anxieties of all kinds; but I'm glad to say that I can look around me and think that you men, ay, and you women and boys, have worked together well, and tried to do your best by me. For certain John, the carter, there, always thinks as the poor hosses are half starved and only half fed, and he grudges Willum, the shepherd, every morsel of corn as he has for them fat, lazy ship of his; and then there's Willum comes and says as the ship always have to put up with most terrible short commons, and nobody can't be expected to do a flock on no vittles. When I spoke to him about killing a sheep for the dinner to-day, he said as he'd not got one more than half fit, but somehow or other, he managed to send us in some very good mutton.' — 'Ay! ay!' and 'hear! hear!' from the men. — 'And then there's Jim, the cowman, as thinks that he never can get enough vittles for his cattle 'cos it all goes to the 'osses and the ship, and he can never get ground to turn his cows in which hasn't, so he says, been quite soured by them ship a-running over it. But for all that, we've managed to get on very well, and I like to have a man taking pride in what he's got in his charge, and being as anxious to get as much as ever he can for 'em so long as he ain't too greedy. Well! well! I won't keep you too long. Here's jolly good health to all of 'ee, every man Jack of you, for I think you all tried to do your best to get the harvest together this time.'

Again the glasses are drained, and again there is much stamping of feet and hammering of tables. Now is James Spencer's turn, and he gets up at the end of the table, hums, haws, and coughs two or three times.

'Zur, I bean't much o' a speechyfier' (that's always the beginning for him). 'We all on us thanks 'ee, too, most uncommon, for a 'nation good dinner.' ('Hear, hear! hear, hear!' from all sides, in the various keys of men's, women's, and boys' voices, amid renewed thumping and stamping as Spencer, scratching his head, sits down to think a bit before continuing.) ''Tis a sad bad job where maister and men doan't quite manage to hit it off atween 'em, I says; and 'tis allus a good un when our maister can come yere and say as we've a-done a good zummer's work for un. I must say myself as I don't think there's ar a better maister not nowheres round here nor our maister be to we' ('Here, hear!' and stamping), 'and 'tis but right that we should try to do our best by un. I proposes our maister's health; long life an' happiness to un, says I.'

Now the great enthusiasm prevails, and the whole company rises and cheers vociferously, and, under the leadership of Willis and Short, sings 'For he's a jolly good fellow.' Mr Hillyard, in due course, returns thanks; and after that the missus's health is drunk, and the young leddies and gentlemen 'who've a-dined along o' we,' to which in return

replies are given. Then quiet settles down on the company awhile, to be forthwith broken by Mr Hillyard, who asks for a song.

'Sam'l, Sam'l,' is the cry; 'now then, Sam'l, war's thy vice? Gie us a zong, Sam'l.'

'I doan't knoaw nurrun,' says Sam'l the carter boy, humbly.

'Dang it! not knoaw nurrun?' cries John the carter. 'Cass'net thee zing nether when thee's to plough fit to be yerd in the next parish. Gie us the "Varmer's Bouoy,"'

With a little more encouragement Sam'l starts the old-fashioned country song, the 'Varmer's Bouoy,' a song which probably extends all over these islands, and which, at any rate, I've heard sung in Welsh to the same tune. Part of the refrain is:

> And to rip and to soow,
> And to plough and to moow,
> And to be a varmer's bouoy.

When the song was finished, and the applause had subsided —

'Now then, Simie, 'tis thy turn,' cries a voice, and Simie, after the usual amount of hesitation, gets up.

I noticed afterwards that it was not the fashion to get up, but to sing sitting down. However, Simie gets up and begins to pour forth, to a somewhat slow, dragging tune, this very varied ditty:

> Oh, what shall I have fur my breckfust,
> Fur my breckfust, fur my breckfust,
> Oh, what shall I have fur my breckfust,
> If I comes whoam to-dai?
> Bacon and eggs fur thy breckfust,
> Fur thy breckfust, fur thy breckfust,
> Bacon and eggs fur thy breckfust,
> If thee'lt come whoam to-dai.

Chorus joined in heartily by all the company when the singer calls out, 'Now then!'

> Oh, I can't come whoam and I wun't come whoam,
> I can't come whoam and I wun't come whoam,
> I can't come whoam and I wun't come whoam,
> Me ship'll go astray.
> The ship'll go 'stray in the weil-der-ness,

The weil-der-ness, the weil-der-ness,
The ship'll go 'stray in the weil-der-ness,
An' I can't come whoam to-dai. Now then!

Then the same question was repeated for his din-ner, his tea-oi, and so on, and the same or similar replies are given. The song has one very great advantage — that of extreme simplicity for short memories.

The next to sing is an old woman with an extremely shrill treble, at times degenerating into a positive squeak. Then Mr J—, the wine merchant, favours the company with a beery ditty, said to be from Derbyshire:

For feyther 'ee loikes 'is beer 'ee does,
'Ee's fond o' drap o' good beer 'ee is,
Let genelmen foine,
Set down to their woine,
But feyther 'ull stick to 'is beer 'ee 'uul.

So it goes on to the other members of the family, the cousins and the sisters and the aunts, all show decided partiality for beer, in preference to the 'woine of genelmen foine'. Needless to say the sentiment is highly approved of, and vociferous applause greets its conclusion.

Then to my mind came the piece of the evening, delivered by the 'Empress,' so nicknamed because she was a Mrs King, and was, too, a fine big woman of very suitable proportions. She gave it forth with energy and gusto; and the piece, coupled with its mode of delivery, so took my fancy, that I prevailed upon the good songstress shortly afterwards to write the whole of it out for me. 'Her wern't no skollard as her'd never bin larned, but 'er darter wur a skollard as 'ad done redy, writy, an' summey, and 'er'd get 'er darter to write it out fur 'er.' This accordingly came to pass; and the original document is now in my possession from which I transcribe the following. There is no title to the song, and it seems to begin certainly 'in medias res' and not very 'à propos.' I must leave the reader to translate the effusion to the best of his ability, only adding, that Mr Hillyard informed me, this was the Empress' stock song, and he had heard it for many years.

The capting gave consent,
And away ter-morrew,
Levving our dear gurls behind,
In grif and sorrer.
Wipe up your briney tears,
An lev aff weapping;
How happy, happy shall us be,
At our next meating.

Once I had gowld in sture,
For to invite yer;
But now I be louw an' poor,
Yer sims to slight mer.
Yer cu-urted me awhile,
Just to deceave me;
But now me heart yer have awound,
Yer gwine to leave me.

Farewell my parients dear,
Father and mother;
You've a loosed yer darter dear,
You have none other.
Tis in vaiin to wep for me,
Foor I be gowin,
To th' everlasting jyse,
Where fountains flowin.

Doun on the ground her fell,
Like one adying,
Spread out her arms abroad,
Sighing and crying.
Thur's no beliaf in man,
Not my own brother!
So gurls if yever you do love,
Love one to tother.

'Twur on one winter's night,
'Twur dark arl ovver,
The moon her gev a light,
Cud just discovver.
Down by the river's side,

Our ships got sailing;
A luvely mead I spied,
Wipping and waeling.

I stepped up to her,
And axed what grieved her;
Her med I this reply,
None can relieve mer,
My luve is gwine, said she,
To cross that hoshun,
My mind is like the sea,
All wavvy mooshun.

[The next two lines are missing from
the original manuscript]

He sent her this gold ring,
Oh! for a token,
You giv it to my dear,
There is none fairer,
And tell her to be kiend,
And luve the bairer.

But when her heard them words,
Her runned astracted,
Not knowing how her'd done her air,
Or how her acted.
Her run'd and tored her air,
Crying in her anger,
Young man, you've a come too leate,
I'll wed no stranger.

We greeted this song with extreme applause, and Mr Hillyard complimented the Empress upon its delivery and the sentiments it contained. He especially recommended her to instil into her daughters the precept that they had better 'love one to t'other' than look after the young men.

'Ah,' said the Empress, 'yer might as well tell the young meads not to yet nor drink as to tell they not to look ater the men-chaps. Thaay allus 'ave a-done 't, and thaay allus 'ull.'

the precept that they had better 'love one to t'other' than look after the young men.

'Ah,' said the Empress, 'yer might as well tell the young meads not to yet nor drink as to tell they not to look ater the men-chaps. Thaay allus 'ave a-done 't, and thaay allus 'ull.'

The ladies of our party now make preparations for retiring from the festive scene; and the carter and carter boys go out to attend to their horses for the night — a job which they know very well they will not be capable of doing at a later hour, if the course of events is at all in harmony with their desires. Soon after the ladies have withdrawn, the fun gets more furious; the morals of the songs are by no means without reproach, while the Empress and the other women are rather given to pouring forth love ditties of a very doubtful character. It does not now require any pressing to produce a song; and when one man has been so far overcome as to sing the same song three times over in about half an hour, each time under the impression it was a different one, Mr Hillyard thinks it time to retire and leave the meeting in charge of James Spencer to finish the barrels and then disperse. This finishing the barrels is a duty which is most conscientiously fulfilled, and which it would be useless to attempt to prevent. When there is no more drink left, the party dissolves of its own accord.

Willis and myself were out for a stroll some little time after leaving the barn, and we encountered one of the day-men on his way down to the village. He had to descend a bit of hill, and evidently his centre of gravity had shifted, for he leaned back as he walked down it as if he were a horse that had to check some cart, or as if some weight from behind were urging him, involuntarily, forward. Seeing us smiling, he brought himself up with a cry of 'Whoa!'

'I bean't drunk, genelmen; noa, I bean't drunk, though yer thinsh so, I knoash; but I'sh tell 'ee I bean't. I'sh a-got just a comf'able dropsh in me. Kearter Johnsh drunk as iver er can holdsh together; 'ee'sh a-fell down mullock alongzidesh 'osses, and there'll bide. 'Tain't no use to muv' un. Good nitsh, genelmen. This yere hill be steiper now nor when I climmed up un 's marning. I wishes as thaay as odds'd un had a-waited till arter I'd a-got whoam.'

Next morning I inquired of my bibulous acquaintance of the previous evening how he had enjoyed himself.

'Ah,' he replied, ''twer a proper good set out, and I thanks the maister for't, you tell un. I wanted jest about another quart o' loshun to meak I in perfect health. When I got up 's marning I had to send along to git I a quart o' cider the fust thing; I couldn't 'a yet no vittles else. I'd allus says to my meats when I's a-moowing, a quart of cider, says I, do allus go down slick a' four o'clock in the marning.'

'That looks like hot coppers[4] the night afore, John, don't it?'

'Maybe it be; we drinks and we works; we works and we drinks! Plenty o' work and plenty o' drink, says I, an' dang the 'ot coppers.'

Mr Hillyard met me as I returned to the house. 'We have,' he said, 'just had a call from one of our yesterday's guests, Mr Z—, who came to report himself as fresh as paint after last night's jollities; but he brought the news that our friend, J— (the wine merchant), was in bed and not at all the thing. J—, it seems, has been telling the doctor that it was the wretched sherry that he had up here which has been the cause of all the mischief.

'"Oh! he says it is the sherry, does he?" said I, turning to Z—. "Yes, that's something too capital. Why, that sherry which you had yesterday was part of a case which I got from J— himself and paid a good price for, because he declared it was something very special."

'"So I understood from you yesterday," says Z—, "but I thought I'd come and be quite certain. Oh, dear! that's much too good! the biter bit[5] with a vengeance! I'll take care he doesn't hear the last of that in a hurry," and I'll warrant Z— will keep his word,' concluded Mr Hillyard, laughing heartily.

It is needless to say that Z— did keep his word, and that J—, who, being a rare good fellow, was pretty well known in the neighbourhood, was unmercifully chaffed by all his acquaintances about Mr Hillyard's beastly sherry.

CHAPTER 9

THE WEDDING

One of the members of Mr Hillyard's household was a young and good-looking cook, who, of course, as is the way with cooks generally, had certain especial followers. The two most in favour were James Spencer, whom I have previously mentioned as taking the bottom of the table at the Harvest Home, he being a kind of head man upon the farm, and Tom Ryall, who was apprenticed to a carpenter in the village. Now Mary the cook found it no easy task to make choice between the two rivals. No doubt James was the more well-to-do, but then he was considerably her senior, was quiet, and had little to say for himself. Tom, on the other hand, was more about Mary's own age, a handsome young fellow, with plenty of go in him, and a lively entertaining manner, with but one fault — addicted too much to the pleasures of the social glass.

One evening James had come to visit Mary in the kitchen. According to his usual custom he had seated himself uncomfortably down upon the chair nearest to the door, had placed his hat upon his knees, and his stick by his side. It would seem as if he had lost courage directly he entered the room, and had therefore been unable to penetrate further. There he sat uncompromisingly upright, turning his hat round and round in a slow, indecisive manner, following with his eyes the cook as she bustled about the kitchen, but not making the slightest attempt to enter into any conversation. Suddenly the door of the kitchen flies open, and in rushes Tom Ryall, without his hat, shouting: 'Mary! Mary! they're a-gwine to murder I!'

'Hold yer nize, do, yer stoopid! yer'll 'ave missus out yere directly,' answers Mary, none too pleased with the duty of entertaining both swains at once. 'Thee git and set down, and don't stan' thur as if thee was moonstruck.'

So Tom, who is considerably subdued by the presence of James, tumbles into a chair on the other side of the kitchen.

'Why iver did yer want to come here a-hollowing out murder like a great booby?' asks the uncomplimentary Mary.

'Tummas have a-been to market,' says James, slowly and sententiously.

'What odds is it to thee if Tummas have a-been to market?' is the angry reply of that individual. 'I war'n if thee'd a-seed what I've a-seed tonight, and if thee'd a-yeard what I've a-yeard, thee'd sheake loike a lif all over.'

'Market is a vine plaice vor sights,' is James's only remark.

'Thee be quiet about the market,' says Mary, 'and let's hear what he've got to say. What did 'ee see, Tom, and whur?'

Now there could be no doubt that the market convivialities had had some effect upon Thomas, as James meant to imply, and there was a decidedly strong tap-room odour hanging about him; and yet there could be no doubt that his disturbed manner had been caused by something more than the pleasures of the tap-room — something which had evidently frightened him.

'Well then, Mary,' he answered, 'I wur a-coming along to here — I 'ave a-been to market, I owns, and it 'tain't no use a-denying of it; but I can't see as that makes any odds in the matter. There's many a good, ay, and maybe bad man, for the matter o' that, as goes to market, and I can't see why if I has to go to bis'ness thur I needn't go 's well as another.'

'Them as goes to market allus does go for bis'ness,' says James.

'Well, and I went fur bis'ness then, 'cause my gaffer had a-sent I down there to see a man about some pig-trows, and I didn't bide there no great time; but as I wur a-saying, when I comm'd up 'ereby, and had got just by whur them there high hedges be, I seed a great white thing by the side of the road, all glowing white, an' a gurt flame a-coming out o' ers mouth, and two eyes a-shining like two gurt stars, and —'

'Oh, Lor', Tom! do be quiet; I shall be afraid to go outside the door after dark,' cries Mary.

'Oh, well, it wur there, and when I set eyes upon it I give a gurt hallo, and I makes for the back gate as fast as I could, and just as I opened the gate I looked round and I seed the thing, and it fired a gun at me.'

'Oh, what nonsense, Tom!'

''Tain't no nonsense then, 'tis true; 'tis true as I be here; just as I opened the gate off went the gun, and I runned away as hard as I could.'

'All thy bis'ness to market ain't made thee very brave-like,' said James.

'Brave! d'ye think I wur a-gwine to stan' still to have the thing a-firing at I? If't had bin a mortal thing 'twoud 'a bin another matter, but a thing o' that thur sort is more'n I can tackle.'

'Thur wur right enow a gun went off just afore thee com'st in, but I thought 'twere one of the young gents arter rabbuts or the like. I never hurd afore,' said James, 'as ghosts was able to carry guns to shoot folks, and, in course, I don't believe it was ar man as fired at thee; I disbelieves yer tale altogether. I tell 'ee, I don't reckon naught o' yer sperits. I know yer ain't a-zeed no sperits outside the "Blue Dragin". If I wur thee I'd be downrigh' asheamed to come here wi' sich tales, and in sich a state. Howsomedever, I'll leave 'ee to it. Good night, Mary,' and James went out at the door after making what was for him quite a long speech. Thomas would doubtless have made some angry reply, and perhaps have attempted personal castigation, but Mary, seeing his intention, told him 'to sit down and be quiet, and not to go and make a hoaf of himself'.

Some few days after this occurrence it happened that Mr Hillyard had a few friends coming to dinner, and that it was necessary for Mary to help wait at table. Mr Hillyard's two pupils, Willis and Short, were present on the occasion. Another person who played an important part in this dinner-party was Mr Hillyard's young son George, who, however, only came in just as the things were being cleared away, prior to the setting out of dessert. As soon as he was seated, George broke out with, 'Father, I'se got such a tale to tell.'

'What's that, Georgy?' said some of the visitors.

'Fire away, George,' says Willis.

'Well, d'ye know,' says George, looking very serious, 'one day father says to Mifter Willis, "Dere's a 'trange tat, Mifter Willis, tomes trew de garden, and I don't lite 'trange tats. Mifter Willis, you must soot dat tat." So Mifter Willis says to Mifter Sort, "We must tate a dun and soot dat tat;" and Mifter Sort says to Mifter Willis, "We must do out at night and loot for dat tat, and soot dat tat." So Mifter Willis and Mifter Sort dey went out to de date of de titchen darden, and dey toot de dun, and dey tied de dun on to de rails by de side of de date, and dey had a long 'tring on to de dun, and den dey went and hided, and bime-by dey saw de tat tuming up de parf, and dey tept twite 'till, and when de tat tame to de date, bang went de dun!' said George, clapping his hands and nearly jumping out of his chair, 'and dey sot dat tat; and who do you fint dat tat was?'

'I'm sure I do not know, my boy.'

'Why, it was Tom de tarpenter.'

Poor Mary, who had listened with ill-concealed anxiety to this story, rushed out of the room in confusion, while a very general laugh was indulged in, especially when the situation had been more fully explained by the elders.

'The best of it is,' exclaimed Willis, 'that poor Tom came into the kitchen almost in a fit and told Mary that he'd seen a ghost, of which he gave the most extraordinary account, and he also said that this ghost had shot at him.'

'You didn't set up any ghost, I suppose,' said Mr Hillyard.

'Ghost, sir? no!' answered Willis. 'The fact is, that Tom had been to market and got well drunk, and I expect the gun going off gave him such a start that he imagined the rest, or else in his drunken state he took old Dobbin's white face peering over the hedge for a ghost.'

Naturally all this talk got round to Mary's ears in the mysterious way by which every little thing does penetrate a household; and it so happened that it did not advance Tom's suit in her favour in any degree; because she felt that he was not only unsteady, but was quite capable of making himself a fool into the bargain. Had James cut in dashingly at this period there is little doubt that victory would have fallen to his share, but James never had very much dash in him. Love-making was a trade at which he was certainly not an adept; and a proposal a matter which he could never summon up courage to make. On the other hand, Tom was in decided disgrace; but as he promised, and it must be admitted performed, amendment, Mary seemed to consider it politic to take him again into a certain amount of favour, especially since James still gave no very definite sign of his intentions.

One evening as James was returning home, he nearly fell over something in the road which he discovered was a man, and to his astonishment and, it must be confessed, delight, he found his rival Thomas as drunk as he could possibly hang together. Thereupon James administered a kick to the carcase of his prostrate rival to wake him up; but as that remedy had no effect the only thing to do was to drag him off the road for safety, and to lay him on the grass at the side. As the place whereon his bibulous friend had chosen to repose was not so very far from Mr Hillyard's house, James conceives the idea of fetching Mary out to view her suitor and his rival. After some little persuasion this is effected; but, as he did not tell her the purpose for which she was wanted to come 'just a little way up the road,' she was considerably startled at being brought up beside the body of a man.

'Thur look, Mary! what d'ye think o' that?' enquires James.

'Oh, but what's the matter wi' un, Jeames, is er dead?'

'Djed! no! beseps djed drunk! That's all the matter wi' 'ee. D'yer know who 'tis?'

'Oh, James, why 'tis Tummas!' she replies.

'Ay! sure enow, 'tis Tummas. Tummas 'a bin away on bis'niss agin, I s'pose,' is the answer.

'Oh, James,' cries Mary in tears.

'Well now, look 'ee 'ere, Molly, just 'ee say which 'tis ter be. Wilt 'a I, or wilt 'a that thur drunken feller in the ditch? Now, Molly dear, 'a I, do!'

The comparison was evidently forcible, and as the result of such an undeniable contrast the matter was settled there and then. Molly, who was afraid to stay out any longer, was led back to the house by the beaming James, who afterwards departed to get a man and a wheelbarrow to help him bear to his home that 'drunken twoad of a Tummas!' One may easily imagine the abounding charity with which he performed this office. No Roman general with his *Spolia maxima* ever entered the city with greater exultation than that felt by James as he passed through the village as sole escort to his rival, a captive to the charms of Bacchus, ignominiously lying dead drunk on a wheelbarrow — the rival whom he had lately vanquished in combats sacred to Venus. Io triumphe! Io triumphe!

The escort increases in numbers as it progresses, being swollen by the male and female elements of the juvenile population. Twenty times at least the procession comes to a halt, and the primitive chariot is stopped, in order that James may narrate the history of events, and thus satisfy the curiosity of such of the village-elders who came forth to meet them in the way.

Some three months after the date of the above detailed occurrences was the time of my arrival at Mr Hillyard's, just previously to the occasion of the Harvest Home Dinner, shortly after which the wedding between James Spencer and Mary the cook was to take place. During dinner on the evening of my arrival, I was put in possession of the facts above related, together with much other village gossip. Tom Ryall, I learnt, had not been able to face the chaff of the wheelbarrow incident, added to the disappointment of missing his chance of such a bride as Mary.

'Yes,' remarked Short, 'not only that, but the ghost story went uncommonly hard against him. I've heard the village boys running down the street after him, crying out: "Whoa, Dobbin! how's the ghost?" "Dey sot dat tat," and all manner of remarks. One rather bigger fellow came along and yelled across the street: "Biss'ness is a dry job, Tom; takes a sight o' wetting to make it work smooth, eh!"'

'Talking of ghosts, though,' said Willis, 'that wasn't a very bad occurrence that took place down in the village the other evening. I heard it from James today, who appeared to relish the joke in no small degree,'

'What's that, then?' remarked Mr Hillyard.

'Well, sir, you know old Mrs Garnet that goes out charing as it's called, went to do a day's work at Farmer Hinders'. During the day one of his daughters notices some coal put in a quiet, out-of-the-way place behind a door, and fancying it was there for no good, she determined to keep a look-out. It was late and nearly dark when the old woman left, and Miss Hinder had taken up a position near this door enveloped in a sheet. Out comes the old woman, makes for the coal behind the door, and gathers it into her apron. As she is leaving, there appears to her a tall, white figure, which stretches out its arms and says in a sepulchral voice: "Thou shalt not steal." With a scream Mrs Garnet lets the coal fall out of her apron, and runs off as fast as she can, crying out at top of her voice: "O Lord ha' mercy, Lord ha' mercy on me, do!" all down the street till she got to her own house.'

'Well, I hope to goodness,' says Mr Hillyard, 'that it will be a lesson to old Mrs Garnet. She's the mother of Dick Garnet, who is a rather discontented sort of man. One day he happened to say to me in reference to Michaelmas-time that he had never tasted goose, meaning to show what a poor, miserable life he led. "Never tasted goose, Dick," I said, "haven't you? Well, would you really like to taste some?"

'"Yes, that I 'ood, maister," he said, brightening up at the very anticipation.

'"Well then, Dick," I said, "all you've got to do is to pull up your shirt-sleeve and take a good bite out of your arm, and you can taste goose any day of the week."

'Dick's countenance fell, but the other men roared with laughter, and rallied him on his meal of goose for a long time afterwards.'

On the appointed day the whole village was early astir in anticipation of the wedding. Mr Hillyard was deservedly popular in the parish, and it was quite enough to ensure success for the people to know he took an active part in the matter. Mary is to be married from his house, and the party are to return there for the wedding breakfast which he has provided, and to which he has asked some friends of his own and of the bride and bridegroom, intending to have the very best of festivity and good fellowship.

Willis, Short, and myself, have been instructed to see personally to the welfare of the bridegroom on this auspicious occasion, and to bring him to church in a fit and proper state of mind. So with a due regard to the responsibility imposed upon us, we start off after breakfast for the bridegroom's house, to make sure that he is not oversleeping himself, or has been seized with a faint-hearted desire to cut and run. We enter the house and salute him. He is sitting in his shirt-sleeves comfortably enjoying some toasted bacon and a dish of tea. I never understood before why some people would talk about a dish of tea; but here was the mystery explained in a most satisfactory manner. The contents of the tea pot had been emptied into the slop-basin, which held about a quart, and stood at his elbow. It served in the place of cup and saucer, with the additional advantage that the fluid therein arrived at a moderate degree of temperature within a reasonable time. Of milk there was none; a tea-spoon was absent; but for the purpose of stirring, the fork or knife-handle served equally well. To quench his thirst he raises the bowl to his lips by placing his thumb upon the rim, and extending his first and second fingers to grasp it underneath. Having drunk, and unmindful of his clean shirt, he, by the force of habit, draws his sleeve across his mouth. Then, remembering his manners, stoops down and finishes the operation with the edge of the table-cloth, as his betters were wont to do before table-napkins were invented. A dish of tea! The phrase is, after all, most appropriate, and sanctioned by present custom. To my mind it had always appeared to refer to the time when certain of my forefathers, who had been presented with a small parcel of tea, then costing twelve or fourteen shillings a pound, had boiled it in water, drained it, and throwing the water away, served it up to table with a little salt and pepper. After duly finishing the dish of leaves they declared that it was no great sight superior to a bit of cabbage. A veritable dish of tea! What digestions they must have possessed!

To return, however, to our bridegroom. Willis and Short had been holding converse with him, and it was decided that we should call again in about an hour's time. He had, he declared, to clean himself, while he also expected the arrival of his sister to do his hair, and to put the finishing touches to his toilet. We took a stroll through the village, being occasionally greeted with cheers by certain small urchins who appeared anxious to find some outlet for their excitement. Then we passed on to the bridge over the river, and decided to wile away the time by sitting on the parapet to enjoy a morning pipe. On returning to James's cottage we found that we were yet before time. He was sitting on a chair in the road outside his cottage door with a towel over his shoulders and his chin well lathered, undergoing the operation of being shaved at the hands of a neighbour. We accordingly pass on, unwilling to disturb so important a rite. When we next return James appears the very pink of perfection. His Sunday-go-to-meeting garments have been brushed with zealous care; a large blue tie adorns his breast; his face is red and shining, the combined effects of soap and elbow grease; his hair is plastered tight down upon his head and has been liberally anointed with pomatum, which trickles down his neck, as the oil did on to the beards of the priests of old. We heartily congratulate him on being got up to the nines, and inform him that the only thing now lacking to complete his equipment is the addition of a button-hole. He acquiesces in the correctness of the observation, and we consequently tell him that the article in question is already waiting his appearance at Mr Hillyard's. Arrived there we take him to the smoking-room, and beg him to be seated; while Willis proceeds to press upon him an enormous sunflower, with the assurance that it is the most correct thing possible. His face is the most splendid picture of uncertainty. He cannot at all tell whether it is merely some of Willis's chaff, or whether it may possibly be the last thing out so to do. However, I take upon myself to relieve his uncertainty, and inform him that one of the young ladies, now staying in the house, has prepared a beautiful bunch for his button-hole. In a few minutes Miss — appears with a fine nosegay of scarlet geraniums set round a yellow calceolaria, and fringed with geranium leaves, the which nosegay she proceeds to pin upon his coat to his great satisfaction. He ventures to ask how Molly – his Mary – does this morning, and is informed that she is quite nervous and shy at the thought of meeting him, upon which announcement he appears to be somewhat taken aback, but observes 'that he's sure 'er needn't be, 'er hadn't used to when 'ee wur a-courting o' 'er,' a remark which does not fail to elicit signs of approval. At this juncture Mr Hillyard enters the room, and greets James with congratulations concerning the fine day for the ceremony, and so forth.

'And now, James, what's the special weakness this morning? he enquires.

'Weakness, zur?' is the answer. 'I doan't know fur 'urn as I's aware of.'

'Well, but, James, you must have summat to keep you up to the mark, you know; you'll never get through in style if you don't. What's it to be, James?'

'Oh, well, I don't know, zur.'

'Ay, but I do, James. Come, Mr Darke, and we will get James a glass of something that will set him as fit as possible for the wedding.'

So away goes the kindly old gentleman, followed by myself. A jug of cider and a glass being brought him, he proceeds to pour into the glass whisky nearly up to the 'pretty,' and to add thereto cider to fill it.

'Why, that'll choke him,' I say.

'Choke him? Oh dear no! James will drink that down without winking. It's most excellent tipple, and will put him as right as possible for the trials of the day.'

We take James his glass, which surely enough he empties with great satisfaction, remarking that the cider therein contained is 'summat different from what he've been used to in the harvest field, but 'tain't none the worse for that.'

It is now time to march to church to await the arrival of the bride; so Willis, Short, and myself form ourselves into a body-guard to protect the gallant bridegroom to that destination. We find that the church is already considerably occupied by a congregation mostly consisting of women and children from the village, who take the greatest possible interest in the proceedings. The blushing bride soon arrives, escorted by her bridesmaids and female friends, and carrying a bouquet about a foot in diameter. The clergyman having come, the knot is quickly tied; for better, for worse, richer and poorer, two more have been joined as one.

Having successfully run the gauntlet of innumerable volleys of rice, the bridal party finds itself seated in full enjoyment of the wedding breakfast. Mr Hillyard rises to propose the health of the happy pair.

'James has got a capital missus, and I think Mary has got a first-rate husband — I don't say master, because that's a matter we don't know about yet. It strikes me they're an uncommon good pair for G.O. harness. If Mary cooks a dinner for her husband as well as she's cooked mine, all I can say is James 'll have nothing to grumble at; and if James looks after his missus as well as he's looked after my bis'ness, why, Mary shouldn't have anything to complain about. I've known both of

them for some time now, and I've always found them straightforward folk, who've done well by me, and I only hope as they'll do well by themselves and by one another. If they ain't happy together, why, it strikes me 'twill be their own faults, for I'm sure they ought to be. I shan't keep you any longer. Here's a health to the bride and bridegroom; may they be as happy as they know how. Here's health and good luck to ye both, with three times three.' Mr Hillyard concluded amid the ringing cheers of his audience, who rose to their feet and drained their glasses to the health and happiness of the newly-married couple.

The subsiding enthusiasm discovers James mopping his face with a large red and yellow handkerchief, and giving utterance the while between his closed teeth to that peculiar hiss which grooms use when rubbing down horses. A dig in the ribs from his wife brings him to his feet with a start.

'Zur and leddies,' he begins; but comes to a sudden stop.

'Hear, hear!' resounds from all sides.

'Well, zur and — leddies, I bean't no hand at speachy-making, but I thanks 'ee, and Mary 'er thanks 'ee all, zur and leddies — and you genelmen,' looking round upon the male members as an afterthought, 'for our health. The first time 's ever I seed Molly – my Mary, I means – her wur a-dressed up a-gwine to church. I'd been out round a-looking at the owld yeows, and as I yeard a futstep a-coming down the road, I looked over hedge and seed her. Her were quite like a pictur', 'er were. That's the theave as ud suit I, says I to myself. 'Twur summat of a mily day, and her wur a-holding of hers dress up smartish, and showed ——'

'Thur, never thee mind what 'er showed,' interposed Mary, 'but get on wi' what thee's got to say without talking of me.'

'Zur an' leddies,' continued James, receiving the reproof with all due humility. 'Us do thank 'ee for the mony good things as you've a-done by we. I allus says as when a maister do do well by ers workfolk, as the workfolk do do well by 'ee. Our maister do do well by hisen an' we's trys t' accommadate 'ee as best us can. If ern on us had to bide to whoam fur a bit as ain't quite the thing wi' the reumatiz, or a bit o' complant in ers inside, our maister do come to see arter un an' see what's wrong wi' un, and tells un whaat to do. Well, zur an' leddies an' you genelmen, we trys to do well by such a maister, an' we hopes as 'ees prosperus, an' we likes un to get on an' be happy. And zur an' leddies an' you genelmen, you see what our maister's a-done for we, for I an' Molly — my Mary, I means; and I tells 'ee, zur an' leddies an' you genelmen, as us thank 'ee — me 'an Mary do — for the way as you've a-done by we, an' us wishes 'ee all happiness an' good fortin', and if so be as there be ar' a man as wants to zay ought agin 'ee, zur, I'd like to zee 'ee cum vorrud — I ood — just. Well, zur, I proposes yer very good 'ealth, us thanks 'ee for all yer kindness, an' wishes 'ee all good luck,' and James resumes his seat amid thundering applause.

It is needless to describe the enthusiasm with which the toast of Mr Hillyard's health was drunk, nor the thanks returned, nor the other speeches made on this momentous occasion. The last I saw of the happy pair was being escorted to the carriage, which drove off amid showers of rice and old shoes.

So the carriage turns the corner out of sight, and as we stand listening we can hear the cheers and shouts of the villagers while it is wending its way to the station.

CHAPTER 10

TWO HUNDRED POUNDS APIECE FOR 'EM

The facts set forth in the following sketch were narrated to me by Mr Hillyard during my stay with him.

'So 'er wants I to come to 'er, do 'er, Martha?' said Mrs Rimmer. 'An' 'er's took mortal bad, is 'er?'

''Er do want 'ee, Mrs Rimmer, very bad 'er do. Me and Mary have a-bin-a-doing arl us can for 'er; but it don't sim no ways right Mrs Rimmer, an' I do hope as yer'll come along an' gie we a bit o' help. Poor thing, yer know, 'er'd ought to ha' the doctor; but 'er can't afford to pay fer urn, and 'tis four mile to fetch un, and a shocking wet night. But you're a'most as good as any doctor, Mrs Rimmer, if yer'll come along an' don't mind the wet; 'tain't so very fur, yer know.'

'Oh! doan't 'ee say no more, Martha, I'll come soon as I can, I will, though I be most t'owld for this sort 'o thing. I bean't what I'd used to be, Martha, yer know. I'se 'fraid I's but a poor sowl now. Time was when I wouldn't a-minded such a job, Martha, but I bean't up to't now; but I'll come tho', Martha. Set 'ee down whiles I gets ready. There's Rimmer, ee'll be back bimeby; fact, I doan't justly know why er ain't 'ere afore, but s'pose he's stoppin' back fer sommat. I mun set the pleace a bit right-like for 'im, Martha, and put things wher er can find 'um like. Er'll want ers vittles when er comes whoam, and er'll find 'um there ready. I'se had a bit and a sup mysel', I couldn't wait for un.

'Tis six o'clock now, Martha, and 'twere one o'clock when er went away 'ere-from. Come on, Martha; blow the candle out. There now, 'er can light un at the vire. Shet the dure, Martha, I can't lock un 'cos of Rimmer; er must bide wi'out; there's nought to tempt no one in there. Gie' us a 'and, Martha; 'tis plaguey dark, I can't see a yard afore me. How the rain do druv agin one! We mun be quick; I must call into Mrs Ring's, Martha, to tell 'er whur I be a-gwine, so she can tell Rimmer when er comes whoam.'

Six o'clock of a mid-winter's evening; wind, rain, cold, and darkness predominate; a shelter, however humble, is a godsend on such a night, and so thinks William Rimmer as he stops before his cottage. 'No light in the winder; missus out, I'se afeard. Whur the neame o' wunder can 'er be such a night as this?'

He enters. 'Hallo, missus! missus, I zay! Jane! Joan! Jine Rimmer, be y'inside? No 'er ain't, I s'pose; 'ere's the candle sot on the table. 'Er wouldn't be leaved 'ere if 'er was anywheres about. I'd best git un lighted and thease 'ere coat off, and get m' a mouthful o' bread and a cup of tay. Wunder where 'ers to as 'er beant to whoam? Mun be sommat queer as calls 'er 'way such a night as this. 'Tain't no babby-job, is't? 'Er've a-give that there babby-job up some time now; 'er be t'owld fur that there, 'er be t'owld; 'tis ter much on't fer er. Wonder whos'n 'tis, if so be as 'tis. Caleb's? Noa, not just 'it, I count. Zadakiur's? Noa, 'tain't hiss'n nether, fur I come down thur bye, and I should 'a seen that there, if so be as 'twere. War'n I know whos'n 'tis! 'Tis Meark's wi' twins, zure as life! a-having a skeandalous bad time on't, and so they've a-fetched my missus. Meark, poor twoad, if it's twins will ha' fifteen, 'od bless un, and two er burried besides. Ay, and I've a-had nine myself, I and my owld 'ooman, but thay be all a-vled here-vrom; I 'ouldn't let nurn on 'um bide about 'ere along o' the varm-work. 'Tain't no use, that yain't. There's too many about now as can't git work. These 'ere times with hard doos fur farmers, and wi' the 'cheenery and zo on, there ain't the volks a-wanted as there'd used to be. What'll come on't, I can't zay; 'bout two men to yeach varm 'twill be soon, and the country will be sad lonesome, and what wi' the great Hill varm as is idle, and they volks a-gwine to leave Squr-Ditch, and

Farmer Weyman a-torking o' givin' up hissen, I doan't see as wur thur'll be work fur we sort of volk soon.'

'Hello, Mrs Ring, be that you? Whur's the missus to, d'ye know?'

'Ay, 'er looked in on we as 'er went along by, and 'er told I to tell 'ee, when so be as yer comed whoam, as 'er'd a-gone down to see to young John's wife, along o' Martha, 'er 'ad.'

'Oh, John's wife; ah, I clean forgot 'ee. I thought must be a babby job, and I says to myself, I says, thur's Caleb's and Zadakiur's, and then I thought 'twarn't they nether, 'twere Meark's. Young John's wife, is't? 'Is wife is but a poor sort o'crittur ad best – servant-mead, warn't 'er, afore John took up wi' she? Servant-mead, in the townd? Ah, they gits too much vittles and too little work to do for the wife o' we poor volks. Whatyever did er want to teak up wi' a poor, finicking, white-faced thing like that fur, I can't a-while to think. Why didn't er teak a buxom, red-faced country wench as 'ud a-done summat for un? 'Er'll allus be plagued, 'er 'ull, 'o thease jobs; shouldn't wonder if this 'ere doan't go most tor'd vinishing o' she, and 'tis the fust un, too.'

'Well, Willum, 'tis to be a-hoped as 'twon't an' your missus, her'd used to be a very good un an' very keind, 'er was, to other volk when 'er was a-wanted. Maybe 'twill be arl right.'

'Yer ain't a-yeard nowt about it since 'er left?'

'Noa, I ain't; 'tain't many volks as do travel abroad sech a night as this un.'

'When did 'ee zay as 'er went 'ere-from?'

'Jest 'bout six it wur.'

'Well, 'tis about a nour an' arf since 'er went 'ere-vrom; an' yer wants to git back whoam, I reckon . . .'

'Well, I'd sort o' better, now, Willum.'

'So I'll jist step down thur a bit an' see if I can yere owt. Maybe as John won't a-mind a-having some one to spake to un just a minit.'

'Er won't mind a owld mon like thee, Willum, as won't git a-meaking no caddle.'

'It doan't rain as 't did,' opening the door; 'but et's as dark as iver can be, I'll light the lanthern an' kear wi' me. 'Twill be better gwine thur-with.'

William steps out into the night, convoys Mrs Ring to her home, and proceeds on his way. Dividing the village into two parts runs the line of railway, across which a pathway leads. William takes the pathway; and as he steps upon the metals, he happens to cast the lantern-light up and down the line. What is that which its rays strike against? 'Tis a woman's dress, and his heart gives a leap within him. He goes up, turns the body over, and casts the lantern-rays on the face. With a groan he lets the head fall; he had looked on the dead face of his wife. She whom he had left, not many hours before, in the best of health, is now lying across the track with her body nearly severed in twain!

The court is crowded, and here into the witness-box steps William Rimmer. He has aged very much lately, and his stoop is more apparent. When a couple have been married nearly forty years, and have lived together, day by day and month by month, a life in which there have been but few gleams of sunshine – a life of toil varied by the fewest possible days of pleasure – that couple, especially when descending the hill together, with no one but themselves for themselves, must become part and parcel of each other's lives. For that couple to be torn violently asunder by a sudden and tragic calamity, is the hardest possible blow to the survivor — a blow whose force can scarcely be lessened, no matter what money compensations he may happen to obtain. William Rimmer was 'a-lawyering' the company. A death had occurred at that crossing some twelve months before; and the company had been severely censured for not constructing a tunnel under the line. William was endeavouring to obtain damages for this neglect. In answer to his counsel, he states:

'My wages be but nine shilling a week.'

'And what did your wife earn?'

'Nought but a trifle; poor soul! 'er warn't able to do a sight!'

Mr Hillyard, who happened to be his master, was called into the witness-box. He saw well enough that William had made a mistake in thinking to get more damages by appealing to the commiseration of the jury rather than making out the best possible account of himself. Questioned as to William Rimmer's wages, he puts them at fourteen shillings a week. Says the opposing counsel: 'You say the man's wages are fourteen shillings a week; he puts them at nine shillings. Don't you think he knows what he gets?'

'And don't you think I know what I pay?' is the retort. 'I've got all the items here. If you want all the ins and outs of the great labour question, I'm ready to give them to you.'

'That'll do; you may sit down.'

William was only getting nine shillings a week at the time; but he had forgotten a rent-free house and garden, his extra money in hay and harvest, his money for piece-work, his chain of 'tater-ground ready worked, his cider all the year round, and his numerous perquisites, and it was the worst piece of work he ever did to try to make himself out a worse-off man than he was. But how much agitation has resulted from that same forgetfulness which didn't reckon as wages anything not paid in cash; and not always that when it was an extra!

Around the village inn that evening is gathered a considerable crowd of people, waiting to hear the result of the day's trial, and eagerly discussing the various features of the case. One side avers that William won't get naught 'cause the woman ought to 'a looked where 'er was gwine, and not 'a ventured on the line.

The other side expresses the amount that will be awarded to him in all figures, the total being influenced partly by their own wishes in such a case, and partly by pure imagination.

A trap is seen approaching rapidly along the road, and one of the occupants waves his hat. A lusty cheer breaks forth from the crowd, for they know that William has won. 'Hurrah for Willum!' 'Stand treat, Willum!' 'How much is't, old man!!'

'Two 'undred pound!'

'Hear that, naybours! hear that!' yells the blacksmith, 'two 'undred pound for ers missus as were runned auver. Two 'undred pound! Willum, thee'lt live a genelman now, and won't 'sociate wi' the likes o' we.'

'Two 'undred pound!' yelled a shrill-voiced virago, noted in the village as the tyrant of her lord — a poor lame little tailor — whom she often pursued out of the house with a good thrashing. 'Two 'undred pound! two 'undred pound! Why, arl the men o' Sholton 'll *meake* thayer wives bide on the line till they be runned auver if they can git two 'undred pound apiece for 'em.'

'Strikes me, missus, as some on 'em will meake 'em bide vor two 'undred pence, and glad, too, if they wur sure o' being shut on'em wi'out no consequenz.'

'Willum,' says an old chum, 'Willum, 'ave 'ee got the quine all safe?'

'Noa I arn't, Garge; they'se bin and 'peeled, lyjer says; but er tells I as 'twill be all the same, and I's sure to get it.'

'Willum, it strikes I as we've hollered a bit too soon. I'm most afeard on't'

And William never did get his two hundred pounds. Acting on the advice of his lawyer, he agreed to settle for one hundred pounds and costs, rather than risk the uncertainty of an appeal. One hundred pounds was the consolation which the poor old man got for the loss of a tried and faithful wife — a loss which is to a poor man — unable to get any other helper — a far harder blow than to a rich one. One hundred pounds! Many there are who do not get as much!

CHAPTER 11

COTTAGE INTERIOR

It so happened that Willis was not a very regular attendant at church. In country districts, where every man's identity is known to all the parish, every action of every individual is commented upon by the neighbours, with a degree of eagerness amazing to, but not experienced by, those who dwell in populous towns.

Such comments, in fact, alternating with the state of the weather, the prospects of the crops, and the ailments of the cattle, sheep, and pigs, form the staple conversation of the majority of rural dwellers; and this conversation is their only way of expressing to one another that they have not lapsed utterly out of existence.

To attend church is a sure passport of respectability. If only he attend church once a week — in the morning especially; the afternoon is not so respectable, for the working classes go then — if only he wear a black coat and a reverent and devout air, he may break all the commandments, except the sixth and the eighth, and yet stand higher in the estimation of his neighbours, than if he kept the commandments and kept away from church.

One Sunday, instead of joining the rest of the party in their excursion to church, I accompanied Willis on an errand which was not unfrequently his wont, namely, to visit some of the sick old people in the village and read to them. Today he went to old Mother Gregory, who was bedridden. How I remember being struck with this visit to Mother Gregory. Terribly thin and shrunken, she lay upon a small bed in one corner of the room, with nothing but a counterpane to cover her. Her daughter, who attended her, had to sleep in the same bed with her at night. The room was small — very small — leaving but little space round the bed; it had only one chair in it, and nothing but the bare boards. The window was high up and unopenable, and there was a piece of paper pasted over the hole which the doctor had made with his fist in order to obtain fresh air. But there was one object above all others which attracted my attention, and that was, the only picture in the room — a large, old-fashioned engraving hanging directly opposite the patient. It represented the fate of the damned. Standing on the right-hand side, on a large ledge of rock, was his satanic majesty, in all the honours of hoof, barbed tail, horns, and a hideous countenance. (I remember another such portrait of his majesty in a neighbouring church-window by no means old; but there they have painted him a bright green, with fish-like scales, and they have made him carry his tail over his arm as an officer does his sword.) In front of him are several smaller imps — imitations of himself — trundling wheelbarrows full of the unsaved, and pitching them unceremoniously over a small precipice, after the fashion of navvies tipping earth for an embankment. Below, about the middle, is a blazing bonfire of large faggots, in which are the victims in all the attitudes of extreme torture. To the right of this are sundry imps with pitchforks, who spear the sinners like carters do wheat-sheaves, and, raising them aloft, pitch them upon the fire. To the left is another collection of devils dancing hand in hand around the fire, laughing, jeering, and mocking at the tortures of the wicked.

This picture was evidently the old woman's pride — a sheet-anchor of her faith — and she called my attention to it. 'There, sir, there you sees what'll come to they as be wicked. When Mr Marsh' (the parson) 'do come in he allus tells I all about that, and how 'twill all happen exactly like that there to them as don't do as they'd ought to. There wur old John Spence — a married man with a sight of childer he be — he got a-carrying on as er'd no business to wi' Molly Green's daughter, and one day as his mussus comed in to see how I wur a-getting on I told 'er, yer knoaw, sir, as how 'twere, and how there wur one of the faces of they there in the barrows 'zactly like hissen, and I knowed as how 'ee wur a wicked man, and that's wur er'd go to. 'Er screamed out terrible, and then 'er up and shook I in the bed, calling I an owld witch, and 'er never bin aneist I sinz; and now 'er do allus call my darter neames when 'er goes down street.'

I should have thought that such a picture had been nothing more than a relic of medieval times, and had I not heard from the parson of this very parish a graphic description of the place, where all but the elected (who, I believe, consisted only of himself and another in the parish) would go to, I should not have believed that such thoughts and ideas could be prevalent among the rustic population at the present day, much less that they should be fostered by the clergy.

When Willis entered the room where the old woman lay, he asked her how she was; but before she could reply, her daughter, who was present, broke in. 'Oh, 'ers very bad today; very bad 'er be. I tells 'er, 'er carn't last out much longer.'

'When it pleases the Lard to call me, I shall be ready,' reverently asserted Mrs Gregory to Willis, who assented.

I afterwards remarked to Willis concerning the strong faith of the agricultural classes, that it would be a sad and sorry day when such faith as theirs should be shaken.

'Were I an unbeliever,' said Willis, 'I should think it a most ungracious act to try and undermine such faith as theirs, and take away the comfort which it evidently brings; but did I hold views antagonistic to those with which the majority of the nation is credited, I should expect them to have the same tolerance towards myself.'

'Yes, mother, that be right,' said her daughter, in answer to her last remark, 'an' 'twon't be long afore He do call 'ee, it seems to I. We be gwine,' turning to myself, 'to get her downstairs tomorrow, all ready.'

'Get her downstairs!' I said. 'Whatever for?'

'Well, yer see, if 'er don't get downstairs while 'er's able, an' if be chance 'er died up here, 'twould be a sad plaguey job on it. There's no coffin as can be got down these 'ere stairs and out into street, so 'tis allus best for we sort of folk to get downstairs to die. I 'low as 'tis time mother wur a-got downstairs.'

I said nothing, being rather taken aback at discussing such matters

before the person principally affected. The daughter, however, continued: 'I've been a-trying to get 'er to say wur 'er will be buried. This
yere house did once belong to Dean parish, an' her folks do mostly rest
in Dean churchyard, which is rather better nor a mile an' a half
yere-from, an' 'er do sorter want to go there 'erself; but I says to her as
'er 'd ought to go to the churchyard of the parish as 'er's now in, as it is
so much handier, yer see. Mother,' she continued, turning to the
patient, 'yer ought to say which 'tis to be; 'twould be plaguey hot this
yere weather for them as got to carr'ee all the way to Dean, let alone as
the parson wouldn't like it.'

'Never mind that now, Jane,' said Willis, 'let me read to your mother
a bit, and then we must be going home.'

Willis commenced reading to the old woman, at which she was much pleased, and thanked him for coming to see her. As he took his leave she cautioned him about going down the stairs, which were very dark and steep, besides one or more boards being 'broke out of 'em' which the landlord had promised to put right this six months, but had not done so. Her warning was, however, quite in vain, for, before he had got halfway down, Willis tripped up, and, swearing against stairs, landlord, and all, went down head-first. It so happened that just at that moment someone was starting to come up; and Willis, colliding with him, drove his head into the other's chest, which happened to save his own skull from forcible contact with the wall. Recovering himself, Willis finds that he is face to face with the clergyman, who had called in on his way from church. He begs pardon profusely; but his reverence was put out — as well he might be — at being utilised as a buffer in such a manner. Furthermore, perhaps, he was not too well pleased to find one who was very irregular in his attendance at church visiting the sick poor in their own houses; and besides this, had not Willis sworn, and that, too, on a Sunday? Making no allowance for the exigencies of the situation, his reverence forthwith commences to rate Willis on the enormity of his sins; but Willis cuts the matter unceremoniously short by making an undignified retreat; while I am perforce compelled to follow suit. I am sorry to say that when we get away from the house, on our road home, we both indulge in a hearty burst of laughter.

CHAPTER 12

PAST WORK

A nicely-built, tidy cottage stood a little way back from the road. Part of its front was hidden by ivy; part by a trailing rose, which also fell in clusters over the small porch. There was a little wicket set in the hedge facing the road; and against it stood a rather rough, straggling yew-bush, which served to partly screen the cottage from curious eyes. On either side of the path which led up to the door were some flowers; and behind these again were the necessary vegetables, for space is too valued to allow much ground to be occupied as a flower-garden. I pushed open the wicket, and, advancing into the porch, knocked against the door, which was opened to be by a woman rather past middle age — though she scarcely looked it — a clean, tidy woman with an honest, kindly face.

'How's George today?' I inquired.

'Ah, sir, he bean't no better, not no better at all; I be a'most afeared as ee'll be took from us. I'se afeared er ain't much longer fur this sinful world; but the Lord knows best.'

'Who's 'ee got thur, missus?' cried a voice from within. 'Who be it?'

'Come in, sir, an' see un,' said his wife.

'Oh, Maister John, 'tis you, is't? I 'a heard as you wur down to these parts, an' thought, mebbe, as yer'd look in. 'Tis a sight of whiles since I set eyes upon 'ee, an' belike I shan't do it agin.'

'Oh, cheer up, George, cheer up,' I replied. ''Tis no use to give in too soon. We must set 'ee right among us with the doctor's help, and have you about again soon at work. But how are you today?'

'Ah, zur, I be turble with the rumatiz — turble bad I be. When I do lift me yand to me yead,' he said, suiting the action to the word; 'it do hurt I most skeandalous — most skean-da-lous. Oh-ho-ho, Lord a massy!' he yelled with pain.

'Well, it is bad, George; but don't lift it up.'

'Oh, it do ketch I turble bad, Maister John. When I be a set here be the fireside, it don't sim nothink amiss; but, when I do lift un up,' again going through the performance; 'it do make I holler. Ho! Ho! Ho-o-o-o!' And again he screamed loud enough to be heard all over the parish.

'Well, well, George, but please don't lift it up; let it stop quiet,' I said. 'I can see well enough that it hurts you.'

'Ah, sir, that's just what the doctor do say,' put in the wife; 'er says, says 'ee, "Garge," er says, as soon as ever er do come into door, "Garge, don't 'ee go fur to lift yer arm up, today"; but sure as life Garge won't mind about it, an' it will lift un up afore 'ee goes away, an' it do allus make un holler scandalous. 'Tis mortal bad fur un, sur; I'se afraid as er won't get about again, to be o' any 'count on fur work.'

'Oh, there's no telling, Mrs Merrit - there's no telling. You must cheer up; doctors can do a great deal nowadays,' I replied.

'Ay, sure enow 'um can; but 'tis in the hands o' the Lard.'

I sat down in an old-fashioned wooden armchair, on the other side of the fire, and talked to George awhile. The room was small but scrupulously neat and clean — paved, as is usual in cottages, with large rough flags — somewhat ill-lighted from a small window, and some of that light taken up by several pots of flowers at the bottom, curtains partly drawn at the sides, and a valance at the top; the draught from the door was screened by an old high-backed wooden settle; in one corner stood the tall eight-day clock, and close to it the stairs leading to the rooms above; on the other side of the clock was a dresser with plates, cups, and saucers; behind George was a cupboard which served as a larder.

We talked of old times — times when he was strong and well, when he was the foremost and ablest man upon the farm, a pattern to all the juniors — times, alas, which I'm afraid will not be his again. Do what I would, the conversation became melancholy, and I could scarce cheer it. Any little joke or pleasantry seemed most terribly forced, and altogether out of harmony with the surroundings. He still had a keen and lively interest in hearing what was going on upon the scene of his old labours — which grounds were to be 'clopped into whate, dy-year' — how many quarters the eight-acre ground had yielded when it was threshed, and what was the weight — and did master get a good price for it, considering how the times was? Many of his qestions took me entirely out of my depth, and I was not able to answer them satisfactorily. He had quite forgotten that I had for the last few years spent nearly all my time in a town. Then he got to talking about the tenant who had taken my father's farm, whereon he had worked years and years ago, before he came to Mr Hillyard's, which he had done after my father had given up the farm and left the neighbourhood. It was there that he first became acquainted with me, and the best gleam of sunshine that came into his eyes that day shone while he was repeating the oft-told tale of some of my boyish pranks.

The day was now drawing to a close, and we could scarce see each other's face; so I got up, and shaking hands with him and his wife, took my leave. George has altered sadly — very sadly — since I last saw him.

What a change in a short time! For, after all, the time which he called long had been but a year or two.

Ah! George! George! there was a time when thou wast a strong and able man — *primus inter pares* — when thou couldst walk without a stick, and even heavy sack-carrying had not caused thy back to bend. Now thou art bowed down, and thy face — erewhile so full, ruddy, and open — is wrinkled, paled, and almost wizened. Then thou wast able to tire out the strongest among thy fellows during the long days of corn-harvest; now some of the tyros would easily be thy masters. Ah, George! how I remember those days in the corn-field when thou didst sit down for thy 'nunchin' in the burrow of the hedge, throw thy old coat around thee, undo the red handkerchief which held thy bread and cheese, and bring out the big clasp-knife. Didn't I, a little boy then, creep up to thy side — I, who had plenty, ay, and ofttimes more than plenty — and beg for that which had cost thee so much toil, for some of that home-made bread, and that blue-mouldy cheese; and didst thou ever grudge it me? No! No! thou wast pleased to have me by thy side, and to share a portion of thy homely dinner with me; and did not I relish that bread and cheese more than all the dainties of a liberal home? And, then, needs must that I should drink; and thou wouldst bring forth the bottle and fill up a 'tot', and I must wish good luck to thee and the rest, and to the harvest. Perhaps my father would interpose — as, perchance, he had before about that bread and cheese — and thou wouldst make answer: 'Noa, noa, sir; let un drink along o' we, do 'ee now; let un have just a "tot"; 'twon't never hurt un; er shan't ha' but just this un;' thus wouldst thou overcome all objection, and I would drink off the 'tot' with pride, and declare that it was so good, though in truth the cider, which was somewhat 'teart,' would draw up my face, and send a shudder down my back. But I thought it brave and manly to drink it; and thou wast only too pleased that I should have a drop with thee. Ah, George! George! those days will come again no more for either of us; and unless thou hast been more prudent than thy fellows the prospects before thee are but gloomy. Sad, indeed, would it be for thee to end thy days in the workhouse. Idleness was never thy vocation; thou didst always seem to delight in work, and now that thou art unable to do anything the days hang heavy and wearily on thy hands. Thou art no scholar; thou canst neither read nor write; and sitting by the fire in the chimney-corner, or going slowly and wearily abroad leaning on thy stick, can afford thee but the poorest comfort, especially if thou art in pain the while. Rheumatism! rheumatism is the curse of the old people in many a country district. I'm afraid that poor fare and hard cider have much to answer for.

On my return to Mr Hillyard's I reported to him about George.

'Yes,' he said, 'I am afraid that George will not be fit for much more work. I am not able to do much for him. I send him down now and again a slice of meat, and a plate of pudding to help cheer him up at bit. The doctor ordered him a little gin, and I managed to get that allowed to him by the union — but thereby hangs a tale! He used to send in for this gin; and, one day when I went to see him, I asked him if he found much good from it. "'Tain't likely as I should," he replied, and called his wife to bring me the bottle. "Just taste that there, sir." I did so. "It seems to me, George, as there's precious little there but water," I observed. "That's about true," he replied; "but that's how 'tis sent out

from the house. I thought, mebbe, as you was a garding, as you'd ought to know summat about that. 'Tain't right of 'em to send a poor man such stuff as that." "How do you get it?" I said. "Oh, I sends Willum's nipper into town for it, and gi'es him sixpence for fetching it. I can't get it no other way." Well, I took the bottle away with me, and sent him some myself for that week. Then I made inquiries the next time I attended the board. Naturally the gin was not sent from them in that state; but I afterwards learnt that either the messenger, or his mother, or some of them, took most of the poor old man's gin and filled up the bottle with water. It was a mean thing to do to a poor man; and it is needless to say that we have managed to find a better way of supplying him with his gin.'

CHAPTER 13

'TATERS

Mr Hillyard had gone to market; Willis and Short were busy on the farm; so, being left to myself, I took a stroll through the village with eye observant and ear alert for rural sights and sounds.

'How do the 'taters turn out, John?' I exclaimed, as I came to a halt beside the wall, and looked over where he was at work getting up his crop.

'Thur they be; I've zeed mony a better lot, an' I've a-digged mony a wuss crop,' he said to me with stolid astuteness, unwilling to commit himself to a definite opinion either way.

John was somewhat of a character. He was not a native of these parts, for his talk had a different sound to that of the other inhabitants. I was not sure whence he had come; but I always credited him with having emigrated from further west. At any rate his speech had a somewhat astonishing broadness. John possessed a rather melodious, deep, and somewhat sonorous voice — it was essentially a chest voice. He had another peculiarity — which I have also noticed in other countrymen — namely, a habit of uttering sentences which had a great resemblance to blank verse. It was no mere singsong. No! it was much more than that. The sentences of broad dialect given off in his sonorous voice — which, perhaps, heightened the effect — had to my mind — at times, not always, of course — the metrical, rhythmical flow of blank verse. In their sonorousness they reminded me more than anything of the sound of the Greek of Homer's 'Iliad'.

Perhaps Mr Freeman might say that such verse-speech was some-what of a relic of the old Anglo-Saxon poetry — of which he has given us examples in his history — just in the same way as most of the dialect words used by the countrymen are pure Anglo-Saxon, whose pronunciation has scarcely changed this thousand years. The town-dweller who hears the countryman talk of 'yeows,' while he himself says 'ewes,' is wont to smile, think himself a superior being, and to imagine that the ignorant countryman does not know how to pronounce his words properly. As a matter of fact the countryman is using almost pure Anglo-Saxon, while it is he himself who is using a finnicking corruption. But I am wandering.

My interrogation to old John led to our entering into conversation concerning the usual rural topics, and John proceeded to unfold to me a tale concerning his crop of early potatoes. The rhythmical, sonorous manner in which these words fell from him, and the, to me true spirit of poetry which they possessed, impressed them on my memory. I made notes of them soon after leaving him; and now am able to reproduce them for others to judge of their quality. The elision of consonants, the reduplication of vowels, and the trilling of the R, which are the characteristics of some country speech, all served to enhance their melody.

I'd's vine a potch o' taeters 's a mon 'ud wish to zee.
A vinner potch nur ur a mon aroun'.
Thaay wur vorruder nur urn; the naaybors nar a won on 'em cud touch 'em.
I cummed whum won neet summat leate vrom mi wourruk,
An' lukk'd at thaay taeters avore y yad mi ta,
Then thinks I, thaay'd awt to be mowded.
Thur'll be a vrost dyneet, Jorn, says I to mysel',
Thee mun git and mowd thaay taeters arter ta.
'Twur a smortish potch to do, but I bockled to the jub,
An' swatted thur a rum 'un at the wourruk.
'Twur deark 's ar the bag avore I vinished o' the potch.
An' I cudn't zee to hut wi' the how;
But I'd nur a thawt o' gieing out whiles won on 'em remained,
An I leaved nar a taeter unmowded.
But the vrost cummed strait drow the middle on 't,
An' cut the potch right clean a-two.
'Er touched nar a won o' narrer zide o' ut,
But ud hut a leane right drow the middle
Zif a mon had mowd a zwor-r-f* wi' a zyve.

*Thoroughly onomatopoetic in the way he used it. One could really imagine the sweep of the scythe and the swish of falling grass as he rolled this word off his tongue.

CHAPTER 14

A DEAD SHEEP

That evening while returning home, I met a man who'd been a shepherd the greater part of his life, but who, having been able to save sufficient money to take a few odd fields, was now busily engaged in losing his small accumulation.

'How goes it today, shepherd?' I said.

'Oh, Master John, 'tis you, is't? I be right glad to see 'ee, 'tis some time since I 'ad a sight on 'ee. Why, things is but middling, yer know, an' there's one o' th' owld yeows a bit middling today.'

'Oh! that's a bad job; will you have to kill her, do you think?'

'I most expects I shall; 'er doan't sim to mend none. an' I means fur to be in time wi' thic un. One time just arter I'd begun to kip a feaw ship on m' own account, one o' the tegs wur a-took middling. Wall, I said to mysel', thee sims bad-like, but p'raps thee'lt git auver it. Onyways I 'ont gie thee a drunch, vur ef so be I should 'a to kill th', 'twud spile the mate. So I let un bide a bit; an' when I comed back to un zome time arterwards, thur didn't sim much odds in un one way nor t'other. I didn't want fur to lose un if I could help it, and didn't want to kill un, if 'er wur like to git roun', yer knaow. Wall, I thought I'd let un have another chance, an' I'd come and see to un agin pretty soon. However, when I comed back to un, dalled if 'er wurn't a-most djed, an' afore I wur able to git out my knife to kill un, 'er'd gone quite off. "Bost thy kearcass," I zays to un, "why iver's thee gone an' died afore I killed thee!" Wall, I wasn't able to afford to lose the mate, so I cuts 'ers throat quick, an' as 'er couldn't say baa fur 'erself, I sed baa vor un, in case thur wur ar-a-one a-watching me. Then I teaks un accross the ground, an' when I'd a-hung un up in th' woak tree, I starts fur

to git 'ers pelt off, an' to dress un a bit. While I wur to work up comes Master Jonas, the butcher. "Hallo, shepherd," er sed, "what's thee got thur?" "Oh! just a bit o' a casalty ship," I sed. "I seed 'er wur a bit middlin' like, an' so I took and killed un, not to lose the mate.' "What's a-gwine to do wi' un, shepherd?" er says. "Get shut on un somehow," I says to un; "there's a plenty o' volk as 'ull buy un, yer kneaow." "What does 'ee want fur un, shepherd, take un as 'er is?" "A matter o' ten bob," says I. "Ten bob!" er says, "fur that thur djed ship." "Djed ship!" I says, "'er yain't a djed ship, I just a-bin a' killed un." "Killed un, 'ave 'ee," er says; "think I can't see as that thur ship wur djed afore you killed un? Look at the mate," er says. "Tell 'ee what I'll do, I'll gie 'ee three bob for un." "I won't sell," I says. Wall, we bided thur and haggled a smart while, and then er says er'd gie I five bob if I'd gie un a tanner out for luck; but I 'oodn't. "Don't 'ee be so 'nation hard in the mouth," er says; "gie a body a chance to make an honest living." Wall, at last as I bided firm er gied I a matter o' three half-crownds fur un, an' I gied un a bob out for luck. "An' what'll 'ee do wi' un, Master Jonas?" says I. "Do wi' un," er says, "why, put un straight away into my trap, an' that thur as th' inspector don't see I'll sell out to the volks, an' th' rest on't shall go round th' townd to th' owld maids for cats' vittles," er sed; that's what er'd do wi' et.'

CHAPTER 15

THE ELECTION

'Holloa, George!' I said, as I met him on the farm one morning, 'how are you going to vote at the election?' (a bye election to take place in his division of the county).

'Vote, sir? I bean't a-gwine to vote at all.'

'Why's that, George?'

'Why, look'ee yere, sir, the first time's yever I voted — an' I hopes 'twill be the last time — I voted yaller 'cos that thur Brummagem Joe[1] had a-promised all we chaps as voted yaller, as us wer to git dree yearkers an' a keow each on us. The blues said 'twurn't true, but 'corse us thought that 'twere only one o' their tricks. Bill Hanks told we volks straight as he knowed the keows were abroad the bote and were to com up to Gloster; but, says 'ee, "I won't tell 'ee which day they be a-commin' 'cos I be a-gwine down thur fust, yer knaow, to ha' m' pick. I means to ha' a roan un," says 'ee. Wall, yer knaow, the chaps quite over-persuaded owld Dan'l Iles as they'd a-come one day. The chaps got a-telling Dan'l quite sollum-like all about et, an' one on un 'ad a-got hold of a keard, an' er gies un to un an' says, "'Ere, Dan'l," er says, "'ere's the keard as the chap gied I to gie thee. This yere keard's a horder for they keow." "'Tis, is't?" says Dan'l, lookin' at et cute like — nurn on 'em could rade, yer knaow — "an' when be I to vetch un?" "Morrow marning, Dan'l," says thaay. "An' 'a you a got urn?" says Dan'l. "Noa! we ain't, Dan'l, not 'et. Thee bist th' owldest man on the farm, an' thee hast to go a day afore we."

'So owld Dan'l, yer know, starts off fur the bowsen, an' fetches hisself a stick for to drive 's cow back wi'; an' away er goes down the road next marning, right's possible. "Hullo, Dan'l," says the gaffer, a-meeting of un, "whur be aff to so sprack's marning?" "I be aff to vetch my keow, measter," says Dan'l. "Thy keow, Dan'l; whur's they keow, then?" "Oh, the keow as the yallers 'ave a-give to we folks as voted fur 'um, 'er's down to Gloster; I got a ticket fur un." "Let's look at thy ticket, Dan'l. I arn't a-seed one of they afore," say the gaffer. "Yere 'tis, measter," says Dan'l, a-pulling un out of ers breeches pokkut.

'Soon as the maister seed un er bust out a-laffing. "Who gied thee thease, Dan'l?" er says. "What, ain't it a horder?" says Dan'l. "Horder! no that 'tain't, Dan'l, not for ar' a keow, but it's a horder as 'ull suit thee well enow. The keard says, "When empty, return to the X Brewery without delay."" "Daze my buttons, measter! that thur order'd suit I down to the ground, but 'tain't a order for ar' a keow. 'Twere young John as gied un to I, an' I reckons as er 'a bin an' gied I the wrong un; I wun't be putt aff wi' this yere un, I'll go back to 'ee an' 'ave the order for my keow." "Don't be a vule, Dan'l. Thur yein't no order for nar a keow fur thee. 'Tis arl a pack o' their lies." "Oh, ah, measter, you be blue I war'n, an' in course yer don't believe in't, but that thur boss o' the yallers, that thur Brummagen Joe, have a downright promised arl we folks dree yekers an' a keow, an' I knows we be a-gwine to git it. But gie I back that thur keard, measter; if I can't git nar a keow-keard I'll kip that thur un. That's plain enow, I war'n, 'cos you've a-read un out. Yempty! 'zif I wurn't allus yempty when thur's ar a drap o' summat a-gwine. I'll teake thic thur keard to X Brewery, an' I'se war'n I 'on't leave un afore they've a-filled I proper." "'Twon't be not no use, Dan'l," says the gaffer, a-laffing, "this yere keard's only aff a beer barrel. 'Tis the barrel, an' not thee as they wants to vill. Dessay thur yent a site o' odds atween 'ee when liquor's consarned, but I reckon as thee'd best go back an' tackle young John 'bout the keard fur thy keow."

'So owld Dan'l er comes back, yer knaow, an's starts on young John about thic keard, an' in coarse arl them tothers as yerd un plagued un most shemful till er gots ers 'ool up about it arl, turble. I kneows though thur wurn't but feow on's as didn't bleeve but what us 'ud git a keow an' a dree yekers a-took away from the farmers an' a-gied to we. 'Twur just what we'd 'a liked, look'ee, an' that was what sort o' done 't.'

'Rather rough on Daniel to chaff him so badly,' I said, laughing heartily. 'And so you really almost believed about the three acres and a cow?'

'Bleeved it? in course us did. Wun't thur a reg'ler fleet of men-folks got up to look like genelmen a-gwine about the country a-telling arl we to vote yaller cause Joseph 'ud see as we had three yeakers an' a keow? T'other side didn't promise us now't an' as I says to our chaps, says I, "'Tis just this 'ere way, look'ee. Ef yer votes blue yer knows yer gits nowt, but if yer votes yaller there be a chance o' summat."'

'And so you all voted yellow?'

'On course us did, an' got nowt. Soon as ever Brummagen Joe got in er sed er'd never a-promised it. Why er couldn't a-sed it afore beats me; an' now Joe's a-gone blue, an' thur's a job on with they dazed Irish.'²

'You don't care for the Irish, do you?'

'Wall, they don't make no odds to I, they bean't no shapherds; but the day-men don't like thaay as comes amongst 'um sometimes and spiles thur price fur work. Thaay be a poor set o' twoads most on 'um's ever I seed.'

We walked on for some time in silence, but presently, 'I suppose,' he says, 'as there's a lot of pay belonging to this 'ere Parlyment as meakes the gentry all so ager to git intoo't?'

'Do you mean that the Members of Parliament are paid?' I asked.

'Ay, they be, bean't 'um?'

'No, most of them ain't, at least, not in money.'

'How does 'em git it then — in vittles?'

'No, some of them that work very hard get made lords and so on.'

'Lords, do 'um? an' thaay gits the quine?'³

'No, they don't.'

'What meakes 'um want to git into Parliament so for, then, when they could bide at home like genelmen, an' look arter their property an' the folks on it, an' do nowt beseps please themselves?'

'Oh, because they ain't satisfied with attending to their own business, they want to attend to other people's.'

'Ah! that's it, is't? I've knowed that 'ere, now, among the wimmin folk. Some o' ourn be 'nation bad uns fur that; spends more time in their neighbours' housen nor iver thay doos in their own, an' arl just for to meake a bit 'o a 'oonderment an' a caddle. Oh! I understands 'bout the gentry folks now; thay bean't content beseps thaay be Members o' Parlyment a-caddling auver other folkses bus'ness.'

CHAPTER 16

A SIMPLE PICTURE

I had stopped at the gate of a lonely roadside cottage, to speak to a woman about her flowers, the weather, and such-like. While so engaged a queer-looking old man came up to us. His clothes hung about him like sacks, and to my mind could never have been intended for him. His face was bloated and extremely deeply furrowed; and upon his head was a most shocking bad hat. He began talking some gibberish of which I could make neither head nor tail. Then he shouted, gave vent to sundry whoops, and jumped about the road.

'Go away whoam, John, go away whoam!' said the woman.

'Go whoam!' he yelled. 'What's to go whoam for?' Then he mumbled for some time.

'What d'ye say, John?'

'Go away whoam? What's to go whoam for? Look 'ee yere, I've had nur a bite this two days, nur a bite, not a mouthfu' o' vittles, and there's noan to whoam. Go away whoam! What's to go whoam for? I'se had some drink, nought else but a drop o' drink, and 'cept for the drink I'm as yempty as a water-tub wi' the bottom out. Yempty, yempty; quite yempty! nar a little bit inside me! What's to go whoam for? there ain't nought ther! Oh! ho! ho!' he cried, as he shook himself in his clothes till I thought they'd part company with him. 'Oh! ho! ho! gie us a y'appenny, maister, to buy bread wi'! You looks full enow.'

'Noa doan't 'ee, sir, er won't spend it in bread, er'll on'y git ut into un. 'Tain't no use t' encourage un,' said the woman. 'Go away whoam, John!'

'Go away whoam? Look at this 'ere owld jim-crow o' mine,' he

cried, with beautiful inconsequence; 'look at this 'ere owld jim-crow,' plucking off his hat, whirling it round and throwing it in the air. 'How d'ye thenk I come by 'ee; how d'ye thenk, now? I seed an owld skur-crow out in Farmer Giles' field as he'd a-put up; I says to un, says I, "Thee's got a sight better yat on the top of thy yead nor ever I 'as, dalled if I 'oon't swop wi' 'ee," I cried. Just then up comes the farmer. "John," says 'ee, "John, what's thee a-doing a-messing wi' that thur skur-crow?" er said. "Maister," says I, "this 'ere genelman," I says, "'ave a-got a dalled sight better yat on's yead nor ever I 'as, an' I wur a-gwine to swop wi' un," I says. "Swop away, John, if yer be so a-minded," er says; "make a swop wi' un of the rest of thy cloathes," er says, and went away laffing! But I 'oodn't ha' nurn but thease 'ere jim-crow. Whaugh! who! ho! yar! What sort o' genelman be you, maister? Missus, who's this genelman, an' wher' do 'ee come from? What's 'ee a-doing yere? 'Ee ain't no good on 'ere. Genelmen should bide away from folks like we as ain't got a sup inside 'em.'

After treating us to sundry other harangues, interspersed with mumblings, the ancient took himself off. I turned to the woman to ask what she knew about him.

'Oh! er's a sad, wicked old chap. He've allus spent all's ever 'ee 'ad in drink, an' none can't gi'e un a copper now but er must get it into un. What 'ee an' ers poor owld missus do live on I doan't know. They never seems to ha' a mossul in the 'ouse, an' theer's hardly a stick or a rag in it. 'Er's got no cloathes, not no 'count, only just a feaw owld rags, bits o' bag-stuff an' the like for to cover 'erself wi'. When 'ee do go whoam, 'ee do sard 'er most sheamful. Er's harmless enow when he comes yereby, er 'oodn't do none mischy, but 'tis oddses to that when er's whoam. When I furst cum yere to live, er frited I most turble furst time I seed un. Er came up yere an' hollered, an' stroked about this 'ere road, an' hopped about, an' figgered wi' ers fistes a rum un; but er's quite harmless. I doan't take no notice o' un now. Poor owld sowl, belike er ain't 'ad no vittles ever so long, an' his poor wife be mor'n half starved all 'er time. They wun't 'low un nowt from the parish 'cos er's such a skandalous owld twoad, er'd drink it every drop; an' ers wife woan't go in to workus, says 'er'd sooner rot else nor go there, for arl as 'ee do treat 'er so sheamful. As fur 'ee, er do go round to the farmers as ee've a-worked for, an' they do get giving on un a drop of drink, an' now an' then belike a crust. A very little drink do get in 's yead an' make un silly, specially when there's no vittles in un. That's what 'ee've a-bin doing to-day, the silly, wicked owld fool.'

This picture is not overdrawn. Now and again in out-of-the-way places, far from the high-road, stowed away out of sight, perhaps behind some wood, you may come across a tumble-down tenement, whose occupants are in a somewhat similar condition to that described by the old woman. It is a wonder how they exist. The man nearly all his time silly with a very little drink and less food, the woman half starved, with scarcely a rag to cover her. Barely any furniture in the house. How they manage to live and pay their rent is a mystery to which they alone have the clue.

CHAPTER 17

IN A
PUBLIC-HOUSE
KITCHEN

Has the reader ever attempted to picture what kind of men and women were the squires, farmers, labourers, and their kith and kin in the days of Elizabeth, and tried to find a parallel to them in the people of the present time? We make rapid progress now. The modern squire is a man far more refined than was the squire of even a century ago, while he lives in greater comfort than did Queen Elizabeth herself. The better class of farmers — the great sheep-breeders of the south and midlands of Englands — are men generally of good education, and in their turn superior to the squires of Elizabeth's time in all that we call civilisation. To find a parallel to the squires and farmers of the sixteenth century, we must now seek it among the very lowest, least-educated farmers, and among the agricultural labourers. Rough in manner and speech, but withal good-tempered and not unkind — fond of joking, practical joking especially, and somewhat unable to appreciate the injury it may inflict on his victims — shrewd and hard-headed in his own way of business, but very often with the poorest, or sometimes with no education at all — fond of alcoholic drinks, and with a strong, firm belief that they are the most nutritious and strengthening article which he can consume — intolerant of anything to which he has not been accustomed, self-opinionated, and almost invariably lamenting the degeneracy of the present times, compared to what they were in his youth — a member of the classes which I have mentioned presents to my mind the nearest social parallel we can at present obtain to the squires and farmers of Elizabeth's time.

Now of what are these remarks *à propos*? A trifling circumstance often turns our thoughts into channels totally unconnected therewith; and so in this case.

If we consider the bigoted religious intolerance of the sixteenth century, when Catholic burnt Protestant, and Protestant burnt Catholic with all the possible signs of most unchristian hatred — when witches were hunted out and zealously sought for — when to do anything at all new would be to incur the imputation of being leagued unto the devil — we can scarcely conceive that we are dealing with the men of the same period which produced Shakespeare. If, however, we consider the type of men who formed the staple population of country districts, if we consider what were their probable opinions and ideas as judged from those whom we have set as their parallels at the present day, we can begin to understand the matter. But again, what a source of wonder it will be to the future historian to consider how little the progress and civilisation of the nineteenth century has affected the almost uneducated countryman, and to know that were he unrestrained by the law of the land, and were the necessary power in his hands, he would probably burn all those who differed materially from him in opinion, and would include in the bonfire everything new that had been introduced since his time, with especial references to the farmer's machinery — reapers, binders, and the like — and would take care not to omit such obnoxious institutions as the School Board, and all its officials, together with the vaccination officer, the nuisance inspector, and any one else who exercises a control upon his indiscriminating liberty! Having by this time probably exhausted the patience of even the most good-tempered reader, I will proceed to narrate the following incident of aversion to anything new. I had planned that I would finish up my holiday by a walking tour, and the weather appearing fairly favourable to my project, I at length took leave of Mr Hillyard and his kind hospitality. I had prevailed on Willis, who was very good-natured, to accompany me on my first day's journey, stay the night, and run back by train in the morning. During the afternoon, in the course of our walk, which lay across some rather open down-like fields, we came upon some fungi, called by the uninitiated toadstools, frogsmeat, or any other appropriate epithet; I knew, however, well enough concerning their good qualities, and Willis himself, having had some training concerning such matters at Mr Hillyard's, was not ready to flatly contradict me upon the subject.

What we found were in fact the champignon, the horse-mushroom, and the large puff-ball; all of which we accordingly gathered, intending to take them to our place of abode, and to have them for our evening meal. We did not, however, make our destination that evening, for we were caught in a violent storm of rain and took refuge in the 'George,' the nearest public of a village, fortunately close at hand.

Here we decided to stop the night instead of proceeding, and therefore made the necessary arrangements. Then we wanted to dry our clothes; we must either dry them on us before the kitchen fire, or go to bed while they were being dried for us, or rig ourselves out in the landlord's spare togs. We chose the former method, went into the kitchen, and carried our fungi with us to see about the cooking.

There were some half-dozen countrymen smoking and drinking beer in the kitchen, which, in fact, served as a kind of bar-parlour. After passing a few remarks with those nearest to us, we turned to the landlady, and asked her about cooking the fungi — mushrooms we called them — at the same time opening the handkerchief and displaying before her astonished gaze our collection of toadstools. Of course, the first idea that struck both her and those of the natives who had crowded up was, that we were two fools of cockneys, who didn't know a mushroom when we saw one. 'Lor' bless 'ee,' was the triumphant exclamatory chorus, 'them thur bean't musherroons, they bean't nought else beseps toadstools.'

'Thur's nur a one of thaay things, sir, as is fit to yet, I assure 'ee; them's not the right sort, them bean't. They'll kill 'ee fur sartin.'

Then up spoke a shepherd with an air of authority. 'Them thur,' he said, pointing to the horse-mushrooms, 'be the only ones as be 'tall like the proper musherroons; but thay bean't the right sort, 'cos thay be

white underneath. Them thur be horse-musherroons, and they be piz'nus. As for that thur puffer, nobody ever ate they, and them there tother things be nowt but toadsmeat.'

Then the landlady gave her opinion. 'Musherroons be very dangerous things, sir, that they be. I be allus afraid on 'um, 'tis allers safest to drow 'em away vrom 'ee.' It was quite in vain I assured the assembled company that I had partaken of all these kinds, and was alive and well to-day to say so. Incredulity was rampant.

'Do 'ee mean to say, sir, as you 'a yet thaay very same sorts as thease 'ere,' was the question — 'the very same?'

'Yes,' I said, 'I know them as well as I do the common mushroom, and they are rather better, if anything, and quite as harmless!'

'I be sure as yer've never yet nurn of thaay,' says the shepherd. 'I knows better.'

'What do you mean?' I said. 'Do you think I want to tell you wrong?'

'You never yet nurn of thaay.'

'Don't you see?' said Willis. 'He means we never ate any of those on the table, because they are not cooked yet.'

A slight laugh was raised, and I ejaculated: 'Very good! Very sharp!'

'Noa, I don't mean nothing of the kind,' he persisted. 'I don't believe as you'd be alive if yer've ate urn of thaay. You be mistook, that's what you be,' and he retired in dudgeon to a corner.

I saw that if we meant to have our feed of fungi, we must cook it ourselves, and so I asked the landlady to let me have the frying-pan, and I'd soon show how to cook 'em and how to eat 'em. 'Oh, Lor', sir, don't 'ee go for to poison yerselves, don't 'ee now,' she cried out.

'Poison ourselves!' I said. 'I'm not tired of life yet, you may be sure; I know what I'm about well enough.'

'I wouldn't eat nurn of thaay if you gied I a crownd,' said one of the natives; 'no, that I 'oodn't.' 'Thaay'll be djed afore morning,' says another. 'You'll have a crowner's 'quest in the house, missus, and thaay'll say you've a-poisoned 'em.'

'Oh Lor',' exclaims the landlady, 'I don't want that. Noa, I can't let 'ee have the fry-pan; I can't let 'ee cook 'em; let me drow 'em away for 'ee.'

'Don't be silly,' I said, 'let's have the frying-pan, and I'll soon cook 'em; I know more about these things than you do.'

'You take 'em away, missus,' said the shepherd. 'We've no bizness to stand here and let they kill theirselves so long as we can prevent it; just think what 'ud be said.'

I thought the chances of our feast looked very small at this moment, and that the edibles would be forcibly taken from us and ignominiously bundled out of doors; but a rescuer was at hand.

He was a big, stolid-looking individual, with unkempt hair and beard, and a knowing twinkle in his eye – he had but one – having lost the other, as we subsequently learnt, fighting for Queen and country in the Mutiny. Being the travelled man of the community, he was consequently revered for the dangers he had passed, and credited with a large amount of experience; hence his opinion on matters discussed at the 'George,' carried, as we found, very considerable weight with it. He was called by common assent 'the gin'ral,' and the gin'ral delivered himself as follows:

'Tell 'ee what 'tis, lads, thay thur as travels about like these genelmen, know what's good to eat mor'n other folks do think on. Isn't it nat'ral as gentry should know more about such tack, nor them as bides to whoam? You let thay alone; thay knows what thay be at, I'll be bound.'

'Here, missus,' cried Willis, 'bring this gentleman a pint.'

It came accordingly. 'Health, sir, and much obliged,' quoth he.

'Same to you, sir,' said my most diplomatic companion. To call him sir and gentleman almost in the same breath, and to give him a pint of ale, was the very height of bribery; a Parliamentary candidate couldn't do a better stroke. 'And now the frying-pan, missus, some fat, an egg, and some bread, and we're set up!' I said.

Opposition had almost disappeared, and the shepherd's suggestion that the policeman ought to be sent for to witness what we were doing, and, if necessary, to prevent us by force should he in his inscrutable wisdom see fit, fell rather flat. 'A policeman's life is not a happy one;' well perhaps not; but to be called in to prevent two persons from committing suicide, by eating fungi, would be preplexing to a member of the rural constabulary. If he sees a man mount the parapet of the Clifton Suspension Bridge, or some other high structure, preparatory to making a plunge for the next world, his duty is to him plain and straight — he would run the culprit in for attempting soosanside! but in the case of two harmless, unknown gentlemen stewing fungi ——

I am almost sorry the suggestion was not acted upon. To be confronted with a member of the rural police, and cross-examined concerning my intentions with regard to those fungi, would have been delightful as a novel experience; but our supper would have been spoilt. There is no greater pigheadedness than in an official who can wield a little authority without fear of consequences, and to show his authority he would probably have prohibited the use of those fungi as articles dangerous to human life, and we might have thought ourselves lucky at not being brought up on a charge of attempted suicide, and only let off because the beaks — who might also be somewhat at sea — thought we didn't do it with evil intent, but merely out of ignorance! Such might have happened, but the course of events ran otherwise.

My companion beat up the egg while I peeled and sliced the delicately white puff-ball. Then, having dipped it into the egg, and sprinkled breadcrumbs over it, and having prepared the horse-mushrooms, I put the frying-pan on the fire with a lump of fat in it. At the sound of the bubbling fat a shout of approval rang out from the other side of the room.

'That's the way, sir, that's the way!' exclaimed an old man, 'you've been at that job afore, I knows,' and crossing the room he came and patted me affectionately on the shoulder. 'Daze my back, but yer knows what yer be abouts, I sees,' he cried, as I gave the pan an extra shake to send the grease around. 'If only my missus cud handle the frying-pan same as yer be a-doing now, 'oodn't I have summat nice fur my breakfust, that's all, 'oodn't I jest!'

The landlord of the 'George' looked on approvingly. He was not a typical landlord by any means — rather out of harmony with the place — not a jovial, fat, ruddy, unctuous Boniface, but a lean, quiet, somewhat cadaverous individual, who left the management of the inn to his wife. However, he must needs deliver himself of his judgement. 'Englishmen,' he observed, 'can allers cook their own grub. I allers says if an Englishman can't cook ers own grub, as er ain't much use on. It's good for a man to cook ers own grub; 'tis so much the sweeter yetting arterwards. A man as can cook ers own vittles, and yet 'em too, that's the man as I likes to see.' I agreed with him there and then, and endorsed his opinion.

The frying was a warm job; and it is needless to state that our clothes were dry long before the operation was finished. All in good time we had a respectable dish fried up ready to go into our sitting-room, and giving instructions that some eggs should be boiled to come in as a kind of topper-up to our feast, we adjourned. Ere leaving the room, however, I happened to ask a beery individual seated at the table, whether he would eat a bit of puffer if I fried it for him. The beery individual assented; and I accordingly cooked him some that was over, and set it before him. The beery individual, who had previously expressed his aversion to such articles, consumed them with approval; but I am told that he expressed much disappointment that we didn't stand him a pint to wash it down with. He had no idea of making a martyr of himself without some compensating advantage, evidently. But this is a detail not heard till afterwards. Needless to say we ate our supper with very considerable relish; we left not a scrap on the dish. When the things were cleared away, their appearance in the kitchen evoked very considerable comment. 'Well, I'm dalled, thur yen't a mossel a-leaved! They've a-cleared their trough of vittles up proper. I ull be queer if they ain't a-tuk middling arterwards.' The occupants of the kitchen adjourned to the street, and the news of the proceedings spread through the village. Small knots of people gathered around the inn, momentarily expecting to hear shrieks of pain proceeding from its rooms. They were doomed to disappointment; but in order to show that we were sound and well, and had, in fact survived the perils of our meal, we deemed it advisable to present our persons to the assembly, and to take an evening stroll through the village streets. We lit our pipes and sallied forth, the objects of many a gaze. We strolled through the village and out into the country beyond, in full enjoyment of one of those pleasant evenings which succeed a wet afternoon. As the shades of night began to creep o'er the landscape, we wended our way back. Some groups were still left, and we could detect as the centre of them the individuals whom we had encountered in the kitchen. We greet the anxious landlady with the assurance that we are not dead yet, we intend to take a glass and a pipe before going to bed, and that we will again adjourn to the kitchen for that purpose. As we open the door a considerable hubbub of voices falls upon our ears, in the midst of which we can hear the landlord saying, 'Let the gin'ral alone, can't 'ee?' to a small man who it seems had dared to interrupt the gin'ral in a long-winded yarn concerning the mysteries of the Indian juggler.

'Well,' said the gin'ral, resting his chin upon his hand, and leering at the spellbound company like a modern Cyclops, 'it's true I'm telling ye for all that. I tell 'ee that that there man would take a sword from any man in the comp'ny, an' putt it right down into the inside of un, till nowt but the hilt were a-left sticking out of his mouth. An' I tell 'ee another thing, I seed a man out there stand on his head on the top of a gurt bamboo cane twenty feet high, an' toss about brass balls, an' ketch 'em again with his hands.'

'Well,' said one of the audience, after a murmur of astonishment had gone round, 'dost mind that man down to Coombe who'd break any stwon you wur minded to gie un, er'd break un wi' ers fist?'

'Ah, that I do,' said his neighbour on the right, 'an' I do mind the time we brought un thuc gurt blue stone to try wi'. That wur a tough nut for un to crack, that wur, but he did it tho' in th' end. But I do mind some years ago when I went to the For'sters' Feet, a Bank Hol'day[1], a man as 'ad a pig — Lord, that was a 'oonerful pig! Ers maester says to un, says 'ee, "Go roun' among the volk an' find the wench as 'a got 'er best bib an' tucker on." Off er starts thur-right an' comes to Jaene who wur as smart as a peeny, an' er nods ers yead at she an' grunts. Then ers gaffer says, "Find the man as ain't a-got a varden[2] in's pokkut," an' aff that thur pig goes straight to owld Joe Blake as wuddn't 'a bin able to git in to see the sports if er 'adn't a-climmed over wall, when none wuddn't a-looking. Then the chap tells the pig to find the man as 'ud sooner ha' a glass o' whisky than go to year the parson preach a sarmin, an' blest if er don't come straight up to I an' grunts. Now I never wur much o' a church-goer beseps o' Sunday marnings when I goes to ring the bells. I allus says as I 'grees wi' parson best when I've a-runned into a brick wall, as then I can send folks to d–nation so well as 'ee. But that thur pig – if I'd a had a knife in my pokkut, he 'uddn't a-gone a 'oondermenting about to no more folk, I felt that ashamed o' myself.'

As we paid our reckoning next morning, I asked the landlady whether she would eat of those same toadstools after our example.

'That I 'uddn't,' she said, forcibly, 'that I 'uddn't! Musheroons is all very well; but yetting o' that thur frogs' meat as wur never mean'd for the vittles o' any Christin, 'tis a tempting o' the Lard, 'tis.'

CHAPTER 18

A DEAD CHILD

I was on the tramp and very hungry, for it was past the usual time for my midday meal. 'Where is the nearest public?' I inquired of a man I met.

'None nearer nor two mile,' was the discouraging reply.

I almost groaned in despair. I was so hungry and thirsty; the day was hot, and the roads dusty.

'Does any one about here sell anything to eat or drink?'

'Yes, be sure they do. My missus do keep ginger-beer and such-like tack on hand, and thur's plenty o' bread and cheese indoor.'

'How far off?' I asked.

'Why, here, just close anent 'ee.'

I was indeed thankful, and accordingly accompanied him into a small cottage standing close to the roadside. The opening of the door let us straight into the kitchen — a clean, tidy room with a most uneven stone floor. Of ceiling proper there was none hiding the joists and boards of the room above — which joists and boards were of a fine brown colour, not suggestive of dirt, but the combined effects of old age and some occasional smoke. Nailed on to the lower part of the beams were different boards in various places; and these served as shelves for any odd small articles. Nails, nail-passers, and such-like, were poked in between the beams and the boards of the floor above. A pretty paper adorned the walls; and on the left-hand side of the fire-place, close to the large, old-fashioned, high-backed arm-chair, the numerous holes in this paper in one particular place betokened which was the old lady's favourite seat, and where she was wont to make her pincushion. The missus greets me kindly, and when my wants are made known to her, proceeds to set out on a nice clean tablecloth bread and butter and cheese. What will I drink, ginger-beer or orange-champagne? they have them both. Always distrusting those highly-coloured preparations, whose nastiness is only equalled by their length of name, I choose the plainer beverage, stuff which is harmless enough — harmless, at least, when it does not — to give it a smack — contain so much acid as to taste like the washings of a sulphuric-acid carboy.[1] I sit down and start on my lunch with a will, being very keen set. 'Would I like a lettuce and a few young onions?' I confess a weakness for the same, and they are brought straight from the little garden at the back. Blessed indeed is the man who — his palate not having become vitiated with sybaritic dainties — can enjoy such a meal. Here was enough to satisfy any honest hunger, but nothing to tempt an aldermanic overgorged system to continue eating beyond the necessities of nature.

The husband went out and left me alone with the old missus, from whom I learnt as much of the village history as she could compress in some half-hour or so of talk, interlarded with various incidents which she read out from the local newspaper. She had lived in that cottage for very many years, she and the old man, who did a bit of hauling and sundry odd jobs to keep himself in pocket. They very often had travellers stop there on their journeyings. A 'bisikle' came down from London once and fell by the way. They went out, picked him up, and brought him indoors. Then when he came to himsself a bit, they would have him take 'summat to eat and drink, but he couldn't quilt it.'[2] He couldn't drink at all, for he was that bad he couldn't swaller naught, and he sat there in the chair same as I was at that moment and as it might be me, with the vittles and drink in front of him, and couldn't touch a drop on't!

How I pitied that poor 'bisikle's' incapacity! Generally such machines are the cause of much consumption of liquor.

'They do say as the poor man had a overtired hisself, and had gone without food too long, for thur be but few publics along this road, although it's a big road, too, and 'tain't allus as a body thinks o' calling in at a cottage like. But Lor' bless 'ee, sir, we likes to do for any one, we does; we likes to see 'em, and have a chat wi' 'em.' I inquired as to the ultimate fate of the 'bisikle,' and whether he regained his capacity to 'quilt,' and was informed that he came to in about an hour's time, 'ate his vittles, and rode off;' but the opinion was expressed 'that folks as is took that way didn't ought to be allowed to ride them there things!'

My hunger is getting satisfied; but I still play with the lettuce and the bread, while the missus readjusts her spectacles and reads me the chapter of accidents from the local paper. This man had got six months for beating his wife. 'Serve him right!' A farmer had lost his horse through eating of yew-bushes. David Smith's little boy had a-bin run over in the street and killed. 'Ah, poor man,' sighed the missus, 'my daughter had a little boy as died — a dear little chap he were. We ain't got no water hereabouts without a-fetching it from a well about 300 yards away. A smart step for any one when they's tired, and comes home arter a hard day's work, to go there with a yoke and buckets for to fetch water to drink. I do think as the folks who do build housen ought to be compelled for to find water for them as takes 'em close to their doors. 'Tain't right as they should have to go so fur for it. This 'ere well was very deep, and we was allers afraid on it for the childer. There was a windlass over it for to haul up the water, but there weren't

ne'er a cover to it. Times and times had we a-telled the landlord about it, but there was never nothink a-done. Well, my daughter's little Bill — that was his name — went off fur to play wi' his sister as was older nor he, but they were both on 'em but little uns. Folks like we can't be a-minding childer all day — we as 'a got to work hard. They was a-telled times and times again not to go aneist that thur well; but they 'oold go, and I s'pose they got at play beside it, and the boy fell in. The little girl, her come back quiet-like home; and presently when her mother seed her — her'd a-been out a bit — her axed her where was their little Bill. Her wouldn't say naught for some little time, and then her said as he was in the well. Her mother come a-rushing up here for the well drags, as my old man do keep; but he'd put 'em away, and he was out, and we couldn't find 'em nowheres. Presently he come in wi' George – that's her husband – and they took 'em and went off. He allus knows where he've a-put a thing, my old man do; but I never can find it if he've a-put it away. George, he dragged the well, and very soon he brought up the poor little chap; but er wur quite dead. It wur sad, sir, I can tell 'ee, to see that thur little chap a-brought up like that by his own father. He did look so innercent a-laid there on the grass, his little face a-turned up, and his father and mother a-knelt down beside 'un to see what they could do; but 'twere no use.

'There was a crowner's 'quest on un, and sometimes the jury do a-gie their fees to poor women like that; but they didn't do it this time.'

'I suppose the well is covered up now,' I observed.

'Oh, yes; the jury said as the landlord was much to blame, as he hadn't seen to it afore, and they said it was to be done, so that it's all safe now; but it's a pity as it couldn't a-bin done afore.'

I shortly afterwards took my leave, being charged sixpence for my repast; the old lady hoping I would call in again.

CHAPTER 19

WHERE THE MISSUS IS MASTER

In the course of one of my rambles I entered a public-house. Meeting the landlord in the passage, 'I want some bread and cheese.'

'There's the missus inside,' he replied, apparently unwilling to have anything to do with me while she was at hand. I accordingly walked into the kitchen where the missus was clearing away the remains of a dinner of bacon and cabbage, and repeated my demand.

'Sit down thur then half a minute, and I'll attend to 'ee soon as I be able,' she replied, as she went on with her work. She was a big, fat, untidy woman, and the whole place was not remarkable either for cleanliness or for tidiness.

'What did 'ee want?' she again asked, when she had put away the plates and dishes. I told her of my requirements in the way of food and drink. 'All right,' was the answer, 'doan't be in no hurry, and I'll fetch it 'ee.' Presently the required articles were set before me, and I commenced my meal. 'What brings 'ee to such a lone pleace as this 'ere?' was the next question; and, in truth, it was a lonely, out-of-the-way place, where strangers were presumably a novelty.

'Oh, I chanced to come this way.'

'Willum,' she called out to her husband through the window, 'Willum just thee get an' dig thay 'taters as I told 'ee about. Thee get an' see to 't straightway. Thee allus wants telling ever so many times 'fore thee'lt do aught. Joe!' to an urchin, evidently her son, who came into the kitchen just then, 'get off into the tallut 'an help the bouoy to clean un, as I towld thee. Doan't thee git to play now stead o'. work, an' doan't thee git a-hindering o' 'ee, or, drabbut[1] thee, I'll warm thee presently.' Then, turning to me, she detailed at some length the virtues of her family, saying how her husband and that 'buouy, were two of the laziest twoads as ever a hardworking soul were a-blessed wi'. Thay'd bide about all day a-doing nowt, an' never move a finger to help a body. How did 'ee find out such a lone place as this 'ere?' she resumed. I did not tell her that the place was marked on the map – a piece of information which she would probably have received with incredulity.

'Oh, I knew the road must lead to somewhere,' I replied.

'Ah, true enow,' she answered, as if that were an easy solution of a really difficult and perplexing problem. 'Truee enow; an' what do you do now, if I may meake so bowld?'

'Oh, just walk about the country and look at the places, that's all,' I answered.

'Ho,' she replied, with a toss of her head, 'nice thing to be like you then, wi' nought to do; summat different to we sort of folks as 'a got to work all day an' every day, an' ain't nur a moment's rest. Oh, summat nice to be o' the like o' you.'

'Ah! missus,' I answered, 'washing dishes and digging 'taters ain't the only kind of work; there's more work than that which is done with the hands.'

'Ah, well, belike that's true.'

Our conversation then drifted into other channels — the weather, the merits of her cats, and sundry other topics. Presently I paid my reckoning and prepared to take my departure. Then, as I was stepping into the yard, her curiosity again got the better of her, and she once more made the inquiry: 'Now, what do you do, if I may meake so bowld?'

To which I replied again: 'Oh, walk about and see places.'

'Ah, that ain't all as yer do do; yer do do summat more besides that.'

'Oh, perhaps so, most people do,' I said. 'Which is the best way to get to the top of that hill?' I asked in continuation, pointing to an eminence just in front of her door.

'Sure I doan't know,' she answered, 'I never was thur. I've a-heard folks say as it's a fine place when you be atop on 't, but I never has time to go thus; thur's allus too much to be done, an' all folk be so dratted lazy nowadays. Why, I doan't go outside this 'ere yard sometimes for weeks together, beseps 'tis perhaps to see if one of the hens have a-laid astray up the road.'

'Well, do you know there's an old camp on the top of that hill, and I'm going to see it; that's what I've come here for.'

'Oh, yer be, be yer! Well, well, I've a-yeard tell as there was a summat up there, an' I've a-yeard as the townsfolk do come a-prying around to look at un; but Lor' bless 'ee, I've never troubled my yead about such things as that thereimy. There's enow for we sort o' folk to do about our own housen, wi'out caddling about what other folks may a-done as is djed an' buried this long while.'

'Well, I'm off there, missus, so good day!'

'Good day! Yer'll find a road up thur somehow or 'nother. I doan't doubt.'

CHAPTER 20

DRINK

Not a very long time ago heavy drinking was the fashion among all classes of society. For a guest to leave the table sober was construed as a most serious reflection upon the host, while it was considered as very poor hospitality not to ply him with drink — it appeared like niggardliness on the part of the host. Less than forty years ago Boniface told a party of naturalists, who had dined at his house and disputed the charges of his bill, that in his opinion, 'A gentleman was him as took his three bottles of wine after dinner,' and as they had been particularly abstemious the inference was obvious. But within even the last few years the quantity of wine drunk after dinner has greatly decreased, and the circulation of the decanter has become extremely limited. Cynics say that it is on account of the depression of trade; while doctors tell us that it is on account of the villainous concoctions which pass by the name of wine being so much more injurious to the system. If the latter be correct, those dealing in the liquor traffic are playing into the hands of the temperance advocates with a vengeance.

I can remember as a boy being taken into the market-room of an hotel in the Midlands. I could scarcely see across it for tobacco-smoke, and when we were able to grope our way through the cloud and discover the farmer we were in search of, we found him discussing his sixteenth glass of gin and water. A good deal of hard drinking is done even now in these same market-rooms by those who go by the name of old-fashioned farmers; but the tendencies among the present generation are much more temperate, and this, I doubt not, is due in a large measure to bad times. Some allowance must be made for such drinking customs among men, who, shut up in solitary country places for the rest of the week, can hardly be expected to meet friends on, perhaps, their one off-day, and to part without some sign of good-fellowship. The glass lends itself to such expression very readily; but when a man's acquaintance is large it is apt to be overdone. With such customs lately prevalent among the middle classes, and in certain cases not be any means eradicated among them, we can wonder that habits of hard drinking still linger among the poorer classes? Intoxication, however, is not so prevalent among the agricultural population as among their brethren in the towns, and this is due in all probability to the absence of temptation. In counties where it is the custom to give larger quantities of beer and cider during hay and corn-harvest, it frequently happens that a mild state of intoxication supervenes every evening when the work is late; but such intoxication is of a harmless nature, more often provocative of comic scenes than otherwise. The quantity of fluid which a seasoned vessel can absorb during a summer's day is almost fabulous. Three gallons was the usual quantity of an old man who declared 'he had drunk sufficient to float Her Majesty's Navy, and was now on for the French 'un.'

The giving of drink in this manner is no doubt detrimental both to the workmen and their masters. The workmen argue that while it is to their advantage to have some drink during the hot days of summer, they could not purchase — with the money which would be allowed them in lieu of it — the same quantity, because the farmer would give them only the wholesale value of their drink, while they would have to pay retail price. Furthermore, it is questionable if in many cases the farmer would give even that, because, while he might be liberal with the drink, he would be close with the coin. Another rather naive argument was put forward once. The man said: 'When we gets the money and hands it over to the missus 'er spends it, and us don't know what becomes on't; but when us gets the drink we puts it inside us, and then us knows whur 'tis.'

Talking of this handing money over to the wife, though, I have come across one or two curious tricks. It is the invariable practice of the men not to hand over all their wages to their wives, but to reserve part for their own special delectation in the village public. One man in receipt of twelve shillings a week only allowed his wife five shillings to keep house upon; another in receipt of a like sum had a wife who was 'as good a man as he,' as the phrase goes, and consequently he dare not keep anything back, especially as he had thirteen children to provide for, while the other had only himself and his wife. But this man — who must have been very much blessed with such a quiverful — was often able to outwit his wife, because if his money came to anything for extras or overtime beyond the twelve shillings — even if only a sixpence — he was careful to obtain that extra sixpence separate; he would not take home ten shillings and half-a-crown. Oh no! he would take home ten and two shillings and a sixpence — but he kept the sixpence dark.

Recurring again to the giving of drink by the masters, but without any desire to discuss the various details of the subject, I will just mention an instructive little incident which happened one afternoon while I was on my walking tour. I was overtaken by the rain, and had, in addition, lost my way. It was a lonely kind of country, in which one might wander for hours without seeing a soul. Not that the fact of the rain, or having lost my way, made very much difference to my temper. The rain did not, because I was fully prepared for it; the loss of my way did not, for I had a fair notion of the general direction in which I ought to turn my footsteps. Still, I was not sorry when I heard some voices behind a hedge. Proceeding along the lane — one of those curious old wide green lanes which one meets with in certain parts of the country — I looked over a gate and saw three pairs of horses with their respective ploughs standing still. Beneath a tree were the carter, the under-carter, and the boy passing round the stone jar of cider. I walked up and entered into conversation. Nothing would do but I should drink. I did not at all want to, and at first refused. When pressed again — and knowing what a sad breach of etiquette it is always considered, and how it is held as a useless exhibition of pride to refuse what is meant in thorough good-nature, and as a pledge of good-fellowship — I consented. The jar circulates during the turns of conversation, till presently I again require pressing.

'Drink, maester, drink along o' we. There's plenty on't, maester, yer needn't be afraid on't. We've another jar under hedge, an' we don't know how to finish un afore night,' says the under-carter.

Then the carter volunteers the statement how last night they had about two quarts left which they couldn't get rid of, so they emptied it away 'under hedge; 'twould never do to teake it back again, because they would not get so much next time if they did, when, maybe, 'twould be a drier day.'

'Get wet inside's well as out, maester,' is the observation as the jar comes round again. Then I offer to pay my footing towards obtaining a drop another time; but they won't accept of it.

'No! no! maester, put it back in thy pokkut, us won't ha' it. We bean't chaps o' that sort, maester, allus a-cadging; no! us bean't. Have 'ee another drink, maester, and don't 'ee be afraid on't. 'Twon't hurt 'ee. 'Tis a bit sharp, but better for 'ee nor that there sweet stuff as is doctored.' Then follows the naive statement: 'If so be as yer don't drink it, maester, we should only ha' to throw it away, so help 's out wi' it.'

But I thought that for one unaccustomed to the qualities of cider, I had run the risk of sufficient stomach-ache for once, and that it was time to depart. So, as they wouldn't take a tip, I shook my entertainers' hands with a hearty grip, and went my way. Shall I ever meet them again? The chances are much against it, or of my recognizing them if I did; but should it so happen, I must stand them a quart, though the cynical should aver that, in giving what they might not want, their generosity was not very great. I prefer to think otherwise — 'twas kindly meant.

CHAPTER 21

A DRUNKEN WIFE

Drunkenness is bad enough in a man, but how much worse is it in his wife! No one could find any excuse for a man who gets drunk and ill-treats his wife – a wife who is perhaps a hard-working, industrious woman trying to keep a home together in spite of a good-for-nothing husband; but what if the picture be reversed, and the wife be drunken? If in such a case she receive corporal punishment, I scarcely think purists should say too much. The verdict of humanity in general would be, serve her right.

Mary Warden was the daughter of a villager who had in his later life been able to set himself up, with the assistance of one of his sons, as a local carrier. At an early age she had been put out to service as a nurse-girl to farmers' families in the neighbourhood. As she grew up in years and advanced in experience, she took a general-servant's place under a mistress who superintended the cooking. Her next step was to go as cook to a small family in the neighbouring town. I cannot say when she first took to evil ways; but such matters usually have small beginnings. However, in less than three months' time, she appeared home unexpectedly, having been found by her mistress one evening in a state of absolute drunkenness on the kitchen floor. She had, during her mistress's absence, abstracted the brandy bottle from the side-board, and imbibed its contents. Her home-coming was not one of the pleasantest to herself or her friends, but on serious promises of amendment, and to keep her out of the mischief which idleness brings, a situation was by some means found for her in a distant part of the county. Excepting for this failing, she was a very good servant, and consequently she now remained in her situation for some time, giving satisfaction. But the dénouement came at last. She had become fast friends with the groom, a married man whose house she supplied with food from her master's table in consideration of his wife keeping silence. During the absence of the master and mistress on market days this man would come into the house, turn the beer-tap with a pair of pliers, and the two would boose in company, sometimes not unassisted by his wife. One evening the master came home quietly alone before his usual time, and, walking straight into the kitchen, found the trio so engaged. Their places were vacant next morning. Mary did not dare face her parents that time, but got a fellow-servant, who had lately married and settled in the country, to give her board and lodging for a while. It was during her stay with her friend that she became acquainted with George Warden; and when he 'axed' her to be Mrs Warden, she consented without much hesitation, for she really was at a loss what to do otherwise.

For a time all went well; but when, during the next winter, her husband was laid up for some weeks unable to work, and the money, and consequently food ran short, while no one would trust them, Mary relapsed into bad habits; and though she could get credit for nothing else, she managed somehow to obtain it for drink. She took toll of the wine ordered for her husband's benefit, which led to angry words between them; and one night she came home for the first time thoroughly drunk, and lay like a log on the kitchen floor, while her husband lay hungry and helpless in his bed upstairs.

It was some little time after this date that I became acquainted with the family, and Mary had by that time three children. She would go on for some time without touching drink; but at other times seemed perfectly unable to restrain herself. Her husband generally bore with her with philosophical good-temper. When she was drunk, he usually treated her with the greatest possible indifference, and took no more notice of her than if she were a log. Now and again she angered him beyond even his control, and the results were unpleasant — for her, at any rate — for she was no match for him when he brought the weighty argument of a fist to meet the sharp edge of her tongue. Her

neighbours, neither male nor female, ever pitied her under the circumstances; in fact, some of the former declared 'that had her been wife to
they, and gone on wi' such 'oondermenting tricks, 'twould 'a bin a case
for 'sizes, 'twould!' a somewhat emphatic manner of expressing the bad
chance which the woman's life would have stood at their hands.

It was fortunate for George Warden that he lived some distance —
two miles — from a public-house, and also that he lived in a rather lone
country place, otherwise I fancy his house had been stripped of all it
possessed. As it was, nearly every portable article had found its way to
the public. One day Mary told her neighbours that her kettle leaked,
and must needs be mended; but they — the women it was, for their
husbands were all at work — shook their heads when she had left, and
one averred that if she brought her kettle back she'd bring something
more with it; while another observed that Mrs Warden would return
'empty-handed, but full inside.'

The latter proved a true prophet. Late that evening, Mrs Warden was
found by the roadside in company with a boon companion – a
paramour, very probably – in a state of insensibility. She was brought
indoors by some men to where her husband was vainly endeavouring
to feed the crying baby. Poor little wretch! it was miserably thin, and
needed its mother now. How could it be otherwise than thin and puny,
seeing that it was nourished by a mother so saturated with gin? Can we

wonder that its feeble existence flickered out a few weeks later! And what of the mother at that time? She had been steadier till then after her last bout. Did she show any grief? I fancy not; but made it an excuse for another visit to the tavern.

When will the melancholy tale end? Not yet, perhaps. Perhaps in the time the husband will join his wife in her evil courses, and both drift into the workhouse.

Are such cases common in the country; as common as in towns? I believe not; not such confirmed intemperance, such ruin of a home. It is to be hoped they may not become so.

CHAPTER 22

AUTUMN

It was one of those fine and bright autumn days, when we experience all the pleasures of summer without its oppressive heat, and I was in full enjoyment of a country walk. The sun was bright and the sky almost cloudless; the view was pleasing, but not too clear; a haze, indicative of continued fine weather, hung over the more distant landscape. On the hills, the beech-trees were fast assuming their glorious autumnal tints. Nearer at hand were the fields, from which, by now, most of the corn had been gathered, though here and there might be seen one in which the stooks or the cocks[1] were still out. Presently I came to one which presented rather a contrast to the others. The crop was still uncut, but it was beaten down almost flat, and the weeds were growing up thickly among the prostrate corn. I leaned on the gate to have a look at it, and then saw that the process of cutting had commenced, but, apparently, the effort had been abandoned.

'Good day, maester,' I heard a voice cry out, and turning my head in the direction whence the sound came, saw some men sitting comfortably under the hedge, doing no harder work than was involved in imbibing the contents of the bottle.

'Good day,' I replied, 'you seem to have a pretty comfortable job; you're fine farmers in these parts to sit under the hedge and drink instead of tackling to work.'

'Comfortable job, indeed. Ah! you'd say so if you'd a-got un to do,' was the reply of Bill, the spokesman of the party. ''Tis all down, and in such a mugglement we can't cut it no ways, and the straw 's so dratted rotten, we can't make a bond wi' it to tie wi'; an' as for pretty varmers, here's the pretty varmer a-comin' down the ground, though 't won't do to tell un so.'

I looked in the direction indicated, and saw the gaffer coming down the field with a very rueful countenance as he surveyed the small progress made by Bill and his mates at the work. The gaffer, as I afterwards learnt, was the muddling occupier of some few acres of land, and owner of a few head of live stock.

'Well,' he said, as he approached, 'how do 'ee get on wi' 'ut?'

'Djowced middling, zur — djowced middling, I can tell 'ee,' observed Harry, while Bill sat silent as if he could not find words to express his opinion thereof. 'We've a-tried un with the zythe, an' we've a-tried un wi' the hook,' continued Harry, 'an' I doan't knaow which meakes the most mess on 't; but,' catching Bill's eye, he discreetly added, ''tis uncommon heavy in the yead — 'tis uncommon heavy — and 'ull come out better nor 'urn in the parish when 'tis dreshed, I war'n.'

'Measter,' says Bill, with sudden energy, as if he had just been able to get his ideas into shape. 'Measter, yer varms this 'ere ground too well, yer do; yer does un a djowced sight too well. When a ground's done so skeandalous well 'tis zure to drow the kearn; and when the kearn's a-drowned yer may knaow as the kearn's 'eavy in the yead on 't. Yer be too gen'rous to this 'ere ground, measter, I tell 'ee. Jest yer mind our naybur,' jerking his thumb in that direction. 'His carn did stand up strait as a schoppek-stael,[2] but 'twern't but half a crop, an' a poor whimbling[3] lot on't then. Here, you've a-got a gurt crap o' carn, an' a gurt crap o' straw.'

'Ah! you know when you hefted one of thaay sheaves o' hissen,' remarked Harry, 'the butt ends did go down to ground straight; but jest 'ee heft one o' theasum, maester,' he says, suiting the action to the word, 'and the yeds do vall down a rum 'un. The job is, as 'tis so skeandalous bad to cut all a-led about; on course we cud a-go in and a-hoggerymaw[4] ut aff and leave 's many yeds on the ground as was in the sheiff; but that yen't how yer do want it a-done, we knaows, and 'tain't to your profit as it should be a-done that way nether.' There was a deal of cuteness, I thought, in all this praise of the quality and quantity of the crop, while they expatiated on the difficulties attending their work. He liked to be thought a better farmer than his neighbours, and was not at all averse to having his pride tickled. As the gaffer turns on his heel to leave the field he says: 'Well, you chaps, you make a good job on't, and do it careful, look 'ee, and I'll send 'ee down a piece o' bif and another jar o' cider to help 'ee with it.'

'Meates,' says Bill, when the gaffer's out of ear-shot, 'that's the waay to treat un. Tell un 'ee's a dazed vine varmer, and he sends we down a bit o' bif and some more cider. It doan't pay to speak the truth to some volks, eh, maester, do it?' he said, turning to me. 'Come and ha' a drink, maester, on the strength on't. It do go down slick 'smarning. You be a stranger hereabouts, bean't 'ee?'

I was of Bill's opinion that a drink would go down slick, so I walked up and consented.

'Didn't we pitch un a tale about this 'ere crap?' says Bill.

'I don't know,' I observed, 'that I ever saw a much worse one, considering the mess and all. Why, we used to grow much better crops in our parts.'

'Oh, up there at Z——.'[5]

'Ah, I knows the please,' says Bill in a meditative way. 'I knows un. I wur never there but once, though, and that was when I wur a-courting her as be my missus and I took her up the church tower; a proper sight of country yer can see therefrom. Then I did meake a cut wi' my clapse knife around my gurt voot and a leetle one inside o't round hern. Lord-a-mussy, how 'er did squeal when I tuk howld o' her ankle to howld her futdown steady on the leads whiles I did cut round un, and the job I had to kip it thur. Ah!' he added, 'I've a-knaowed times since, when her've a-wanted her own way a bit, as her've been ready enow to put down that thur voot o' hern.'

The tot of cider circulated again, when Bill burst out afresh:

'Ah, yer knaow, when I wur a-coortin' o' 'er thur wur a young feller in them parts as had a-cum to larn the varming, and he tuk a-hanging around arter she. I knaowed as 'ee wur arter no good wi' 'er as I'd a-yeared o' one or two as had a-got into trouble wi' un; but jest so long as 'ee wur about, my lass 'oodn't ha' nowt to say to I. One even I caught my genelman a-comin' away from her door, and I says to un, I says: 'Yer black-hearted scoundrel, if yer don't promise to leave that there lass alone, I'll gie 'ee a durned good dreshing,' I said.

'"Who the d——l be you," er said, "and what odds is't to thee?"

'"I do kip kompany along o' she," I said, "and I won't ha' you a-muddlin' wi' 'er."

'"I'll do just as I be a-minded," er said.

'"I'll be dalled if yer do," I says to un; "will 'ee fight?"

'"Noa, I 'on't," er says, "I 'on't fight such a country lout as you be," er says; that's what er called I.

'"Yer be a gurt coward," I said to un, "that's what yer be; and if yer wun't fight," I said, "I'll catch 'ee some day in the village and gie 'ee a durned good hiding afore all the folks."

'"Yer gurt clodhopper," er says to I, "yer gurt clodhopper, if thur's ar a quiet place about I'll fight 'ee till 'ee can't stand."

'"Come along o' I," I says; and I led un to a lone place, aneist a hayrick, and we whipped off our clothes and fell to thur as vierce as a pair of bulldogs. We hommered away at one another wi' our fistes like vlails a-dreshing on a barn flure. He knowed better how to fight nor I; but hard work and hard vittles 'ad a-gied I a hide as tough as ar a bit o' leather, and I ne'er felt ers blows a mossell. We ne'er stopped not for no time for to get our wind, as yer do read on in the paper about the fights nowadays; we had to catch our wind when's cud, an' I cud last out longer nor 'ee. Arter we'd a-been hommering away for ever so long, he did git waker, and I cud hit un well then, I cud,' said Bill, with triumphant reminiscence. 'Ah, I knocked ers two eyes very nigh into one, as er cud scarce see out o' 'em, an' I flattened ers nose for un skeandalous. Oh, Lord! he wur a sight — an' so wur I, for that matter. Well, at last I knocked un clean off ers legs, an' er fell down an' cut ers yead ag-in' a stone, an' didn't git up ag'in. I thought at first as I'd killed un. Up cummed the varmer an' wanted to know what I'd a-done to un, an' I telled un. "Er'll git auver it," er sed; "thee lend a hand an' let's carr' un whoam." I said I wurnt a-gwine to carr' un whoam, we'd carr' un to public. Howsomever, as we went along the road one o' my butties cummed up and I gets un to teak my place, and they carr'ed un whoam on a hurdle, an' put un to bed, an' sent fur the doctor fur un. Oh! thur wur a vine caddle, an' er talked o' summonising I; but they telled un er'd better not. I never seed no more o' my genelman, for er left they parts soon's ever er cud dare shew issell abroad. My lass wur sweet enow on I when er 'eard how I'd a-fought for 'er, an' 'twarn't long avor we got hitched up together.'

CHAPTER 23

THE CLOSING SCENE

One last little episode concludes the events of my tour, and, in consequence, of my sojourn in the country. The last day of my walking tour I fell in with a friend also on a holiday, and on the tramp like myself; but combining these with the pursuit of geology. I journeyed awhile with my stone-breaking friend, and presently we came to some quarries. Seeing a boy minding sheep near them, and wishing for

information as to the ownership of these same quarries, my friend stepped up to him and said:

'My good boy, can you please inform me to whom those quarries belong?'

'Dunno,' replied the boy, somewhat vacantly.

'Always the way,' my friend observed under his breath.

'I say, nipper, who do the volks teak thaay quarrs off?' I interrogated.

'Oh, Mr So-and-so, as do live down to thuc big house,' was the answer.

'What sort o' a genelman be he?'

Whereupon we could have had the history of the neighbourhood had we been desirous to obtain it.

'We have got our information,' I observed to my friend, as we turned away. 'The person from whom they rent the quarries is, of course, the owner.'

The moral to be learnt is, if you wish to converse with the natives, you must be able to speak their language.

COTSWOLD CHARACTERS

At the Cup Final   No 2.
Slaughter. 9-4-21.

CHAPTER 24

THESIGER CROWNE, THE MASON

Leaning with arms folded upon his garden gate by which hardly anybody ever passed, Thesiger Crowne bade me good evening. His cottage was in a bylane of a village that is in itself in an undiscovered pocket of the Cotswolds. He was a widow man, as they say, and one elderly daughter lived with him. He looked very handsome this evening. He had a stout frame, tall, and he was rather a dandy, with the dandy's proper respect for natural tradition. He was a yeoman villager some generations deep, and he would have scorned to confuse his class with any other. He had been into the market town to-day, so that his dress was as it might be Sunday, with a lay touch of difference. His boots were of the sort in which he had years ago learnt to walk as many miles as might be, daily in all weathers. His corduroy trousers, originally buff in colour, had been bleached by repeated washings. Over his cotton shirt, set off by a linen collar with no tie, in place of a coat he work a sleeved waistcoat, the sleeves of lining cloth, the rest of a dark honey-coloured velveteen. His very white hair and whiskers surrounded a very red face, ample but well shaped, and, as though to remind some of us who play at being countrymen what the real thing is, he wore a hard black bowler hat of rather fasionable shape.

'Good evening, Mr Crowne,' I replied. 'I hope you're well.'

'Well, that I baint so much. The indigestion it is. I do have often to sit

up in bed of a night.' I commiserated with him. I asked him if he had
seen a doctor.

'Doctors — no. I've made a shift to do without they so far, and that's
a deal of time. It's a rest I do want. If I live, I shall be seventy-seven
come Ciceter Mop.[1] I've done a deal of hard work in my time, and I
think it be about time for I to take a rest. Not that I should be surprised,
mark you, if I did live to be a hundred and two.' Presumably the record
for the village was held at present by a hundred and one.

A deal of hard work in his time. He was a mason, one of the old
Cotswold breed, and his handiwork is in every town and village within
twenty miles of the hamlet that had been his home for seventy-seven
years. Even beyond that, for the builders recognized his skill, and he
had been known to travel on his trade into the further midlands, into
Sussex, once even far across into Norfolk. At sixty-six, he told me, he
had had a job that for eighteen weeks meant a six-mile walk in the
morning, a day's work, and six miles home at night. He had never been
out of England, and I talked to him a little of foreign countries. 'Did
you ever go to China, sir?' Thesiger had a gift of irony. I had to confess
that I had not been there. 'It must be a rare place, China. But no man
can go everywhere. That's how I look at it.'

He had a grandson living in the village, one who had fallen from the
high craft of masonry to miscellaneous jobbing. Thesiger remembered
that when he himself was a boy he used to go with his father to work in a
near town. His own wages were sixpence a week, and his father drew
seven shillings, a considerable share of which was paid in kind — pig's fry
and chitlings. He remembered his mother washing them at the spring and
selling them to people on the spot. Now his grandson, born and bred in
the same place, had been asked for an estimate for whitewashing four
cottage rooms. No painting or other work was to be done. His estimate
was nineteen pounds. Hearing of the prices that were being paid, he had
lost his head and estimated wildly, it is true. But nineteen pounds for, at
most, three days' work, and his great grandfather sixty-odd years ago at
seven shillings a week, partly paid in kind. It is a fantastic epitome of the
wage madness that has been besetting the world.

One of his cheeks was furrowed by a deep scar, an honourable wound

from a somewhat strange action that made history in the village forty
years since. On an outlying road had stood an ancient pest-house, which,
during an outbreak of smallpox in a town six miles away, the urban
authorities had decided to appropriate for the severer cases. Indignation
in Thesiger's village at once rose to determined fury. The first van was
met by the inhabitants, the horses turned on the road, and the driver
threatened into retreat. One of the patients died on the return journey.
Open war followed, and the van came back with a strong police escort.
Thesiger led his fellows, indignation now in full cry, to the pest-house,
and in a few minutes the building was in flames.[2] The charred ruins are
still there. The police saw that no more was to be done, but in a scuffle
before they left, Thesiger took the mark of a truncheon on his cheek for
life. And he and four others helped to make the reputation of a defending
counsel, since famous in legal history, at the next Gloucester assizes.

Thesiger had a turn for reading. His was a mixed fare of out-of-date
history books and the wilder kind of romance. Out of his learning he
had developed a curious but rather proud little self-deception. He told
me he was descended from Oliver Cromwell. He offered no explanation of his dignity, merely asserting it. But tactful enquiries in the
village did not result in any support for his claim. Indeed, it appeared
that it was the effect rather of a general affinity for the great of name
than of any particular kinship. It seemed that at times he would transfer
his ancestral honours to the Duke of Marlborough, sometimes to Wat
Tyler, and on one uproarious occasion at the Chippendale Arms he had
been heard to declare with circumstantial fervour that he was in the
direct line of descent from Robinson Crusoe.

Somewhere back in his family history, a centry and more ago, had
been a tragedy. There had been a case of sheep-stealing, a broken-
hearted daughter, a betrayal, and a drowning. I fancy to myself that it
was Nan Hardwick, Mr Masefield's Nan. Thesiger reckons that those
were callous times anyway; you had to be built of hard stuff then. For
himself, he earned a pound a week until he stopped regular work. Now
he is seventy-seven, and to-morrow morning he will walk across to the
far village to draw his weekly old-age pension, ten shillings. Time for I
to take a rest, indeed. But he looks good for his hundred and two yet.

CHAPTER 25

SIMON RODD, THE FISHERMAN

Simon Rodd's name was a lucky accident. He was eighty years old, and lived in a small shop at Laneton, a little market town on the fringes of Oxfordshire. The shop was now managed by his son, Simon being deaf and not so keen of sight as he was. The establishment dealt in variegated stock — stationery, cheap jewellery, popular literature, quack medicines, peppermints, photographic views, gimcrack ornaments. In these and their like Simon had long since ceased to take any interest. They were the chaffer-wares of necessity, and had never been in his line. But a pile of cardboard boxes at one end of the counter always kept his attention. From the inner parlour, where he sat for long hours in vacancy or meditation, he would keep an eye on them. When he saw a customer's hand move towards them, he would get up and step by step drift into the shop. He was a sleeping partner in the business now, it was true, but no one else really knew about those boxes. They contained artificial flies. As he watched one lid after another being taken off, displaying a glorious range of coloured wings, ginger-quills and iron-blues, nut-brown alders, snowy-white coachmen and black gnats, his faded eyes would lighten with an old eagerness, and he would bide his time.

For Simon Rodd was a fisherman. Not like Simon Peter who caught his multitudes crudely in nets, nor as those who go out with floats and worms, tired anglers, but one of the elect, a fly-fisherman, and dry-fly at that. Laneton is famous for its chalk stream, running midway across the town itself, and when he was twelve Simon had cast his first fly. At seventy-five the hand had grown infirm, and he could no longer see the cocked wings floating down the stream towards him. So that now he had retired to the parlour, listening to ignorance in the shop beyond, making his occasional excursions into publicity when the fly-boxes were in play. And then if you behaved with proper humility, he would respond and give out of the store of his experience.

I turned up at Laneton in May-fly time, an unbroken novice. Everybody, I knew, was looking amusedly at my new rod, my new bag, my new waders and brogues. The Boots at the hotel was a diplomat, assuming that all my old gear had been worn out in hard service. I took the bold course, and confided in him that it was my first equipment, which he very well knew. Sitting in the garden at tea, I struck up an acquaintance with an old hand who had flies sprinkled about his hat. Him too I let into the secret, and showed him my fly-box, splendid with an assortment of plumed and speckled May-flies from London. He looked rather coldly upon then, but spoke civilly. These fellows are not bad sorts, they remember sometimes their own green days. He recommended a visit to Simon Rodd. 'He ties a special fly for the stream. Get the old man himself if you can. He knows ten times as much about it as his son.'

I stepped across the road to the shop. A young assistant was serving, and I asked him for some flies. He slid the boxes along the glass counter towards me, and left me to my choice. I lifted a lid, and saw nothing very likely. Had they any May-flies? An under box was pulled out, and there, wing and hackle, lay a profusion of dark, silver-grey beauties. Were these particularly good for this river? Yes, they were the Laneton Marquis. I put a few on the palm of my hand, and made a pretence of critical examination. As I did so I was aware of somebody standing in the shadow of a door behind the assistant, waiting. I looked up, and saw an old man in a shiny black alpaca coat. He observed my critical air with a courteous indifference.

'Is this the Laneton Marquis?' I enquired, by way of an opening.

'Yes,' said Simon Rodd, 'that's it.'

'I'm told it's very good for the Chedd.'

'I've done pretty well with it, sir.'

Seeing that for more than fifty years he had taken an average of something like four brace of fish a day with this fly during the May-fly season, it was not too much to say. I capitulated at once. 'I'm afraid I don't know anything about this job. What do you advise?' Immediately he was all grace. Near the town I was to use the winged variety, further up-stream, above the hut, he would suggest the hackle, the natural fly generally being rather spent there. In the evening the hackle all along the river, though then sometimes an alder was good even while the May-fly was up. Would I mind being shown what he considered the best way of tying the fly to the point? I should be very grateful. With trembling fingers and straining eyes he threaded the gut, deftly made a loop, gave a little tug, and handed it to me. 'You'll find that after a day or two you can do that in the dark.' Sceptically I thanked him, took my flies of his selection, and went out. 'If you want to know anything, perhaps I can tell you more than some of the others.'

He could have told me, but I could not have learnt. He had lived dry-fly for sixty years, and I must hope for half of that to learn half that he could tell. For he could not now be said consciously to know anything, it was all nature to him. Sometimes in the evening, when the fishermen had come in, I would see Simon Rodd walking, with hurried short steps, without infirmity towards the river, walking-stick in hand. One night I followed him idly in the dusk. He came to the river-bank and stopped. He looked up and down, his eyes covering by habit the water that he could no longer see clearly. Then he moved on slowly, measuring the stream, here and there leaning out towards bushy channels, sometimes peering intently at what seemed to be a sucking at the surface of the water. Presently at a fast-running pool below a stretch of stone wall he paused again. He looked across for a few moments. Then his right elbow went to his side, the walking-stick was raised and, beautifully timed by his wrist, went to and fro — one, two, three, four — and then the cast was made. I knew how the gut flew full out to the end, the rod well up, how perfectly that imaginary fly fell thirty-five feet away just above the rising fish. He was about to strike when he saw me. In the fading light I had come up nearer to him than I realised. I begged his pardon. He was not at all put out. 'There was always a big one there,' he said. 'I know, but I find it difficult to get my fly over so far.' 'Difficult,' he answered, 'why no — it's like this' — and again the walking-stick flickered in the dusk, and again the fly fell two feet above the rise, as livingly plain as though the line were truly running through its rod firmly held in the hand that could never be firm again.

CHAPTER 26

RUFUS CLAY,
THE FOREIGNER

One evening as I was walking down the road with Thesiger Crowne, we passed a long-striding, heavily bearded man, wearing a slouch hat, baggy coat and trousers, and shabby black leggings falling well down on to his boots. He was carrying a gun, and beside him trotted a large retriever dog. I had not seen him before.

'Who is that?' I enquired of Thesiger.

'Rufus Clay,' he answered. 'He's a foreigner.'

Signs of red hair at birth may have encouraged his parents to call him Rufus, but it certainly turned out to be a misnomer. His full beard was black, and his complexion swarthy, but I thought the man looked English.

'A foreigner? What is he — a Spaniard?'

'Spaniard?' said Thesiger. 'No. He come from Pinswick.'

'You mean he lives there?'

'No. He do not live there. He do live here.'

Pinswick is a village seventeen miles away, on the other side of the county. I was puzzled.

'But you said he was a foreigner.'

'Yes, he be a foreigner. He's a Pinswicker.'

'But how long has he lived here?' I persisted.

'Oh, not above ten or twelve years.'

I had been Thesiger's neighbour for eighteen months, and I came from five counties away. As he spoke, I supposed that he must look upon me as something out of the sea at least, though we always seemed to be very good friends. I discovered that nothing short of two generations of unbroken tenure constitutes native rights. Settlers, if only from the next parish, are foreigners, and openly called so. For casual pass-the-time-of-the-day acquaintance, even for neighbourly talk, this is no particular disability, but if you come with the intention of carrying on business, you are likely to be disillusioned, as Rufus Clay learnt.

A few days later I found his house. It was buried behind high walls, not visible from the road. There was nothing mysterious about it, but unless you had special occasion to go in, it was out of sight and out of mind. Rufus had set up as a cobbler, coming to the place when he was between forty and fifty, with a small bag full of savings. On a broken board over the wall door was written, 'Rufus Clay. Cobbler. Repairs neatly executed.' But in a month he found that for trade he might as suitably have gone to a city of the dead. Why he had stayed on for ten years nobody enquired, and he himself did not seem to know. I was told that he had a large kitchen garden, and sold some of the produce on the rare occasions when anybody wanted to buy. I went in now and found him digging. I asked him if he could let me have some onions. He looked at me without saying anything, did not move for a few moments, then stuck his fork into the ground, and pulled up as many onions as he could hold by the tops in two large hands, and gave them to me.

'How much?' I asked.

'Oh, a penny.'

'Only a penny?'

'It doesn't matter. Tuppence if you like.'

I paid him, sorry that he had not asked more. As he put the coppers into his pocket, he remarked, 'Your're a foreigner too, aren't you?' He said it a little sadly, with a touch of bitterness.

'I suppose they would call me that,' I answered.

'Yes, they would. Unnatural I call it.'

'Don't you get on with the folk here?' I ventured.

'Get on — how the darnation can you get on? I don't know them, and they don't know me. Never will. It isn't civilized.'

'You've been here a good many years now, haven't you?'

'Eleven years too long,' was the reply. 'I'm a gowk to have stuck it.'

I asked him to have some tobacco, which he did. I wondered why he had stayed so long if he did not like it. It seemed that in the winter epidemic of 19— he had lost his wife and two children at a stroke, and had left Painswick forever. He had settled down into his new quarters not hopefully, but without misgiving. The prejudice against 'foreigners' had surprised him. He had not spirit to fight it, nor heart to move on. So that with his few pence saved and the help of a garden he had drifted along in a sullen but not actively resentful lethargy.

While we were talking, the retriever that had been on the road with him that evening lay on the earth among a not very prosperous crop of cabbages, at full stretch in the sun. He had taken no notice of my arrival, but as I bade Rufus good-day and turned to go he was at my side in an instant, spiny-furred and growling. His master called him to heel, and as he did so the affection in his voice was clear. It was the first sign he had given of any sustaining human warmth. 'He's ten years old. He's all I've got,' he said. 'Him and high walls.'

I found in the village that there was no antagonism towards Rufus Clay. He just didn't exist. What might have happened if he had been the sort to persevere in advances I can't say. After the first month or two of failure he had made none, and for all the thought he was given he might as well have been within the churchyard walls as his own. Now and again I went to him on some small marketing errand, and once in a while I would meet him on the road at nightfall, his gun on arm, and his one friend behind him. I never heard his name mentioned but once. On a late August evening in the Chippendale Arms there was a meeting to start the local football club on its way for the coming season. There was some difficulty in getting a sufficient number of willing and eligible people to serve on the committee. During a lull a youth, for want of something likelier to suggest, said, 'What about Mr Clay?' There was a rustle of disapproval, and I thought I heard a murmur of 'foreigner' from the corner where the chairman, the Chippendale Arms host, was sitting. No other notice was taken of the question.

Then once again his name was spoken. Late in the following spring Thesiger Crowne, Tom Benton, Isaac Putcher, Rawson Leaf, and myself with some others were standing by a gate at the village end, gossiping of nothing in particular. Beyond the gate a path ran some three-quarters of a mile, straight down through four meadows, to the bank of a derelict canal. A few yards along the bank to the right could be seen a disused lock. As we were talking, we saw the figure of Rufus Clay in the distance, walking along the bank with his dog, towards the path. No attention was paid until they reached the lock side. Then the retriever came to a sudden halt, barked excitedly, and in a moment disappeared over the side. We could see the man's agitation even at that distance, but still the talk was hardly interrupted. Then a strange thing happened. Rufus stood upright a moment, seemed to quiver, and plunged after his friend. At once we were in full flight down the field. It was too late. What had drawn the dog in, whether a rat or what else, no one knew. But the lock with its water fifteen feet below bank level, was a death trap. Both dog and man were past our help. It was an hour before they could be got out. And then Thesiger Crowne said, 'A bad job that. Rufus Clay. These foreigners do never learn their way about.'

CHAPTER 27

PONY,
THE FOOTBALLER

I do not know what his other name was, or even the real one that was given him at his christening. Everyone in the village called him Pony. He was a grown youth, twenty years or so of age, large, with a handsome face but a rather dull eye. He had assiduity without direction. He was ostensibly the wheelwright's assistant, but he was hardly known to assist. He bustled about ardently, but no result came of his bustling, as no plan preceded it. If he was sent out on two errands he would return proud in the accomplishment of one, having forgotten the other. Like the clown in the circus he contributed an amiable disorder to the work of the world, but what was art in the clown was nature in him. Being told by his mistress to post some letters and feed the fowls, he deposited the letters in the cornbin, did his feeding, and went happily home. His was not the abstraction of the poet; he just wasn't equal to the complex demands of life. Friendly, willing, honest, he had neither initiative nor reliability. He was born to sit in the sun, but, with a living to be made, his best hope was a job with no uncertain humours in it, stone-breaking or leading plough.

To have to do with Pony was generally to be vexed with him, yet nobody disliked him. Even his master, who betongued him in an infinite series of terms, had no thought of dismissing him. He was glad not to be disliked, and far from indifferent to the ratings that he daily earned. He had, somewhere in the shadows of his mind, a wistful longing for efficiency. He wanted very much to be as clever as other people, realising forlornly that he never could be. His master, the masons, Mr Thorn the baker, Philip the shepherd, who always seemed to contrive a fold full of healthy lambs at the right time, Mrs Murgatroyd at the Post Office, who could register letters and reckon up about insurance stamps and money-orders, Roger Stone, who drove a traction engine — all seemed miracles of competence to him. Watching them, he would make little resolutions to himself, but they faded always.

Pony had heart but no brains, and that was an end of it. Sometimes his vagaries had a spice of the unexpected in them, but for the most part his was a routine of uninspired stupidity. Once he got into disgrace, when, with native ineptness, he chose Felicity Pratt, the constable's daughter, for an amatory impulse, and kissed her. His ears were boxed, but no worse came of it. He relapsed into his uneasy obscurity. And then his day of glory came.

It was a Saturday at the end of February. An unwonted crowd had assembled on the village football ground. The local team was to meet Edge Albion, their rivals from across the valley, in the semifinal of the Cotswold Cup. Not for years had athletic excitement run so high. Both teams had had a highly successful season, and were neck-and-neck for honours in the Ciceter League. The winners of this afternoon's match were almost sure of the cup, neither of the other semi-finalists being fancied for a chance. It was thought that the advantage of ground would just about see the home team through, but half an hour before the kick-off several hundred Edge supporters made it clear that their favourites were not going to fall through lack of support. At twenty minutes past two the Edge eleven, in blue jerseys and white shorts, came on to the ground to try their paces. They were greeted with a roar. Then, to a thunder of cheers, seven or eight of the home team followed, green and black, and gave a turn of their quality at the opposite goal. The ground was bubbling with excitement, which became particularised as it was seen that the home captain with his vice-captain and another leader of the team were in earnest discussion with the club officials outside the wooden shanty that served as pavilion and dressing-rooms. A minute later a rumour was flying round the ground. Bob Duckers, the inside left, had suddenly been taken ill and could not play. A strong second eleven was away from home, and difficult as it was to muster twenty-two players at any time, there were no reserves. Consternation was abroad.

Now, Pony was a footballer. Not that he had ever played in a match, even for the second eleven. But he had cut down an old pair of trousers, somehow come by a discarded pair of football boots, and every Saturday appeared on the ground, to join in the kick-about before the match began.

Once, in a practice game at the opening of the season, he had been allowed to play full back, when he twice kicked the ball through his own goal, and in a collision with his fellow back, who was captain of the first eleven, he brought that Olympian so heavily to the ground that he was unable to play in the first two matches of the year. But, although he could but have a stray kick, Pony loved the game, and he eagerly followed the fortunes of his club, the half-crown subscription to which he saved with great diligence each summer. Every member of the team was to him a hero 'sans peur et sans reproche', and today they were all dedicated to a cause in which gods would be jealous to contend.

On so august an occasion, Pony had not ventured on to the playing area, but he was there, dressed as by habit, though wearing a shabby overcoat to hide what he feared might be taken as a presumption. As the rumour reached him, he was sick with apprehension. Bob Duckers was one of the cracks; this was altogether too bad. He hated Edge more than ever. Then some nerve of almost dead ambition was startled in him. Little by little he sidled towards the group of arguing players and officials. He could hear them talking. 'We can't play ten men — it will throw all the balance out as you might say.' 'It's no good — the doctor forbids it.' 'He were perfectly well this morning.' 'We ought to have scratched the second eleven.' Pony was trembling as he listened. Then the captain's eye fell on him. Something was said, which he could not hear. 'Pony,' the captain called out, 'you'll have to play.' Then he was instructed. He was to be inside left, and he was to interfere between the centre and the outside as little as possible. He took off his coat, and went on to the field. As he appeared there was a shout of laughter from the home spectators. They could laugh themselves silly for all Pony cared. He had gone to heaven. He heard the whistle blow.

It was a terrific struggle, on a slow, slippery ground. Pony did as he had been told, and hardly touched the ball. At half-time no goal had been scored. The Edge supporters were in high spirits. If they could make a draw here, they were confident of the result in the replay on their own ground. Early in the second half, which began in a light fog, Pony came to grief. The left half presented the inside right with a perfect opening. The forward was about to take it, when Pony, who had nothing whatever to do with the movement, was off-side, and the chance was lost. The captain remonstrated, and there were angry ejaculations round the field. Then, a few minutes later, the centre forward, with the ball at his foot, found himself beautifully placed. He poised himself to shoot. As he did so, Pony, who was out of position, dashed, impelled by some devil of mischance, excitedly across the goal mouth. The centre had made no mistake; the ball flew from his foot far out of the goal-keeper's reach, driven towards the open corner of the net. Four yards from the goal it landed fairly on the small of Pony's back, and bounded high over the cross-bar. An exasperated howl, coming from players and spectators alike, rose on the foggy air. Tears of rage were in Pony's eyes. He felt that life was death and damnation.

The game went on, furiously, and still no score was made. Ten minutes from time a thicker bank of fog came across the field, and the players flitted like phantoms, their movements drawn, as it seemed to the spectators, into slow, rhythmic abstractions. In the higher circles of the game, the referee might have called a closure, but we do not allow these niceties. Five more minutes passed. Edge stock was very high indeed. Then upon Pony the glory descended. He seemed to be alone. A few players, hardly distinguishable, drifted about the fringes of the fog-ring that circled him. Suddenly the ball rolled before him, someone just behind it. It was the referee. Catching his foot on the ground, Pony gave the ball a kick, so that it went a few yards only. He ran after it, and gave it another kick, wild now, but again mistimed. Again he rushed in pursuit, and, as he reached it, a figure loomed up in front of him, not three paces away. It was the Edge goal-keeper. He was aware, in that tremendous moment, of ranks of straining faces beyond. He kicked in frenzy. The goal-keeper flung himself at full length, only to turn the flight of the ball a few feet as it passed into the net. One of the Edge backs, followed by a medley of players, crashed into Pony, and drove him back on into a goal-post. The referee's whistle blew, and the cries of pandemonium went up. The fog was lifting. Pony, stunned and shaken, was carried off the field. The ball went back to the centre, was kicked off, and time was called. We had gone into the final.

Pony, dazed but recovering, was the centre of enthusiasm such as was unknown in the history of the club. He was carried round the field, the team singing behind him that he was a jolly good fellow. The captain gave him a green and black jersey on the spot. The rector, who was president of the club, invited them all to supper at the Chippendale Arms that night. Pony was toasted, and was called upon for a speech. He stood up, and said that he thought the supper was a pretty good one, and that he hoped Bob Duckers wouldn't mind.

His glory did not come again. In fact it was forgotten in a week by all but himself. A fortnight later the final tie was played on a neutral ground, six miles away. Pony walked, wearing his colours and the overcoat. But eleven men were there this time. He saw them win easily, by five goals. He saw them take the cup away, and on Monday he went to look at it in the parish room. He stood in front of it for a long time, by himself. And with it were eleven silver medals, each with a name engraved upon it, but his was not among them.

CHAPTER 28

JOE PENTIFER
AND SON

Thatch becomes rare in the Cotswolds, the young men finding it too slow and grave a craft to learn. Joe Pentifer was the last of the great thatchers. His long, stormy beard, and his thick hair, itself thatchlike, not so much white-seeming as bleached by many winds, made him a figure such as Blake might have added to his visionary portraits. Ezekiel or Aaron he should have been, but he was, he held, christened Joe, not even Joseph. He was a slow philosopher, mysteriously counting the numbers of the stars from old newspaper cuttings, or reminded by the sickle that he carried to his half-acre at harvest time that life too was but a span. Then he would be a little prolix, stroking his beard with patriarchal deliberation, so that people in a hurry would avoid him. Whatever wisdom may have been within, the world for others did not lighten under his scrutiny, and his discourses, not very justly perhaps, were commonly accounted dull. But no one ever disputed his one mastery. He knew the ways of straw as Praxiteles did of marble or Cellini of gold and silver. The yellow thatch worked under his hands to swift and even order, material as truly used, with a skill as personal, humble though it was, as that of those artists of a higher calling.

As he grew old, Joe left the business more to his son, who, to his lifelong chagrin, was named Aesop. His heir had from early youth been bred to thatching, and had some proficiency in the job. But he was a continual scorn to his father, who was only forced by the necessity of the case at length to allow 'Joe Pentifer and Son' to appear on the small bill-headings that a new generation demanded. Joe himself had always taken a pound a week for his work, never more nor less, and word of mouth and a hand to hand transaction had been good enough for him. With the coming of Aesop the old order had changed, but Joe accepted the new ways without approval, and partnership had no reality for him. Aesop was not a bungler, but he knew nothing of the secret magic, and his father saw no compensation for middling technique in an increased wage. The difference between the senior partner's handi-work and the junior's was a thing for fine perceptions only. Aesop, for all his father's care, was not aware of it. Sometimes when, sorely against his will, Joe had to relinquish a piece of work to his son, an untrained eye, or even a trained eye of the duller kind, would hardly detect the transition from genius to common talent. But Joe detected it, nor was it fancifully. The difference was there, plain enough to a sense sufficiently alert. It was as David Cox to Tom Collier, Worcester paste to Coalport.

For some time the hostility threw no sparks. Joe considered silk purses and sow's ears, and gave up trying to show the duller wit of Aesop what it could not understand. Aesop was aware of subtle and unspoken reproaches, and resented them, but there was nothing he could shape his tongue to. When there was a special piece of work to be done, the old man kept control, deputising only when poor roofs were to be patched or new ones laid in secluded or impermanent corners. Aesop could not afford to quarrel about it. The business was not a rich one, but it was too good to lose, and his father had as well a snug reserve of two thousand pounds or so that had drifted to him from an intestate brother who had gone to New Zealand chiefly because he could not abide his family. So Aesop did not cultivate pride, being rather a politic man, as was remarked sometimes at the Chippendale Arms when the best was being said of the village. But disaster came nevertheless.

Sir John Toppingham was rebuilding his stables, and, because of the latest increase in cost of tiling, decided for thatch, giving the contract to Pentifer and Son. It was a long row of buildings, forming one

boundary of the Green alongside the churchyard, a show site. Joe took
the work in hand as a matter of course, and carried it on without even
consulting Aesop until two-thirds of the roof was done. Then he
slipped on the ladder and wrenched his foot. It meant lying up for a
week or so, and as Sir
John was in a hurry there
was nothing for it but to
let Aesop go on. Joe had
put all his virtue into the
work. He was getting old,
and another chance of this
size and importance might
not come his way. He had
meant it to be his
masterpiece, and now . . .
It was exasperating. He let
Aseop see that it was
exasperating.

At the end of the fourth
day he hobbled out with
two sticks. As he came
into the Green the morning sun was in full flood upon the bright straw.
At once his worst fears were realised. To you and me the thatch might
have seemed to be of a piece, but to Joe Pentifer the division of Aesop's
work from his own was as marked as though someone had drawn a
clear black line down the straw. He stared, and Aesop, busy on the
ladder, did not know that he was being watched. Joe could see the
fingers working wrongly, with no finesse. He loved thatch, he never
knew how much until this moment, with the sun showing what the
beauty of its perfection could be, and Aesop showing what perfection
was not. For minutes he stared, and then he cried out — 'Come down
here. Stand back and look at it, and be ashamed.'

Aesop looked round and came down.

'What's that you say?' He had heard plainly enough, and now
resentment was on top. 'Look at it, and be ashamed,' said Joe, lifting

one of his sticks and pointing with indignation at the long, glowing roof. 'Some folks can't tell between thatch and stubble, it do seem.'

Aesop snatched the raised stick from Joe's hand, and laid it in one sharp stroke across his father's shoulders. The old man looked at his son, saying nothing, nearer to Blake than ever, took back his stick and hobbled away. In the evening Aesop offered a formal but not insincere apology. Joe did not reply.

Thereafter the incident was never referred to. Aesop did his best, and Joe thought as little of it as formerly. But as the senior partner's infirmities grew, more and more work came necessarily to Aesop's hand. A few people observed a lowering of the firm's standard, but by most it was unnoted. Aesop settled down comfortably to authority, and cherished schemes of advancement when he should be sole proprietor. There was the two thousand pounds, and but his mother to share it with him for her lifetime, he supposed, and one sister. There was a hay and corn business in Ciceter that might . . .

These were the days now for Aesop with every prospect pleasing. And then Joe died. His will was read, thus — 'To my wife, Sarah, one thousand pounds and my household goods, and my two-thirds share interest in the business of Pentifer and Son, for the term of her life, and thereafter to my daughter, Ann, to whom also I leave one thousand pounds. Should my daughter predecease my wife, Sarah, then these bequests shall pass to my nephew, Barnabas Pentifer. And to my son, Aesop, I bequeath the stick with which he beat his father.'

WILLUM
WURKMAN'S
WIT AND WISDOM

CHAPTER 29

WILLIAM INTRODUCES HIMSELF

'Hast lost thee woy then, you?'

I had not quite lost myself, but I was not certain which was my best way back home being a stranger in these parts. I had been taking stock of the country and mentally calculating which would be my easiest way, when these words fell on my ear. They were spoken by an old man of anything between seventy and eighty years of age. He was I should think a perfect type of the old-fashioned Gloucestershire agricultural labourer. In height he was a little under the average; thin and straight as a poplar; his few white locks peeped out from under the brim of a hat which was probably as old as its wearer. He was dressed in corduroy trousers and a smock frock, and as he approached, without claiming the powers of a Sherlock Holmes, I was perfectly certain that he had been at work amongst animals, especially pigs. He carried an appreciable part of the Cotswold Hills on his heavy boots. The expression on his face was that of a man very satisfied with himself and not averse to a little inquisitive interest in those he encountered on his way home. I had noticed him several times in my evening walks, but apart from the usual 'Good-night' he had never addressed me before. This night I rather encouraged the old man's conversation.

'No,' I replied, 'but I want to get over to yonder hill.'

'Wot might your name be then, zur?' — apparently there was no shy reserve about the old chap.

'Bagster,' I replied.

'Bist thee Billy Bagster's bwoy as kum whum t'other day?'

I gently declined this honour and told him I was a stranger.

'I've zid thee walking about — whur dost live then?'

There was not a trace of rudeness in the old man's manner; he apparently believed in asking straight questions and getting straight answers. I told him where I lived, adding that my days up till the beginning of the summer had been spent in London.

'Zo, thee'st knaw Lundun — a beg place yent it?' I assented.

'My old 'ooman,' he continued, 'wants to go a galivanting about up thur to the Exhibition. My eldest bwoy he alived in Lundun these twenty yur. Doost knaw 'Ammersmith?'

'Yes,' I said.

'Then thee'st might a met Jarge Wurkman; he lives at a hundred an' two Zizziter Strit.'

'No,' I had not met him.

'He's a good bwoy is Jarge,' said the old man, 'only them thur Zozialists a got 'old on 'im. Do'ost know wot I'd do wi' um — I'd make um kum down ere and plow thuk thur veeld.' He pointed to a very large and awkward looking field which we were passing. 'I warned as that 'ud knok it out of 'um.'

'You are not a Radical, I expect —'.

The old man turned on me. 'Wot, I a yaller! No, thee doesn't knaw Willum Wurkman or thee 'oosn't ax that thur questyun. I be a blue, I be, true blue.'

The old man was getting quite warm. I said 'In the place I come from blue is the Liberal colour.'[1]

'Zo twas whur I kum from,' replied he. 'When I woz a bwoy o' vawr yur my old veythur zed to I, "Willum, my bwoy, wotever thee bist when thee dust grow up thee be a blue." He died when I woz twelve yur old and 'is last wurds as vur as I remember woz "Willum thee be a blue." So I woz a blue; not as I knawed wot it meant, you mind. Well when I woz about twenty yur old I kum to live down hyur and got 'ired by Varmer White at Zizziter Mop and I a been wi' un ever zince. Varmer zays to I wun day, "Willum, bist thee a yaller?" "No," I zays, "I be a blue." I didn't know azactly wot he woz but I a'vound it best to alluz zay stright out wot I be. Well, I vound out ater as Varmer was a Liberal and a yaller, but he never zed nothing to I at 'lection times and wun day, let's zee, why it'll be varty yur ago kum the time, cause twas the zame yur as young Varmer was barn, old Varmer comes to I and zes, "dang my eyes," he zez, Willum, I thenk as thee bist right ater all, I be agwoing to be a Blue the zame as you." "That's right, zur," I zays, "I knawed as I woz right."'

The old man had got into quite an introspective frame of mind as we walked along the lane and I felt quite sorry to interrupt him, but I was not certain that the way we were going was the way I wanted to go. So I said, 'Where does this lane lead to Mr ——' I was going to say 'Mr Workman,' not feeling quite sure whether the old fellow would like me to call him 'Willum' on such a short acquaintance. He saw my indecision and said 'Willum Wurkman, that's my name, and the voke do allus call I Willum.' 'Reminds I' — and he was off again into his recollections of the past — 'Reminds I o' my yungest wench's nipper. Pason zays to I, "Wot's yur grandson's name, Willum?" "Ted," zez I, "only we do call'n Ethered in shart."' The old man chuckled at the remembrance.

We had reached a cottage by this time at which Willum, as I felt I could call him now, stopped. ''Oot kum in and 'ave a glass o'beer?' he said.

'Thank you, not to-night,' I replied, 'I want to get home now, but perhaps another night.'

'Oi,' said Willum, 'glad to zee thee any time.'

I made up my mind to have many a chat with the old man. So I shook hands, and having received his directions for getting home I started on my way down the hill.

CHAPTER 30

REMINISCENCES OF PIG-KEEPING

I met Willum at the usual place a few evenings after that to which I referred last week.

'Good evening, Willum,' I said; and the glibness with which I brought out the old man's name reminded me of an incident which occurred in our village during the summer. Old Betty Turner had got her eldest daughter's son down from London, and being desirous of obtaining that Gloucestershire delicacy called 'chitlings' sent her precocious grandson to the bacon factory for some in the raw state. The boy was a typical Cockney. He asked the man at the factory for a 'bucket of inwards.' The slayer of pigs cast a look of disgust on the lad and it was not for some moments that he gathered what was wanted. But the bucket which the boy carried assisted his perceptions. 'Doost thee myen a bukkut o' innards?' he cried. The boy concluded that it was even so, but in telling me the incident he naively remarked, 'They do talk funny down hyar, don't they?'

In reply to my query as to his health Willum said, 'O! I be a' right, but not just as sprack as I shud like, these blamed east winds a' gid I the rumatiks.'

I suppose it must have been the recollection of the above incident, or it might have been the odour arising from Willum's boots; at any rate my thoughts turned to pigs. 'Everybody seems to keep a pig,' I remarked.

'O! Oi,' said Willum, 'but peg kipping yeny wot it usent to be. Now

I a' kep a peg ever zence I woz married and I allus reckon to have a zide o' bacon to cut at. But Lard bless ye thur yent dree men in the villij as knaws 'ow to cure a bit o' bacon now, and zence old Dan'l Jones died I a' had a rare old job to cum across anybody as could even kill a peg.'

I said I had been told that it did not pay to keep pigs in these days.

The old man was quite vicious as he replied: 'Pay! A' coorse it dwunt pay. Thur's Nalus Pickwick kep a peg and got a book called — Lar' bless my zawl what was thuk thur book called — why "Zyentific Peg Kipping." Nalus used to cart that thuk book about wi' un and spend zumtimes as much as a zhillun in Stroud for zum zart o' stuff as the book zed ud make the pegs vat. Wun day he comes to I and zays "Willum," he zays, "do 'e come and look at our peg." Well, I went and looked at un and I zed, zays I, "Nalus thee'st better kill un or else her'll be a d'yed un." Nalus went off down the bottom to get a butcher, but avoor they cood get back the peg was d'yed. But they killed thuk ther peg all the zame and I dwunt thenk as Nalus lost more than half a zuvrin by un.'

I joined in Willum's laugh, but not very heartily, for I wondered how many pigs killed after they were dead I had partaken of.

'You zee tis like this ere,' continued Willum, 'if you kips a peg zo as to ave plenty o' bacon to cut and kum agyen at, the peg pays. But nowadays evrybody zells thur pegs an' lets them as buys um make all the profit. Now thur was Jakob Tanner. Jakob used to kip his couple o' pegs and did vurry well oot on um as long as the childurn woz yung and ad to yet wot woz put avoor um. But when Jakob an' his missis was left alone Jakob got the lumbago wun day and the missis had to tyuk the pegs thur vood. "Jakob," her zays, "if I a' got to veed the pegs I be agwoing to 'ave sum o' the profits." Zo now Jakob a' got to buy the missis a new hat or zummat when the pegs be zold. Natral enuf thur yent much profit left for Jakob now.'

I suggested that pigs were very dirty animals, and I wondered how we could so enjoy our bacon for breakfast.

'Now that's wur you do make a gurt mistake,' said Willum, 'Ther yent a cleaner animal than a peg when they be properly looked ater. I suppose I a' had to do wi' zum thousands on um in my time, and I never knawed wun as vouled his sleeping place, an' that's more than you can zay o' most animals. Why Lor' bless yer, zur, a peg is more like a human being than any other theng as lives. Old Doctor Vizzik as died last yur used to tell I as thur insides were nearer like ourn than any other animal. An' I a' noticed the look in thur eyes an' if you'll believe I thur wuz just the zame look in Ted Robert's eyes when the doctor told un he wuz a' gwoing to die as I 'av zid in the peg's eyes when the butcher was in the garden. An' when the zow a' had a litter o' yung uns why I 'av zid just the zame look in her eyes as my old 'ooman used to 'ave when our yung uns was barn. Bless 'e, zur, pegs and we be vurry much alike.'

We had reached Willum's cottage by this time, but the old man stood and talked.

'Talking o' pegs,' he said, ''minds I o' wot the missis was rading tuther night in the "Stroud News" about zum doctor or other as zed as 'ow we ought to tyuk a male o' sand zumtimes. When Nalus Pickwick, as I was a' telling ye on just now, had got his fust peg and was a'trying to brang un up on "Zyentific Peg Kipping" the peg wun day 'oodn't stand up and his tail wuz as straight as thuk thur spout. Nalus dosed un up wi' wot the book zed, but the peg's tail 'oodn't curl no'ow. Zo Nalus kums down an' zays "Willum, wot dust thenk I'd better gi'e the peg to make his tail curl?" "Why," zays I, "thee go an' get half a bukkut o' small coal and let the peg yet it." Nalus thought as how I wuz a joking at fust, but ater a bit he went an' got a han'ful o' small coal and looked over the sty and zed "Chuk, chuk." But the peg only grunted and 'oodn't get up, so Nalus goes inzide and put his hand to the peg's snout. Her vurry zoon skrunched up the small coal and looked for zum moor. Ater about the zixth 'andful her got up, and avoor night her tail was as curly as a corkscrew.'

With this little reminiscence Willum turned towards the door and I wished him good-night.

CHAPTER 31

ELECTION STORIES

'But 'ant you ever been down hyur at 'Lection time?'

I was enjoying my third stroll with Willum and we had been discussing the result of the last bye-election. Willum had told me that feeling was inclined to run high in the Stroud Division when an election was proceeding, and was surprised when I told him that I had not had the pleasure of witnessing a contested election in the Division.

'Then you a' got a treat in store, that's all I can zay,' said Willum, 'I allus thenks o' the time when I axed the yaler candidate a questyun as he coodn't answer.'

'When was that?' said I.

'Well, twas like this ere d'ye zee. The yalers had got a loyer chap aputting up. Now wot were he's name; 'body ood thenk I woz agetting old for I be jiggered if I can recall thuk chap's name. Twas Trimmer or Brimmer or summut like that. Any'ow his name dwunt matter. I was in at the Twelve Bells one night agetting a pint o' beer vur zupper 'cause our barrel had run out. Reuben Young happened to be thur too. He zays, zays he, "Hast thee yerd as the yalers be agoing to have a meeting to-night?"

'"Nah," zays I.

'"They be," zays he, "sh'at go?"

'Now carding to count this yer Trimmer or Brimmer or whatever his name woz co'od talk like one o'clock. Zo I zed to Reuben, "If thee oot go zo'll I." "Right you be," zays he. Zo by'n'bye we went down to the meeting. True anuf thuk chap co'od talk. He put I in mind o' our em'ty beer barrel at whum, for you co'od tell a woz em'ty be the noise a gid out. Auld Butcher Jenkins was churman and presently he ups and zays, "Anybody got any questyuns to ax?" The skool-gaffer – he az been d'yead these fifteen yur, he axes a lot o' vurry good questyuns and the Yaller chap answers um as slik as anytheng. Then twas quiet vur a bit, and as nobody zeemed inclined to ax any more questyuns I thought as how my time 'ad kum to ax wun. Zo up I gets. Butcher, he zays, "Wot! you got a questyun, Willum?" "Yus," zays I. "Out wi' un then" zays he. Zo I zays, "Well Mr, wot I want to knaw is whether you can tell I the diff'rence atween the woy a cow gets up vrom the ground and the woy a hoss gets up?" 'An if you'll believe I if thuk thur carpet bagger of a vellow didn't go as red as my missis's vlannel petticoat and zed, ater 'umming and 'a'ing vur zum time as Rally 'e didn't thenk it woz a questyun as mattered a girt deal. Ater that I allus put he down as being like auld Squire Atkin's zun. No doubt you 'ave yeeard wot he rote to the bailee?'

I said 'No, I had not.'

'Twas like this ere,' continued Willum, 'the auld man died in Lunnun bout Mikklemuss time, and yung squire as woz barn and lived in Lunnun all 'is time told bailee as thengs woz to go on as usual. But the bailee wanted to zee the yung gaffer and kep on riting for un to kum down. But he oodn't kum. At las' bailee wrote and zed if the yung guv'ner didn't kum down thuk wik he didn't knaw wot he zhood do 'bout the lambing, and squire wrote bak and zed the lambing had better be put off a vyow months.' Even I could appreciate this. I had not dared to laugh about the question the old man put to the candidate for I felt quite unable to answer it myself.

Presently Willum started again. 'Yuss we do 'ave it to down here at 'Lection times I can tell 'e. Thur woz a 'lection once — why it must be nearly varty yur ago. Auld Zam'l Cook woz alive then. He woz 'bout the only chap in the villij as cood put his hand to paper, and enybody as wanted to zend a vyow lines used to get he to write um. I woz at a Yaller meeting one night, and the yung chap as woz aputting up made a spach, and then he zed as he 'ood answer any questyuns, zame as chap did as I woz atelling 'e on just now. In them days twas pretty zafe to ax vur questyuns cause nobody 'ood ax eny. But Zam'l 'e got up and 'e zays, "I shud like to ax 'e, zur, the right woy to spell mangul wuzzle?" We cood zee as Zam'l 'ad got un, but he woz pretty sharp he woz, and he zays, zays he, "A'right, my man, I will spell Mangul wuzzle when you can pronounce it right." Zo he slipt out on't alright. But twas wot vollod 'bout two yurs ater as caused the fun.'

'What was that?' said I, quite interested in these old stories of byegone days.

'Well, you zee,' the old man continued, 'the Yallers wun that time, but thur man broke 'is nek wun day ahunting up Zizziter woy and thur woz anuther 'Lection. This time they didn't get zuch a smart chap and wen he kum down hyur we thawt as 'ow we 'ood try and get un on to mangel wuzzle agyen. But I be agetting avoor me tale. I awt to 'a told 'e as the Yallers had got a meeting in the clubroom one night. In the aternoon we got auld Zam'l's gran-zun to try and 'tice the auld chap down to axe a questyun. Yung Tommy got the old man into the Twelve Bells and gie'd un a pint o' beer. Presently Tommy zays, "I zay, grampy, be you agwoing to the meeting to-night?" "I dwunnow," said Zam'l. "You'd better go and ax un to spell mangul wuzzle?" said Tommy. An' just as he zed that who shood kum in but Baker Bunting and he hyers wot Tommy zays. Now Baker woz gwoing to take the chur at the meeting so we thought as how we had let the cat out o' the bag, zo we didn't zay anything more while 'e woz thur. Bi'mby when Zam'l had had 'is beer 'e gets up and zays he shood go to the meeting. We zed as tood be no good as Baker had heard wot we had zed. But Zam'l zed he shood go all zame. Zo we all went to the meeting to zee wot 'ud happen. Lawkamassy thuk Yaller chap was about the poorest hand at a speech as I ever yeard. When he finished the Churman zed as any questyuns 'ood be welkum. But nobody got up and I cood zee as the yaller chap was jolly glad as thur warn't any questyuns to answer. Just as we 'ad gid up all thoughts of a joke up gets Zam'l. I zid the Churman pull the yung chap's coat and whisper zummat in 'is yur. Then he turned to Zam'l and zed, "Well, my man, wot questyun do you want answered?" "I wants to knaow the woy to spell zooper-vossut,"[1] zed Zam'l. Everybody was as quiet as a mouse to see what the candidate 'ood zay. He puts up 'is glass to 'is left eye and zays, "Ha, ha!

yes, yes! well! well! it ain't a plitikal questyun, but – aw! just to oblige
you I don't mind spelling the word for you – it is – aw! let me see –
M-A-N-G-O-L–" But avoor 'e had got as vur as that even we as didn't
know much about spelling zid wot had happened and nearly bust our
zides alaffing, and Baker Bunting woz as savidge as a bare wi' a zore
bak.'

We had by this time reached Willum's cottage, where I left him and
proceeded homewards.

CHAPTER 32

WILLUM AND HIS FAMILY

As I sauntered along the leaf covered road to meet Willum at the usual place of meeting I saw in front of me an old, old man. He was quite a patriarch in appearance, and it would not have surprised me to hear it was Willum's father. On these Cotswold Hills people seem to live to be as old as Methuselah. I was speaking to quite an elderly man a few days ago and he casually mentioned that he spent his Sunday evenings as a rule by 'running down to veythur's vur a vyow hours.' I said, 'But surely your father must be a very old man?' 'Lar, bless 'e no,' was the reply, 'he's only aity dree an muther's vive yur older'n 'e and as sprack as a lark. Her comes up most wiks and gets her bit o' bacon.'

The old man in front of me met Willum as he came out of the farmyard and I was very much interested in the salutations which passed. 'Hullo! Jarge,' said Willum, 'how bist?' 'I be,' said Jarge, 'how's you?' Then they stood still but did not look at one another. After contemplating the sky for ten seconds Jarge said, 'What's thenk on't?' 'We shall ha' zum rain avoor marnin,' said Willum. There was another silence. Then Willum said, 'Well, zo long, I must be agetting whum.'

I had been hearing about Willum during the week. I never like to inquire into family matters, for I have found that if there is one thing more than another which the British working man likes to keep to himself it is his own home affairs, so unless information is volunteered to me I never inquire about things concerning the family of any person I meet in these parts. But I had heard that Willum had had twelve children, of whom nine were still living, and I must confess I was very interested to know how such a large family could have been brought up on what must have been a very small income. So I said, after we had asked and answered the usual questions about our health and remarked on the weather, 'The children look very healthy about here, Willum.'

'Oi, Oi!' was the reply, 'they dwun look zo bad, but they yent as beg and strong as they used to be. But thur, tyent to be expected. Wot wi' this yur eddication as kips um at school now till the' be ver' near growed up, and doctoring and messing wi' um, why childurn now yent half wot they woz. Molly Phelps was atelling I tother day as her yung un had got consols in the throat, wotever thuk might be.'

The old man looked at me inquiringly, but I could not tell him. I have ascertained since that the child was suffering from her tonsils.

'Now, how many yung 'uns do you thenk I a' brought up?' continued Willum. Without waiting for me to answer he went on. 'Why nine, and we a' burried dree. Zo I knaws zummat about it. But thur, voke dwunt have the vamilies the' used to.'

The old man shook his head. 'I can't zay,' he continued, 'as I be much of a skollard, but I 'ave tuk stock o' two or dree thengs in my time and one on um is that all the best men as you do rade on do kum o' beg vamilies. Thur was Lard Zolsbury, the vinest mon as ever lived. Zee wot a lot o' bruthers and zisters he had, and then look wot a vine vamily he had hisself. Then thur woz Billy Gladstwun. Putting politiks azide vur a minnit I thenk as he woz a man as anybody 'ood a' been proud to a vathered, and he woz one o' a beg vamily. Then luk at the Keng. You can't zay but wot he woz one o' a beggish vamily. No, zumtimes I do thenk as the rason why times be zo bad and the country be a gwoing to the dogs or the Zozialists, 'tis all the zame, is drew thur being too many zmall vamilies.'

I ventured to hint that it must have taken much economy in money matters to have brought up Willum's large family.

'Yuss,' said Willum, 'We didn't have much to chuk awaoy on butcher's myet. When our vust babby kum to town I was agetting leven zhillins a wik an' I never earned more than thurteen. But then d'ye zee I had me house vur nex to nuthing an' we never had to spend anytheng on taters and green stuff, and as I woz atelling 'e tuther day I allus kep a peg. But thur's a lot of truth in wot Maister Goddard used to zay.'

'What's that?' said I.

'Maister Goddard used to zay,' continued Willum, 'as ow childurn woz all vurry well when th' woz yung and zucked the muther, but when um got old and zucked the veythur twaz nation unkid.'

We walked on some distance in silence after this. Willum seemed to be thinking deeply.

Presently the old man turned to me, and I was astonished to see a large tear on each furrowed cheek.

'Talking o' childurn,' he said, ''minds I o' my yung marrid days. We only lost dree o' our yung uns and two on them woz when the fever woz in the villij. But the missis and I woz atalking 'tuther night about our vust little un as died at zix munths. "Willum," her zays, "we be both on us agetting old, and the Almighty ool zoon take wun or 'tother on us; 'ool you be able to reckernize our little Billy when you zees un?" And do you knaow we both on us tried to rekelect wot the little chap woz like and we coodn't' — and the old man's voice trembled — 'no we couldn't. Now wot do you thenk, zur,' — and the old man looked at me with swimming eyes — 'do you thenk as our little Billy 'ool agrowed up or 'ool he be just a babby as wunt knaow his own veythur and muther and they wunt know he?'

I thought some moments before answering and then I said 'Willum, these things are beyond you and me. I can only tell you what a poet once wrote on the subject. It has comforted many and may help you. Speaking of his child who died in infancy he says:

> "Another child I have; his age I cannot tell;
> For they reckon not by years and months
> Where he is gone to dwell."

We walked on in silence till we reached Willum's cottage. The rain had been falling for some minutes.

'Zett in vur a wet night, I count,' said Willum.

'I think so,' said I, as I bade him 'Good-night.'

CHAPTER 33

WILLUM'S GRANDCHILDREN

In my walks with Willum nothing has impressed itself more on my notice than the easy and direct way which people in this neighbourhood have of inquiring the destination of those they meet on the road. I recall one particular incident.

Two boys met as I was bidding Willum 'Good-night' last week. Said one to the other, 'Wur bist gwoing, Joe?' 'Byent gwoing nowhur,' said Joe. 'Yuss the' bist,' was the rejoinder. 'No I byent,' replied Joe, 'I be acoming baak'. To which, of course, there was no reply.

It was getting dark as Willum and I met for our stroll this week. I remarked to him that the intense darkness of the nights was one of the features of country life, to which I found it difficult to get accustomed.

'Yuss,' said Willum, 'we do get it darkish down hyur, and when the parish lantern yent alight tis as dark as black 'ool.'

'You are fortunate to have a parish lantern,' said I. 'I suppose it is hung outside the Churchyard; was it a Jubilee memorial?'

'Lar, bless 'e, the parish lantern's the moon,' said Willum.

I felt foolish.

Willum continued, 'Thur's several thengs as we do call after the parish. Now this yur road as we be a valling about on' (the road had been covered with large chunks of local stone since last week) 'is covered wi' parish gravel.'

I could not help saying that I supposed the parishioners did not suffer from corns or they would improve the quality of their gravel.

'Talking of carns,' said Willum, ''minds I o' my son Dick's youngest nipper. He kum down an stopped wi' his grannie for a wik or two last autumn. Wun night her said to I, 'Willum, we be agwoing to a' zum rain and I must cut me karn.' Little Dick run off and got a old zikle as I woz atelling on im a day or two avoor as I used to cut the karn wi'. "Hyur you are, grannie," zays he, "come on, I'll help you."'

'How many grandchildren have you, Willum?' said I.

'Ha! Now you a axed I wun,' replied Willum?' with a laugh. 'Ef you'll count um as I do tick um off we 'ool zoon vind out. Now Jarge, that's my eldest, he got zix, I know. Dinah, that's my eldest wench as married Billy Perkins over at Driffield, her a only got a pidgin pair.'

'What's that?' said I.

'Why a bwoy an' a girl,' replied the old man.

'That makes eight,' I replied.

'Sarah a got — now I shall a to go drew um — thur's Etherd and Willum and Patience and Abijah and the twins; they be named Hugh and Double Hugh, leastwise thuk's woth thur veythur calls um. Then thur's little Timothy and the babby, an' I byent zure as thur won't be another by the time as I gets whum,' laughed Willum 'lets zee how many's that?'

'I make it sixteen,' said I, 'but I'm not sure that I didn't drop one'.

'Ha! that's wot Martha, my next daughter, did wi' her fust and the little chap is lame to this day. They call un "Little Jim" ater his veythur's mother, whoose name was Jimimah. He a got two brothers and one zister.'

'That makes twenty,' said I.

'Now my next wench yent married. I never cood make out why her didn't pick up wi' zumbody, but I be vurry glad as 'tis as 'tis vur her's the best o' the lot and a rael good daughter. Pason zays as how her's a "unhappropriated blessing." Her have promised her muther to gie up her place an' kum whum whenever we do want her to look ater thengs. 'Tool be better to 'ave won o' yur own vlesh an blud than zum skaramoucher as 'ood be a briviting about into thengs as didn't consarn her.'

'That leaves three of your children,' said I, to bring him back to the subject, for we were now within sight of the cottage.

'Yuss, thur's Richutt, and Zaul and Betsy. Richutt a got vive yung uns.'

'That makes twenty-five,' said I.

'Ho! thur's a lot more yit,' said Willum. 'Zaul he a got, well I'm jiggered ef I can azactly remember how many 'e a got. But thur's Reuben and Job and Nalus.'

'What?' said I

'Nalus, short for Karnelius,' said Willum, 'and David and Margrett and Tom and Dorothy, and I thenk thur's wun or two as we ant zid yet, anyhow I can't put me tung to thur names just now.'

'That's thirty-two at any rate,' I remarked, I hope your youngest daughter hasn't many or I shall lose count.'

'No, Betsy a only got two at present,' said Willum. 'Her married the skool-gaffer at a place up near Lunnon, a vurry clever chap he woz too, and had bin to collij. Their two be named, I knaw you'll laf, but tis as true as I be a standing hyur, they be named Zokrateez and Plato. We do call um Socks and Crocks when thur veythur yent wi'in hyuring.'

'Then you have thirty-four grandchildurn an' I lives in opes as thur'll be more shartly.'

We stood talking for a little while, for the moon had risen and it was quite light.

'Did ye hyur wot happened avoor the magistrates when Teddy Burton axed vur his license tuther day?' queried Willum.

'No,' said I.

'Well, the Clurk zed to Teddy avoor the Court begun, "How many childurn have you, Mr Burton?" "Ho! Wun the right zide of a duzzen," laughed Teddy.

'Presently the Churmun zays to Teddy, "I unnerstand that you hav leven childurn, Burton?"

'"Ho," zed Teddy, "then wot's bekum o' tuther uns."

'"You told me you had eleven," said the Clurk. "I knaw I didn't," zed Teddy.

'"But you did," zed the Clurk, "you zed you had one the right zide of a dozen."

'"Well, zo I have," shouted Teddy, "I've got thirteen."'

'Good-night, Willum,' said I.

CHAPTER 34

THE CHRISTMAS GHOST

I met Willum on Christmas Eve last week. 'Are we going to have an old fashioned Christmas, Willum?' said I.

'Now, I wunder wot you do myen by a old fashioned Christmuss,' replied Willum.

'Oh!' said I, laughing, 'I mean a Christmas-card kind of Christmas — robins, and holly, and snow and skating, and all that sort of thing.'

'Ho! Is that wot you calls a old fashioned Christmas?'

'Well' — and the old man looked over the hills with a weather wise air — 'it might, and agyen it mightn't snaw avoor Christmuss, but ef the wind do stik whur 'tis now we shall ave zum valling wether zhartly, but thur wunt be much ice vur zumtime yet, an as vur holly I dwunt thenk as I ever knawed it zo poor.'

'It means a mild winter when there are no holly berries, doesn't it?' asked I.

'Ha' You a yeeard thuk yarn ave ee,' laughed Willum. 'Now I can gie you bout vifty yurs' axperiyunce o' thuk. I thenk twas in vivty eight as I determined to vind out whether thur woz anytheng in't or not. Zo I zed I ood drive a nail in the byem as runs auver our vireplace every time as it kumd right. And how many nails do you think thur is in thuk byem at this minnit?'

'I give it up,' said I.

'Well, thur's just two,' continued Willum, 'zo I dwunt thenk much o' them thur tales as you do rade in the papers. As vur as I can judge thur yent any woy o' telling wot kind o' winter we be gwoing to ave, but I a noticed that nearly allus when we ave had a hot dry zummer we do ave a smartish sharp winter. But I dwunt go zo vur as to zay as wun depends on tuther like. I laves thengs like that to thay as do write in the papers' — and the old man looked at me with a twinkle in his eye.

'Now, Willum, 'tis Christmas to-morrow, so I am sure you will come down the road to the Twelve Bells and have a glass of port with me?' said I.

'I'll kum and ave a glass o' beer ef you likes,' said Willum.

'Very well,' said I.

We entered the old inn. A wood fire was blazing in an old fashioned grate. The room was low roofed and the windows did not open. The fumes of Shag tobacco were at first overpowering. There was a wooden seat with a straight back running round the walls and here and there it was divided into what I can describe best by calling cosy corners. The beams in the ceiling were black with age and dirt; the floor was of stone, covered here and there with sawdust freshly put down. Two men were lazily drinking their beer and talking about old-age pensions as we entered.[1]

'Hullo! Willum!' said one of them, 'how bist – aint zid the' vur auver a wik?'

'I be,' says Willum, 'how's you?'

At this point four or five men came in. Seeing me, practically a stranger, they all retired into their shells, just nodding to Willum by way of salutation.

'Gentlemen,' I said, 'will you do me the pleasure of drinking with Willum and myself? Landlord, bring in a quart or two and some glasses.'

The beer was brought. Whether it was Clissold's or Carpenter's, or Stroud Brewery, or Godsell's I can't say, but it was very good, and soon we were all chatting away as if we had known each other for years.

'Now, Zakky, les ave "Down at the Old Bull and Bush." said Job Gardiner, as I found his name to be. 'Aye kum on' said another, Billy Wilkins I think his name to be.

But Zakky wanted a lot of urging. At last he said 'I'll zeng "Bull and Bush" ef thee'll zeng "Varmer's Bwoy," Job?'

'Right you be,' said Job.

I cannot say that the voice was musical or that it was in tune. The first few lines hung in the air somewhat and I thought the song was going to be a failure, but presently we got to the chorus. By the time we had shouted 'Bush! Bush!' in the last line Zakky was a different man, and the succeeding verses went with gusto, and the last chorus shook the rafters.

Then Job let us have 'Varmer's Bwoy.' There were now about a dozen of us distributed in easy attitudes round the room.

'Les ave wun moor,' shouted Job, 'now then lads,'

> 'Vur to plow an to zow,
> 'An to rape an to mow,
> 'An to be a vermer's bwo-o-y,
> 'An to be a vermer's bwoy.'

Then Job turned to Willum and said, 'Now, Willum, thee cans't tell we a yarn, casn't?'

'I dwunnow,' said Willum. 'Kum on,' said Job, 'tell us bout Pason Hood an hees Nanny Goat,' said somebody. 'No, no, you a yeeard ee too many times,' said Willum, 'but I tell ee wot, I'll tell ee a ghost story.'

All were quiet as Willum begun.

'Zum on ee 'ool remember auld Varmer up yonder' — and Willum hooked his thumb over his shoulder — 'well, when I vust worked var'n I used to zlip up in the cock loft in the varmhouse. Wun night just avoor Chrismuss the missis was agieing I me drip o' beer vur zupper an her let the cup down and smashed un all to likkuts. "Lar, Willum, zummatt's gwoin to appen," her zays. I awt to tell ee as her woz a Carnish 'ooman and believed in drames and warnings and zuck like. I've zid her kum down in the marnin' and go straight to the winder an luk in her drame book an then turn round and zay, "We zhall zure to ave a visitor to-day vur I dramed about cats last night." Sure nuf we uzurully did, but I thenk they 'ood akum wi'out her adraming about cats. But I be vurgetting me tale. Well I went to bed thuk night and bout twelve oklok I yeeard zuch a banging o' the vrunt door as never woz. "Dal it all," zes I, "Who can thuk be at this time o' night." I didn't get up very sprak I can tell ee vur twas nation cold. Thenks I, I'll ave a luk at you avoor I goes down. The parish lantern was alight, zo I pops me yed out o' the winder and luks down to the vrunt door, but be jabers thur wuzn't nobody thur tho' the old knocker was a jumping up an down like a parched pea in a kullinder. It gid I quite a start I can tell ee. I got back to bed agyen and thought I must a been draming. I hadn't bin athur many zeconds avoor thur kum the knocking agyen louder'n ever. This time Varmer yurs un and I yurs un a shouting, "Willum, who be thuk at the door." "Nobody," zays I. "Yuss tis," zes he, "just you run down and zee who tis." I didn't like it a bit, but anyhow I went down an jolly glad I woz as the old dog Jack kum running up behind I when I got to the bottom of the stairs. I unchained the door and acoorse thur woz nobody thur. "Who is it?" shouts Varmer. "Nobody," zays I. "Well thas funny," zed ee, "didn't you hyur the knocking, Willum?" "Yuss," zed I, "I yeerd un twice." I bolted and chained the old door and woz just got back to bed agyen when thur was such a banging agyen as never woz. Warmer gets his gun and missis her begins to skweel. "Kum on, Willum," zed Varmer, "les go and zee who tis." Off we went down an Varmer goes up to the door and shouts out "Who's thur?" Nobody answered, an Varmer zets to wurk to unbolt the door, and the missis begins acrying vrom the top o' the stairs, "Don't ee go out, me dear, don't ee, I knaws tis a ghost or else Jack 'ood bark. I knawed zummat was agwoing to appen." But Varmer's temper was up and out ee goes, and I behind un. The dog run sniffing round, but thur wozn't a zawl to be zid cept a donkey in the home piece. Thur woz nothing to do but to go back to byed. I spose we hadn't been upstairs more'n two minnits avoor the row started agyen. I thawt the auld door was akumming down. I luk'd out o' the winder and thur woz nobody thur, an the old Neddy was a veeding as peaceful as anytheng. "Thur's nobody thur" zed I to Varmer vur he had yeeard it agyen acoorse. "But thur must be, mon," zed he, "the blamed door oodn't knock hisself." Well, off we went down agyen and went drew the zame performance but thur woz nobody to be zid.'

The old man stopped for breath. 'Wet thee whistle Willum,' said Job in quite a chastened voice — 'darned ef I yent angshus to knaw wot twos, woz it a ghost, or did ee vind out anytheng?'

The old man went on. 'I shud thenk as we went down to thuk door as many as zix times. As soon as we did get downstairs twas all as quiut as the grave, but the minnit we did get back to byed the row did begin wuss'n ever. At last Varmer zays, "I be gwoing to bide down yur." "Oh! me dear, dwun ee," zed missis. "But I be," zed Varmer and down he zets in the armchair in the kichin and old Jack the dog krept under'n an I went back to bed. We didn't yur any more noise thuk night.'

'And didn't you vind out anytheng?' asked several voices.

'You wait a minnit.' said Willum, who quite enjoyed working his hearers up to this excitement. 'Thuk performance went on every night for nigh on a wik and the village got to hyur on't and everybody said the place was haunted. Meyster woz as savige as a ber with a zore back, and missis woz expecting to hyur every day as her veythur and muther was dyead. But nothing appened except Chrismuss. We all had a jolly good time, and wether twas the beer or the plum pudden I dwunnaw but I coodn't zlip and bout 12 I had to run down stairs. We adn't yeeard the knocking thuk night up till then but just as I got to the vut o' the stairs the zame old row begun on the vrunt door. It made I vurgit all about beer or pudden. And then I zid wot twas.'

We all hung on the old man's words.

'Yuss, I zid wot twas, and bust out alaffing. The missis had putt down a zack bag at the vrunt door and old Jack was a zetting up on hees haunches an a skratting hisself vur all 'e woz wuth. His back was agyen the door and acoorse the old door zhuk like billy-ho. The dog did run to we when we did kum down the stairs and go back agyen when we did go to bed and start his skratting agyen when twas all quiut.'

'Well, ef thuk yent a good un,' said Job, and everybody commenced to talk and take up their neglected glasses.

'Now, Ezra, les have Woszayul' said Job.

Ezra did not want asking twice. Whether I can remember the song exactly I cannot say, but this is something like it:

Wozzayul, wozzayul, awl auver the town,
Our yur it is white, an our ale it is brown

Our baouwl it is made o' the maplin tree
We be jolly vellows and we drenks unto thee.

Hyurs luk to me meyster an to his right eye,
May God grant me meyster a good Chrismuss Pie,
And a good Chrismuss pie as we may all zee,
We be jolly vellows and we drenks unto thee.

Hyurs luk to me meyster an to his right arm,
May God grant me meyster a good crop o' karn,
And a good crop o' karn as we may all zee,
We be jolly vellows and we drenks unto thee.

Hyurs luk to me meyster an to his right leg,
May God grant me meyster a jolly vat peg,
And a jolly vat peg as we may all see,
Wi' me woszailing baouwl I'll drenk unto thee.

Now butler, kum breng us a baouwl o' the best,
We 'opes that the zaouwl in 'Even 'ool rest
Bur ef thou dust breng us a baouwl o' the small.
The down go butler, baouwl an all.

Willum had finished his beer and got up. I gave him Good-night and
Merry Christmas at the door. But the others were wound up and I
could hear their voices for a long distance as I walked down the hill.

CHAPTER 35

CURES FOR RHEUMATISM

It was a dull January afternoon and the cold pierced to the bones. The sky was heavy with snow clouds, and the wind was north-east; a depressing day, a day when there seemed no bright side to anything.

Willum complained of the 'rheumatics' as we started for our little stroll. Now rheumatism is one of the ills of the flesh of which I am most happily entirely ignorant. But I have learned to sympathise with an old man when he complains of the 'rheumatics,' and I have charged my memory with some dozens of alleged cures. So I said, 'Have you ever tried anything for the rheumatism, Willum?'

'Well, to tell'ee the truth, I ain't got no faith in them thur cures,' said Willum. 'My missis was arading tuther night 'bout a old mon as was cured by carting a tater about hi his pokkut, an' I woz vool enough to try thuk dodge, but it 'oodn't wurk wi' I. Then my bwoy Jarge, he thought as 'ow he'd got rheumatics, and went and bought a gallivanic reng, I thenk he called it, and zure 'nuf karding to 'ees account he got rid on't, and he zent the theng down to I. I wore un for nigh on a month, but I coodn't get shut o' the pain. Then Varmer's wife her zed, "Willum, you get zum Epsom zolts and putt um in a bottle o' gin wi' zum zulphur, and have a couple o' tablespoonfulls fust theng in the marnin." Well, considering as her found the bottle o' gin I coodn't do no less than try, but ater the vust dose I had to tell she, if her didn't mind I'd rather have the rheumatics. Then old Billy Smart told I he cured hisself by zukking lemons, so I zet me tith on edge vur a wik a zukking them thengs as be as zour as barges, but the carkscrews still kep' turning in me knees. Then thur waz a Lunnon chap as kumd down hyur, an' he zed "All you wants to do, Mr Wurkman, is to exercise the limb and get the wife to massij it, or summit like that." I told un my old limbs had had anuf massijing in thur time, an I didn't thenk as thuk 'ood do any good.'

Willum paused, and I began to think I would not announce my cure.

'Lar' bless 'ee,' continued the old man, 'when you do get to my yurs you'll thenk you be let off mighty light ef all you a got to complaim on be a touch o' rheumatics. Besides,' — and the old man turned to me with a laugh on his eyes — 'the Lard knows we can't afford weather glasses, and zo He zends we the rheumatics to let us know when tis gwoing to rain. You mark my words if we don't 'ave zum wet avoor to-morra night.'

I am writing this several days after I saw Willum, and I am bound to say the old man was right.

We were passing through the wood which lies near Willum's cottage. The old man stood still in the road.

'Do you see thuk ellum tree?' said he.

'Which one?' I asked.

'Thuk 'un thur, just aside the beech.'

'Yes,' said I.

'Now, do you know, I oftin thenks as thuk old tree do suffer mortal bad wi' the rheumatics. You just luk at his twisted limbs, and the gurt lumps on his jints. Zumtimes when I do go by un I can yur he acrying out like, and I do allus thenk as he agot a touch o' the screws then. You kum an' putt yur ear to un now. I warnd as 'e agot um to-night.'

We went and stood under the tree, and true enough I could distinctly hear a faint moaning as if the soul of the tree were in pain.

'Thur you be,' said Willum, 'the poor old theng agot um to-night, zo we be sure to 'ave some wet.'

I was mystified for the time being, but having seen the tree since in a better light I can now explain that the noise was caused by a telegraph wire which passes under it.

As we went on, Willum said, 'Zeems to I as thurs a lot o' human natur in trees and vlowers, if we be only zimple anuf to look for't. I can't zay as

I allus thought zo, vur though I wurked on the land all me life, I didn't take much stock o' thengs till I woz agetting on in yurs, and then I zeemed to get nearer to understanding um. What vust set I athenking 'bout it woz one spring when one o' my gran' childurn was down yur. I woz doing zum hedging out in the vifteen acres, an' little Jinny, as we did call her, brought out a bit o' cooked dinner to I. I zed to her, ater I had yet me dinner, 'Now, me maid, you run and play, an' don't 'ee get into mischif.' Bimeby, I begun to wunder whur her had got to. Zo I went to try and vind her. I had to go across the veeld avoor I cood yur her purty little voice. Then I zeed as her woz tuther zide o' the hedge. The ground was soft and her didn't yur I akumming, zo I stopped an' listened an' I yeerd her zaying, "You pretty ickle fings, I loves 'oo, yes I do." I peeped drew a hole in the hedge and thur was Jinny on her knees. The zunlight was shining on a little place as woz in the burrow, whur a root o' daisies woz a blossoming. Jinny was looking at um an' talking to um as if they woz babies. "O! poor ickle daisy," her woz zaying, "did somefink break your leg; let me twy and make it well." Then all on a zudden she putts her purty little head down an' kisses the daisies an' zes: "I loves 'oo ev'ry one, yes I do." Then I walked softly awoy an' left her; but ever zence I 'ave thawt as vlowers an' trees can understand we more than we do thenk.'

We stood outside the old man's gate. A serious mood had fallen on both of us.

'Now you luk at them thur trees,' said Willum, 'how old an' twisted they do look. If you didn't knaw, you 'oodn't thenk as nex' May they 'ood be covered wi' green leaves, an' look fresh an' young. I offen 'as me thoughts about it, an' I thenks as we shall be like they. Yur be I agettin' old an' twisted an' wore out, but the Almighty 'ool make we old voke fresh an' young again when the time comes.'

The old man turned to his door with a quiet 'Good-night,' and it seemed like a benediction.

CHAPTER 36

A MIRACULOUS CURE

'We a' bin laafing vit to split our zides in the villige zence I saw you las' wik,' remarked Willum, as we plodded through the dirt and wet this week.

'What about?' I asked. It had seemed to me to be a week devoid of any smiles. Even Nature, who usually at this time of the year gives us a smiling day or two, had frowned and scowled, and pelted us with hail and snow, and bound us fast with frost and ice.

''Tis rather a long story,' answered Willum. 'Perhaps you a' yeerd o' Liza Beesley?'

No, I had not heard.

'Well, her and her old man, Teddy Beesley, a lived hyur all thur lives. You must a' zid the little cot wi' a gurt vossil stuck auver the door.'

'Yes,' I said, 'I have seen that; it is just by the post office.'

'Yuss, tha's it,' replied Willum. 'Well, Teddy an' his wife 'ave lived thur ever zence they woz marrid. Teddy come in vur a bit o' money zum yurs back an' he made a offer to old Mother Bishop, as the cottage belonged to. Teddy zed, "I'll pay you vive zhillin' a wik as long as you do live vur the cottage." Atween you and I and the gatepost Teddy had got to know as the old 'ooman woz in a bad woy wi' her heart or else I dwun thenk as he 'ood a made the offer. Well the old wench thawt it auver and zed, "Vurry well." Zo Teddy got the cot as he thawt on the chip. But that woz at least ten yur agone an' Mother Bishop be as sprak as ever an' luks like gwoin on vur another ten yur. But tha's another story. Tyent about thuk as we a' bin a laafing, thought I might tell 'ee a vunny theng amout thuk vossil as you anoticed. Teddy have done a nice bit o' quarring out at the back o' 'ees house an' made a pound or two by selling the stwun. He allus had a eye to thengs did Teddy, an' one day he dug up thuk vossil and thenks tood look nice stuck auver the porch. Zo I puts un up thur. One day a old gentleman went by. I spoze he had got a tile loose or zummat, acause we 'ad zid un knocking about in the quar down at the bottom wi' a little hammer, an' putting bits o' stwun in 'ees pokkut. Howsumdever the old chap comes back an' knocks at Teddy's door. Liza went and lifted the latch. "I begs yur pardun," zes the old gentleman polite like, "but I see you have a Ammonite over the door." "Then 'ee agot thur zence dinner time," zes Liza, "the young scaramoucher!" Her woz agwoin to run out but the old man stopped her, "I am avraid you dwunt unnerstand," he zes. "Yuss, I do," zes Liza. "Mr Crawly zed in his zarmon las' Zundy as the Ammonites an' Jebusites wiz still in this land o' ourn. I didn't blieve un at the time but I spoze he was right. You let I get un an' I'll gie un Ammonite." I ought to tell 'ee as Teddy an' 'ee's wife be Plymouth Rocks or zummut o' that zart.'

'Plymouth Brethren,' I laughingly interjected.

'Well tis all zame,' the old man continued. 'Anyhow Liza got the mop and went out to look auver the door. Acoorse thur wuz nothing thur except the old vossil. "I can't see no Ammonite," zes Liza. "But look, my dear woman," zes the old toff, "surely you can zee that lovely specimen?" "Oh! is thuk wot you do call a Ammonite," shouted Liza, "well, I never yeerd a oonderment like that called a Ammonite avoor."

Willum stopped. Presently he went on: 'But I shan't tell 'ee wot I was thenking on at vust if I dwunt look sharp. 'Bout a month ago Teddy Beesley got tuk ill. The doctor kum round and zed as Liza had better kip the old man in bed vur a day or two. He didn't want much kipping vur nex' day he coodn't get up, and avoor the wik was out the doctor zed as he had got the yaller janders. I went and zid the old chap an' thenks I thurs no need to call um yaller acause the man 'ood be colour blind as coodn't zee that vur hisself for Teddy was a yalla as mustard. The doctor kumd every day, but Teddy didn't get no better, an' Liza was wurrid smartish. Zum o' her Plymouth vrends did kum in an' cheer her up a bit, an' speshully Mr Crawly, who 'ood rub his 'ands and zay as the Lard luvd them as He chasened. An' still Teddy got no better. Thengs went on vur a wik or more and Crawly was abeginning to reckon on having a nice bit o' ham vur the funeral. Las' Mundy he zes to Liza, "Mrs Beesley, our afflicted brother can't last another day, by to-morrow marnin' he will be gone." An' Liza bleeved un, an' made up her mind as her'd 'ave a couple o' tops and one black skirt. Her wuz allus frugal was Liza, an' a good manager. But in the aternoon old Quakky Piper from 'Hampton happened to come in. When he zid Teddy he bust out a laafing. Liza was quite upset. "Doosn't knaw as the mon's adying," her zed. "Dying, be blowed," zed Quakky, "Ted 'ool be out an' about to-morra if thee't do what I tells th'. Now look 'ere just go down to the blacksmith's shop an' ax 'e to let th' 'ave a dip out o' the water as they do cool the irons in." Liza went off and wuz vurry soon back wi' about a pint o' dirty water. "Now, then, Teddy, my bwoy, just thee drenk this 'ere," zed Quakky. Zum'ow or 'nuther they got it all down Teddy's throat, an' then Quakky had to start vur whum. Nex' marnin' shure anuf Teddy woke up veeling almost well agyen. Zes he to Liza, "I be off to wurk." "But th' bisn't vit vor't," zes Liza. "But I be," zes Teddy – "tennyrate I'll go to dinner-time." An' up he gets an' the missis putts a bit o' cold bacon and a connobber o' bread in a 'ankicher vur 'ee's brekfust, an' off he goes. Bimeby round comes Mr Crawly. You med be sure as Liza woz a feeling pritty up an' down like, hardly knawing whether to be glad or sorry when her thawt o' they new clother. Crawly rubs 'ee's 'ands and putts a vyow tears into 'ee's voice an' zes, "How is our poor bruther smarnin." "He's gone," zed Liza. "Ah! I knew it would be even zo," zed Crawly, "an' what time did he depart?" "Bout 'alf ater zix," zed Liza, "an' he tuk 'ee's brekvust wi' un." The reverend gentleman thawt as trubble ad touched Liza's brain zo 'e zes, "Ah! poor man! poor man! an' wens the funeral?" "Funeral, be blowed," zes Liza, "thur yent going to be no funeral vur 'ee's coming whum to dinner." What happened ater I ain't yeerd yit as we a laafed too much to inquire,' concluded Willum as we reached his cottage door.

I had a good many quiet chuckles as I recalled the story on my way home.

CHAPTER 37

LETTER WRITING

'Good-night, Willum,'

'Good-night, Tommus; the days be agetting out vine byen um?'

It was the village postman we passed. He was an undersized man with the suspicion of a hump on his back. He had a beard which was not a credit to him, and his teeth were prominent and stained with tobacco. He carried a stick which was characteristic of the man, for it was rough and gnarled, and appeared to have few qualities besides strength and a consistent objection to appear graceful.

'I should think a postman's work on these hills must be very tiring and monotonous,' I remarked to Willum.

'Yuss, I spoze tis,' replied the old man. 'And yet agyen tis a'right in the zummer and when the weather's mild. Acoorse tis a bit unkid when thurs snaw on the ground. But Tommus he abin at it vur thurty yur an' I'm jiggered if he do look much diffrunt vrom wot 'e did when he started. 'Tis this yur air as I've tawld ye about. I do offen have a chat wi' Tommus about thengs. He wuz atelling I tuther night as tis extraornary the number o' letters as he got to deliver now; bout dree times as many as when he started. An' he tell'd I, too, as tis quite vunny to notice the diffrence in the woy they do address um. Yurs ago if old Abslum Looker over at Rodmarten had a letter vrom 'ee's zun in Amurrika thur ood be just "Absalom Looker, Rodmarten England," on't, but Tommus zes as now tis allus "Mr A Looker," and zumtimes "A Looker, Esquire." Zeems as if they be avraid of a good old Bible name like "Abslum." An' tyent as if old Ab had changed mind you acause he's just the zame as he allus wuz, which minds I as I had a letter come tuther day addressed to Willum Wurkman, Esquire. I was a bit skeerd at vust, and when the missis put her specs on to rade it, bless my zawl if zum chap didn't want I to buy a theng as looked like a babbies belly-band. He called it a gallyvanic belt or zummit like that. Ever zence then I aint zet much account on letters as do call I Squire, I allus knaws as them as write um byent ater no good.'

'I expect you get a lot of letters from your children, Willum?'

'Well, thurs none of um as be much o' 'ands at putting pen to paper. The do vollo thur veythur in that. Lar' bless 'ee, I only wrote two letters in my life. One o' them wuz to my old 'oomun when her went agallivanting up to Lunnon. "Willum," her zes, "thee must drop I a line to let I knaw how th' bist or I shall be a worruting." "Aright," zays I. "But be jabers when I got started on th' job I vound as twaz wuss'n breast-plowing in the' 'lotment. You med hardly blieve it, but I didn't knaw what to call the old girl. When I got "Dear Wife" down it looked zo cold like an' zo I started avresh on anuther sheet o' paper. An' I writes "Dear Mary," but that sounded out o' place seeing as I hadn't called her Mary vur nigh on twenty yur. Zo I shuved in "My" in vrunt an' that spoiled it, acause I knawed her 'ood zee wot a job I had had to start. Zo I got anuther sheet o' paper, an', thenks I, I'll just call her wot her used to call I when we wuz acoorting. An' I writes down "Dear old duck." But that looked zilly on paper, tho' it zounded a'right when her zed it. I thawt as I 'oodn't spoil any more paper zo I just wrote down all as I cood thenk on an' made up me mind to choose the one as zounded best. Zo I villed a page almost wi' "Dear Mother — an' that made the tears come in me eyes vur I 'adn't wrote them wurds zence I was a bwoy — "Dear old girl," "Dear partner," and a lot more as I vurgits now.'

'What did you choose at last?' I asked.

'Well ater about a 'our's thenking I decided as "My dear Wife" 'ood have to do, though it zounded mighty vunny. But when I had got that down on another sheet in the pakkut an' that 'ood 'ave to do wether or no. Zo that settled it. Then I went on wi' th' letter. I tried to thenk how my old dad allus wrote to 'ee's eldest bwoy. As vur as I rekerlect twuz zummat like this. "I now takes up me pen to writ to you hoping as you be quite well as it leaves we at present, thank God for it. We killed the peg last wik and the sparrib 'ool come by the carrier. The mice 'ave yet all our 'taters so the casn't have none. Mother be allright an' 'ool zend the breeks nex' wik if we do have zum drying wether. So no more at present from thee loving veythur."'

'What did Mrs Workman think of her letter when she got it, Willum?' I asked.

'Ah! now I coodn't a tawld 'ee that a wik ago,' replied the old man. 'How vunny as we shood be atalking about letter writing,' he continued, talking, it almost seemed, to himself.

'Las' Thursday night I zed to the missis, "Whur dist putt thuk old 'ankicher o' mine as I wore at Jarge's wedding?" "Wos want 'ee vor?" her sez. "Well, I thawt as I 'ood putt out to air agyenst nex' Zundy," sez I. I aut to a tawld 'ee as I wuz upstairs an' the missis wuz ironing in the kitchin. "Oh I can't be bothered now," her sez, "I'll vind un to-morrow; 'ees in my box zumwhere." I didn't say no more, but the thawt struck I as I 'ood vind un. Zo I goes to the missis's box, a theng as I don't recall ever doing avoor. I opens the box an' on top thur wus a lot o' wimmen's tackle, dresses an' zuch like. I lifts them out, but I coodn't zee the 'ankicher, so I goes on looking. Bimeby I comes to a neat little parcel done up in a bit o' shiney paper out of a pakkut o' tay. Thenks I thas the 'ankicher. Zo I opens the paper. An' wot do you thenk I found?'

The old man turned to me almost in tears.

'I don't know,' I softly answered.

'Vust o' all thur wuz a bit o' our little Billy's hair, soft and brown; then thur wuz a vew strands o' long gray hair as I guessed wuz her muther's. Then thur wuz my old letter. As zoon as I zid that I just putt ev'rything back as quiut as a mouse an' went downstairs an' zed no more about the 'ankicher.'

In the silence that followed we reached the cottage.

The door opened and a voice, which was that of an old woman, called out, 'Come on, Willum, I agot a bit o' peg's vry in the pan and 'tis done to a turn.'

'Good-night, Willum,' I said.

CHAPTER 38

THE
'EARL O' SIPLAS'

I was not alone as I waited for my old friend this week. There were three of Willum's grand-children, who had come to stay at the cottage for the Whitsuntide holidays, walking along the lane to meet their 'Grampy'. I tried to make friends with them, but like most children they were shy, and it was only the eldest child, a girl of about twelve, who would speak.

'Do you like being in the country?' I asked her. 'Not 'arf,' she exclaimed; from which I gathered that her home was London.

'And what do you like best down here?' I continued.

She paused awhile before she replied. Then she said: 'I like to see the green fields, and the birds' nests and the bees.' So I gathered that, in spite of or perhaps on account of, her Cockney blood the love of Nature was strong in her.

'You must mind and not get stung by the bees or wasps?' I said.

'Jimmy was stung by a wops' — how soon a child imitates our county pronunciation I thought — she answered. 'He was sitting on the garden wall the other morning when the sun was shining. Presently he called out "I say Lil, come and see!" "Lummy, Chorlie!" I said, when I saw the wops on his leg, "it's a new kind of floi" (fly). Then Jimmy shouted "Crikey!! Ain't his blooming feet hot." And Grannie got the blue bag because the wops had stung him.'

'Here comes Grampy,' shouted one of the others. They all three started off running, but presently the eldest girl stopped.

'Aren't you going to run with the others?' I said.

'No! I don't fink!' she replied.

'Why?' I asked.

'Well, Grampy haven't shaved since Sunday.'

'Whatever has that got to do with it?' I exclaimed.

'You see,' she said. I waited. I saw the other two children cling round the old man's legs, and I heard the old fellow say, 'Come on and be bearded.' He took each child in turn and rubbed his scrubby chin on the little pale faces. And although they laughed and jumped with delight I soon saw why the elder miss was not anxious that her soft cheek should be scrubbed by Grampy's stubby beard. The sensation must have been like rubbing one's face on a file.

'What a nice rain we have had, Willum?' I remarked.

'Yuss, and now the voke be acrying out as we be gone back to winter agyen. I never knawed zuch a hungratevull lot as we be. A vyow wiks back here we wuz tellin' the Almighty as thur ood be no hay if He didn't luk zharp and zend zum rain. And now old Varmer Tibbutts be agrowsing acause we byent being burned up wi' th' zun. I hope tyent wikkid vur I dwunt mane it to be, but I do zumtimes veel wot a bad time zum on us ood have if the Almighty wuz just a ornary mon like you an' I. We shud try to plaze ev'rybody and ood vinish up be plazing nobody. But He do just plaze Hisself, an' you med be zure as tha's how tis as ev'rytheng wurks together vur good to they as loves God. Acause if they do lov wot plazes He, ev'rytheng as 'appens is wot He plazes an' zo they be plazed wi' ev'rytheng as 'appens.' The old man stopped, quite surprised, I thought, with himself — and perhaps feeling a little mixed.

After a pause Willum commenced again; the children were running on ahead chasing butterflies.

'I agot a vuny bit to tell ee,' the old man said. 'Jarge's wife abin stopping wi' we vur Whitsun. I thenk I tawld ee as her be a Cockney. Well, tuther day her wuz out in the villige an' got achatterin' wi' old Muther Timms. Perhaps you anoticed as a good many o' th' publics round here have changed hands lately. Thurs a new landlord at the "Twelve Bells," and down in bottom "The Tin Duke" —'

'"The Tin Duke," Willum?' I said, 'where's that?'

'Dwunt you knaaw the "Tin Duke?" Oh! ah! acoorse tis put up "The Iron Duke," now I kums to thenk on't.'

'Oh! I know that,' said I.

'Well, thurs a new mon thur. Jarge's wife be the darter o' a publican an' natral anuf her tyeks a lot o' hinterest in the publics round hyur. As I wuz azayin' her got atawking to Muther Timms an' the old oomun tawld her about the changes. Said she, "Thurs Mr Jones gone vrom the 'Twelve Bells,' an' Mark Sibly he agot the 'Cradle an' Coffin,' and John Vowles have got the 'Duke o' Yark', and — do you knaw Lizabuth Howard," went on Muther Timms. "Wot her as marrid my husbend's bruther?" zes Jarge's wife. "Yuss," zes Muther Timms — "well, her agot the 'Earl o' Siplas.'"

'The what?' I exclaimed.

'Wait a minnit,' laughed Willum. 'Jarge's wife kum whum and started tawlking to we about wot Muther Timms had tawld her. "Farvah," her zes, "where's the 'Earl of Siplas?" Like you I zed "The wot?"

'"The Earl o' Siplas," zes Jarge's wife. "Never yeerd on't," zes I. My old ooman zes, "Thur yent no public o' thuk nyem round about hyur." "Who did her zay has got it?" I axed. "Lizbuth Howard," zes Jarge's wife. "Lizbuth Howard!" zes my missis, "why, I knaws as that yent right acause Lizbuth be at whum wi' th' erysipelas."[1]

'Then I laffed out loud,' went on Willum, 'vur I zid wot 'ad happened. Muther Timms had tawld Jarge's wife as Lizbuth Howard had got the erysipelas, an' her being a Cockney didn't unnerstand as that wuz wot wuz myent by "Earl o' Siplas."'

The children were waiting for us at the garden gate. 'You are fond of children, Willum?' I said, as the old man stroked the curls of the smallest girl.

'Aye, that I be,' said Willum, 'thur yent much poetry as I do knaw, but thurs wun vuss as I learned an' I be vurry vond on't acause tis about childien.'

'What is that?' I asked.

'Ye are better than all the ballads
That ever were sung or said,
For ye are living poems,
And all the rest are dead.'

repeated Willum.

And the three children gazed at the old man in wonder; they had never heard Grampy recite poetry before.

The pretty picture of the old man with one work-hardened hand on the curls of a little child and the other holding a little boy by his tiny fist while the eldest girl stood looking on, remains with me as a very pleasant memory to this hour.

CHAPTER 39

SHEPHERDS AND SHEEP

It must have been bad weather for the lambing this year. Even I, who knows as much about lambing as a shepherd knows of trigonometry, could tell that, and as I waited in the lane for Willum this week my thoughts wandered to shepherds and sheep, for in the field behind me there were a few ewes and lambs, and their incessant 'Baa! baa!' reminded me of a saying I once heard from a dear old Gloucestershire man, who has lain quietly these many years by the side of his loved and cherished wife under the shadow of a Gloucestershire village church tower. At dinner-time on Sundays, when the children were inclined to talk too much, and when the maternal warning that children should be seen and not heard was unavailing, there would come a rap rap on the table from the handle of the carving knife, and in the silence which followed this pithy sentence fell from the old man's lips, 'Every baa loses a bite.' As children we did not understand the exact meaning of the words, though we understood quite well the look which accompanied them. I am not sure that I thoroughly grasped the import of the remark until I watched this week how the cropping of the grass by the sheep was only interrupted by the effort necessary for baaing.

I suppose everyone has laughed at the absurd solemnity of an old ewe's 'Baa!' and the happy treble of the irresponsible bleating of the frisky lamb by her side as it, to use a word I have never heard outside Gloucestershire, 'bunts' up against the dam informing her in lamb language that she is thirsty and would drink.

I was busy with these thoughts when Willum appeared.

'When are we going to get some warm weather, Willum?' I asked.

Now I have noticed that if you ask an old sailor a question about the weather he will first of all spit and then fling his head back and take a comprehensive look all round the horizon before replying. But if you ask a Gloucestershire old man what the weather is going to be, he first of all looks at you, then at his own boots, then he stands stiff and sniffs: he will then tell you, that 'he dwunt thenk much on't, an' tool only hauld up 'slongs the wind kips igh.'

Willum answered my question. 'I wunt go zo vur as to zay as we shall shartly have a change, acause my old bwuns ain't a tawld I thuk much, but the missis zid the cat wi' 'ees back to the vire las' night, an' her tawld I as her carn was araging las' night, too, zo I thenks as when the moon changes we shall have it milder; and not avoor tis wanted either. Shepperd was atelling I as he had to be out all night more this yur than ever avoor in 'ees life.'

'A shepherd's life must be a hard one at times?' I queried, for my thoughts were still wool-gathering among the sheep, and I wanted the old man to talk about them.

'Well, you zee, it yent ev'rybody as knaws anuf to be a shepherd, and if I might zay so it yent book-larning as a shepperd wants. Thur's old Matt Robins, one o' the vinest shepperds as ever I zid, an, why, Lar' bless 'ee, Matt can't zo much as zay 'ees letters, an if you axed un how to spell 'ees name why he 'ood tell 'ee to axe the missis. But when it comes to luking ater the yows (ewes) in lambing time or shearing um later on, well tood be a good un as 'ood byet old Matt. An' that minds I o' wot one o' my granchildurn axed I tuther day, an' blowed if I cood answr'n. Praps you can tell I, vur thaough I 'alived among the ship all these yurs I never noticed it avoor?'

'What is it?'

'Well, young Jarge, as is bout ten yur old, an' won vust prize vur zifering at school, axed I why when we zed a leg o' mutton baaing in a veeld we called un a ship an' when 'e wuz on the table we called un mutton. Now I never thawt o' thuk avoor an' zo I had to zay as I didn't knaw, an' I can tell 'ee I dwunt like telling these yur young uns wot a lot I dwunnaw acause they can't hide their veelings an' I can zee by thur eyes as they thenk thur old grampy a rare old ignoramus.'

'I expect, Willum,' I replied, 'there are a lot of people besides you who cannot answer that question. So far as I can I will tell you the reason, but I am afraid I am almost as much an ignoramus as you yourself. The reason is this: Years and years—

'Donkey's ears,' laughed Willum.

'Yes, long years ago, when England was not the important country she is now, there came from across the sea a race of men called Normans, and they conquered the people who lived on these hills and plains of ours. These people used to keep sheep principally for the wool they yielded. But the Normans took their sheep and ate them, and when the cooked joints came before them on the table the Normans called them mutton. And so, now that we are partly of Norman blood and partly of Saxon, we still keep the distinction and call the living animal a sheep and the same animal, when cooked, mutton.'

'Oh! is thuk the rason,' said Willum. I thought he was not very convinced.

Presently he said: 'Pason was atelling we the tuther Zundy as they do call the Twenty-third Zahm the Shepperd Zahm. Now d'you knaw if thurs one Zahm as I do like more'n anuther tis thuk un. He zeems to touch I mor'n any on um, an' I 'ave yeerd lots o' old country men zay tis the zame wi' they. But Pason was asaying, an' I coodn't help thenking what a dollop o' thengs thur be as we do never thenk about, as when they come to putt thuk Zahm into the language o' zum o' the niggurs, as they coodn't zay as the Lard wuz theur Shepperd acause they didn't knaw what a sheep wuz, thur being only goats in their country. An' tood be no good zaying "The Lard is my Shepperd" if they didn't know what a shepperd wuz. It never struck I what a job it must be to maake zum voke unnerstand thengs.'

I concurred.

'D'you knaw,' continued Willum, 'twaz in 'ees zarmun on thuk Zahm as Pason zed one o' the thengs as I do remember best o' all the zarmuns I 'ave yeerd, an' I 'ave listened to a vyow in me time. He zed as out in the East the shepperd goes in vrunt of the ship and calls um all to come ater'n, but if thurs one as is inclined to wander awoy the shepperd gies un a crack on the leg wi' 'ees kruk and lames un a bit so as he can't wander vur awoy. An' Pason zed as zumtimes the Almighty do do that to we. He just gies us a good hard blow and while we do thenk as He's vurry hard, if we only knowed all about it we zhould zee as He was rally kind acause if it hadn't been vur thuk blow we shood awandered right awoy an' got lost praps.'

I pondered on this after I had bidden the old man 'Good-night.' And it seemed to me to explain many things.

CHAPTER 40

SPRINGTIME

'O! to be in England
'Now that April's there,'

So sang the poet Browning, when basking in the sunlight of Italy, and as I walked to meet my old friend this week I too sang with the joy of existence. There are times in our life when we vaguely question the wisdom of the Power which presided over our birth. And there are times, too, when our heart, if not our lips, asks the question: 'Why was I born, if my life is only to be a long drawn out tale of misery.'

But when Easter comes with its message of resurrection; and the glorious sun wakens into freshest green the brown and sombre trees, and puts a new song into the mouths of the birds, as for very love they chase each other through the golden sunlight, then the human heart bursts into joy also, and can, without reserve, say those wonderful words of our Church's General Thanksgiving — 'We bless Thee for our creation.'

It was with thoughts like these that I waited for Willum this week.

'Yuss, a vyow vine days like this ool make a lot o' diffrunce to thengs,' he remarked in reply to my reference to the springlike weather. ''Ave you ever noticed,' he continued, 'how nigh together life an' death be. Thur's Good Vriday when we thenks o' death, and a kupple o' days ater we be a thenking about life an' zenging joyful hymns. Twuz only yes'day as I wuz azaying to old Martha Bennett as praps tis meant to tach we as death is only just a bit shart o' life, and when we be aweeping an' awailing acause zumbody's dyead, why, they may be azenging acause they be come to life.'

The old man paused. Suddenly he pointed to the hawthorn hedge, which in one sunny spot was breaking into the sweetest of all shades of green. 'Now do you thenk as thurs a prittyer colour'n that?' he asked.

'No,' I said, 'it always seems to me to be by far the sweetest and most restful colour to the eyes.'

'Tha's jus' wot I do thenk too,' said Willum. 'I spoze the Almighty knowed as we 'ood get tired o' looking at the zame colour allus and zo he made thengs change so as our eyes might get a rest zumtimes. But talking o' green minds I o' zummutt as I wanted to axe ye.'

'What was that?' I said.

'Well, praps you a'yeerd down in these ere parts when anybody tells a rather tall story the one as be a lissening 'ool pull up 'ees eyelid and zay: "Doos't zee any green?" Now I 'ood like to know wot is th' idea o' thuk?'

I could only say that I supposed the idea was that as green represented the young and innocent, it was a sarcastic reference to the fact that the listener was too old in the ways of the world to be caught by any unlikely story.

'But, Willum,' I asked, in turn, 'perhaps you can tell me what was meant by the lady in the shop near the Church —'

'Wot, old Mother Barnard as kips the jumble shop?' interjected the old man.

'Yes, I think that is her name,' I said. 'The other day when I was buying a few sweets a man came in and started telling the old woman a long tale about how he had been in America—'

'You myens Braggy Butcher,' said Willum.

'I didn't know his name,' I continued, 'but as he went out of the shop the old lady turned to me and said, "Did you hear of a shabby funeral the other day?" I said "No," at which she laughed. I did not like to ask her why, but I have thought since it might have been a joke.'

'So twuz,' exclaimed the old man. 'Her myeaned as Braggy's trumpeter was dyead, and zo he 'ad to blow 'ees own trumput.'

'Oh!' I said, and I am now beginning to discover that there exists a fund of humour in the people I meet on these hills, which I never suspected before.

A little further down the road we passed several young fellows, and I am compelled to say that they were indulging in very bad language, which appeared to me to pollute the sweet pure air.

Willum shook his head. 'It wants old Dr Brown back agyen,' he remarked.

'What would he have done?' I asked.

'I'll tell 'ee wot he did do once,' replied Willum. 'He yurd a yung veller acussing and swurring in the road one day and zo he goes up to'n. The yung chap knowed the doctor and wuz mortal feerd on him. Doctor takes un on one zide and zes to'n serious like, "Let me look at yer tongue?" When 'ee had looked, he zes "Ah! just as I thawt — a bad attack of profanitis" — or zum zuch wurd as thuk. "You call round at the surgery at zix o'clock and I'll give you a mixture." That chap tawld I ater as he never had zuch a mouth wash as the doctor gid un thuk night. When he had tuk it the doctor zed, "All you do want now is a pinch of refinement mixed up wi' a teaspoonful o' good manners and taken several times a day and you'll soon be cured." That chap never swore agyen, and I could tell 'ee who twuz only I hadn't better.'

Two of Willum's grandchildren were waiting at the cottage door as we came in sight.

'Here's Grampy,' they cried and raced to meet him.

CHAPTER 41

CURIOUS EFFECTS
OF WEATHER
CHANGES

It was a day that whetted the appetite; a clear, frosty day; the sun had shone from dawn to setting in a sky of blue; not the deep warm blue of mid-summer, but the cold steel blue of winter. To breathe the keen Cotswold air was to treat the lungs to draughts of sparkling champagne. Not often do we get such days in mid-winter. Nature, ever jealous in the keeping of her choicest treasures, seemed this day to be in a mood of self-admiration, for she had enlivened her robe of sombre winter grey with brilliants, bright beyond sparkling diamonds or flashing rubies.

I felt as I waited for Willum that even the pigs, of whose near presence my nostrils told me, were poetical. And I wondered whether any poet had ever dedicated an ode, 'To a pig.' If not, thought I, it seems to me this worthy animal is more deserving of such honour than the louse to which Burns dedicated one of his best known pieces, that poem in which occur the oft-quoted lines:

> 'O' wad some power the giftie gie us
> To see ourselves as ithers see us.'

On Willum's arrival we seemed quite naturally to fall into a talk about the beautiful weather.

'The Almighty do knaw just wot we poor mortals do want,' said Willum, 'it allus makes I savidge to yur voke agrowling about the weather. Pason Harrison zed in one o' 'ees zarmons as wunce on a time thur woz a mon as went off wun marnin' an' zumbody zed to un, "I hopes the't 'ave good weather vur thee journey," an' he zed, "I be zure to have good weather." "Ow dost knaw?" zed his vrend. "Why, I knaws I shall 'ave wot weather the Almighty zends, an' He never zends anytheng as yent good, zo I shall be zure to 'ave good weather."'

'But surely, Willum, such cold as we have had is very trying to many old and ailing people?'

'Well, I s'pose 'tis,' answered Willum, 'that's whur I do get a bit wrong zumtimes. You see I aint never velt ill meself, an' I can't quite unnerstand why old Mother Barnard should get as grumpy as a ber wi' a zore back when the wind be in the east, and Dan'l Stubbings goes on the booze when the moon be at the vull, an' little Missis Smith vlengs thengs at Smith when the vrost do break. Do you myen to tell I as 'tis the weather as causes them zart o' thengs?'

'I really cannot say,' laughed I, 'do such things happen?'

'Lar bless 'e, ah,' zed Willum, 'an' I could tell 'e a lot more just as bad. Why old Squire auver yander do never go hunting when the wind be in the east, although he be as strong as a hoss. An' I remember a old mon as allus had a bilious bout when it began to snaw. An' thurs many a 'ooman as leads her husband a vine old dance when thurs thunder in the air.'

A sudden thought came to me. 'Do you remember the earthquake of some years ago?' I asked Willum.

'Oh! Ah! that I do,' replied the old fellow, 'not as I knawed 'twas a earthquake. I allus laughs when anybody talks about he.'

'Why?' said I.

'Well, 'twas like this 'ere. My old 'ooman had gone auver to Tetbry vur the night an' I woz left alone in the house. Zumtime in the night I woke up an' velt as if zumbody was pulling I out o' bed. "Tha's wun o' yung Billy Jobbinses tricks," zes I to myself, vur Billy — tha's the cowman's son — was allus vond o' playing jokes. Zo I calls out, "Ow dist get in then, Billy?" Acoorse thur wasn't no answer, zo I turned

---

auver an' went to zlip agyen an' thawt no more about it till Reuben Thomas zes to I in the marnin' "Didst veel the earthquake, Willum?" "Earthquake," zes I, "wot earthquake." Then 'e tells I all about it. Thenks I whur agnorunce is bliss 'tis folly to be wise as Dick Roberts used to zay when thur woz sosingers vur dinner. I durzay as I zhood abin vrightened if I had knowd 'twas a earthquake acause I 'adn't run agyenst yun o' them thengs avoor. But when I thawt was Billy Jobbins I didn't mind a bit, vur Billy woz a harmless zart o' chap. Which minds I — did you ever yeer the tale about Billy 'aving 'ees yur cut?'

'No,' I said.

'Well, you zee, 'twas like this. Billy married a 'ooman as allus looked twice at every 'apenny avoor her'd spend un, an' her didn't zee as thur woz any cause vur Billy spending tuppense every couple o' months or zo having 'ees yur cut by the barber. Zo her zays to Billy, "Thee gie I the tuppence an' I'll cut thee yur." But Billy 'oodn't let her do't. One night, however, Billy kum whum a bit the wuss vur likker, an' when he woke in the marnin' he vound as the missis had putt a pudden bason on his napper an' cut his yur to match. You may be zure as he got it nex' day. "Hast had the county crop, then, Billy?" mor'n one zed to un, an' at last poor Billy lost his temper. "Who cut thee yur, Billy?" I zed to un when I met un in the strit. "The missis," shouted Billy, "but her 'oodn't a don't if I'd been thur."'

We had reached the cottage so I could hear no more of Willum's stories that night.

CHAPTER 42

GOOD FRIDAY POTATO PLANTING

'We shall soon have Easter with us, Willum,' I said, after we had shaken hands.

'Yuss, an' I shan't be zorry neither,' replied Willum, 'vor this abin one o' the longest winters as I do reckerlect, and one o' the wust, if the number o' new gravcs in the Churchyard be anytheng to go by.'

The old fellow seemed in a rather solemn mood so I endeavoured to bring my talk into harmony with his feelings.

'There has becn a lot of illness in the village, I expect.'

'Tha's true,' he answered. 'Old Willum Painter's bwoy he catched a chill an' the doctor zed it turned to pumonia, anyhow it killed yung Ted, an' he a chap o' only thurty an' wuz athenking o' getting marrid. Then Richutt Harris wuz tuk bad out in the veeld wi' the plow a vyow wiks back an' had to be tuk whum in a cart, an' he wuz dyead un inzide the wik vrom — le's zee, what did doctor call't, angelina pickup, or zum such name.'

'Angina Pectoris,' I suggested.

'Ah, tha's it — I never could manage them thur long-winded names; 'minds I o' Watty Biship —' and the old man laughed.

'Watty had bin chucked auver by 'ees gurl, an' her name wuz Belle Perkins thaough her muther allus called her "Belly" — wot vor I dwunnow, acause tyent the zart o' name as anybody, speshully a

ooman, ood like to be called avoor voke — well, as I wuz azaying her
gid Watty the go-by an' shartly ater 'ees muther noticed as he went off
'ees feed, an' zo her purswaded un to go an' zee the doctor. Old Doctor
Brown was alive in them days. He stuck his stitchoscope —'

'His what?' I exclaimed.

'Well, you knaws the theng as the doctor pokes into yer ribs an'
shuvs 'ees ear agyenst.'

'Stethoscope, Willum, stethoscope,' I laughingly said.

''Tis all the zame — you knaws wot I myens — he stuck his — his
'ood you mind zaying on't vur I can't git me tongue round it —'

I obliged.

' — into 'ees chest,' continued Willum, 'an' ater a bit he zes zart o'
quiyutly, "Me man, d'you knaw wot you be suffering vrom?" "No,"
zes Watty, "tha's why I cum'd to you!" "Then I be zorry to tell you as
you be suffering from Angina Pectoris." Watty told I as he blushed all
auver an' coodn't zay nothing vur a bit. Then he blurted out, "Quite
right, doctor, quite right, but that yent her name."'

I thought the old man had overcome his solemnity, but I was
mistaken.

'We shall 'ave Good Friday hyur nex' wik,' he observed, 'and I shall
'ave to make up me mind whether I plants the black kidneys an' yets the
up-to-dates or whether we shall yet the kidneys an' plant the tuthers.'

'It seems quite a custom to plant potatoes on Good Friday, Willum,' I
remarked, 'how is it?'

'Well, you zee, we do none of us to to wurk Good Vriday, an' as the
days be getting out 'tis a vairish long day. I minds the time when I cood
plant all me bit o' 'lotment on Good Vriday if 'twas vine. Zum yurs ago
thaough we had a new pason come and he went on smartish 'bout
planting taters on Good Vriday. He wuz a vurry good mon an' cood
pray wi'out a book, which is more'n a good many of um can do. But as
I tawld un – I zed "Zur, you can afford to pay Tom Vowles to plant
your garden any time, but we agot to do our planting ourselves, an' if
you axes I my opinion I thenks 'tis betted to plan taters quiyutly by
yurself than to go off to a tea fight an' bun struggle like zum o' these
yur chappelers do." "But, Willum," 'ee zes, "coodn't you kum to

Church?" "Acoorse I cood," zes I, "and I myens to go in the marnin, but I shall do me bit o' planting avoor sarvice, and in the aternoon." An' tha's wot I did, an' have done vur many a yur now. The yung gentlmun, he wuz just out o' Colledge, I spose, an' didn't unnerstand old-vashioned ways — tuk it a'right, and the way he spoke about it

Good Vriday marnin' wuz vurry good I thawt. He zed as he wuz only yung an' praps didn't unnerstand quite zo much as we did bout the necessity o' planting taters on Good Vriday — by the woy I never quite fathomed whether he wuzn't a bit sarky when he zed that — but if it was really necessary then we 'ood praps try an' thenk a bit about serious things while we wuz aputting the taters in. Zo I tried to thenk as I wuz degging the ground, 'bout 'ow zum day the ground 'ood be dug vur I, an' my old carcass 'ood be planted just like I wuz planting the taters, an' then I wondered whether me body 'ood change like the zid (seed) taters do, and I should kum up later on yung an' fresh agyen. An' I thawt too as God wuz a beg Gardner an' 'ood plant I just when His right time came. An' then I thawt agyen — and praps you 'ool thenk as this is silly — as praps I had already been planted an twuz 'bout time vur I to be garnered in. Zo tha's the kind o' thawts as I do 'ave when I plants me taters on Good Vriday. But I shood like to tell ye a story as my bwoy Jarge tawld I when he wuz down hyur las' zummer — if you 'ood care to yur't.'

'Go on, Willum,' I said.

'Well, thur wuz a yung pason up 'Ammersmith woy as Jarge knaws an' twuz he as told Jarge about it, zo I knaws 'tis true, though you mightn't blieve it. This yur yung clergyman was tawld one day as a poor old 'ooman lay adying up in a garrutt down a slum. Zo he vound her out. Nobody else 'ad zeemed to trouble about her. He cood zee as tood be all auver avoor long zo he zed, "My poor woman, do you know what day this is?" "No," her zes. Zo he tells her twuz Good Vriday, but her didn't zeem be unnerstand. "Don't you know what happened on Good Vriday?" he zed. The 'ooman zhuk her 'ed. "Then I'll read it to you," he zes. And he read out o' the Gospels all about our Saviour on the Cross. When he vinished her wuz acrying. Her looked at the yung pason — an' my bwoy Jarge zes 'tis Gawspel truth — her zes, referring to wot he had bin arading — "Poor Chap — 'ow he must 'ave suffered — I be glad as it ain't true." An' twuz a long time avoor her cood be made to zee as it all happened.'

We were both silent as we approached the cottage gate, where I bade the old man 'Good-night.'

CHAPTER 43

A VILLAGE
ROMANCE

'William,' I said, as I trudged among the fallen leaves with my old friend this week, 'I have been wondering if you can explain to me a rather peculiar inscription on a tombstone in the Churchyard. I noticed it on Sunday and have asked several for an explanation, but nobody seems to know anything about the people to whom it refers; even the Vicar is ignorant about them.'

'Avoor you goes any vurther,' the old man broke in, 'I knows wot you be a referring to; 'tis the Cross over the grave o' John Lock and Lucy May.'

'You are right, Willum,' I said. 'I was very much struck by the inscription, "Sacred to the memory of John Lock and Lucy May who died" — I forget the dates — and then this text, "They neither marry nor are given in marriage, but are as the angels which are in Heaven." If there is a story about that tombstone I am sure you can tell it me.'

'Yuss, I can,' replied Willum, 'an' kum to thenk on't I be bout the only wun as cood tell 'ee thuk tale now. Lard howe! I be agettin' old' — and he sighed heavily. He did not at once commence the tale, and I could see I had awakened memories of other days for the rays of the setting sun sparkled on the tears in the old man's eyes.

'John Lock,' Willum began — and I let him tell his story without interruptions — 'John Lock was a good mon if ever thur wuz wun. He an' I ood abin about zame age if he had alived. I didn't knaw much about until the autumn o' zixty vawr when I vell off the waggin when

we wuz acarting the karn. Twuz a wonder I wuzn't killed, an' I zhood
abin if it hadn't bin vur me old billycock hat as I happened to be
wurring at the time. He tuk off a good bit o' the force o' the vall.
Howsomedever I wuz in bed vur nigh on a month wi' conscrushion o'
the brain and the vust theng as I axed when I got me senses agyen wuz
"How about they thur taters up in the lotment." The missis her zes
"Never thee mind bout the taters. John Lock a zid to they," and I
vound out ater as he had got um all up an' oodn't zo much as have a
bilin' o' greens vur 'ees trubble. Natral anuf he an' I got a bit vrendly
when I got better. He wuz a tall quiut mon an' a bit of a skollard in 'ees
way. He wuz wun o' dree bruthers. The tuther two, Bill and Adam,
had got marrid an' sad to zay both on um had got trubble wi' thur
vamilies. Bill's dree chidurn wuz all deaf an' dumb, and Adam's bwoy
and wench was sawny like.'

The old fellow paused a minute here. I thought it was to get breath,
but it wasn't. 'Poor all John! Dal it all twuz hard lines,' he reflected, and
I could see that his mind was dwelling on the sadness of the story he
was about to tell.

'Aliving up at tuther end of the villige at thuk time was Missis May
and her daughter Lucy, as nice a wench as you cood wish vor. Her did
help the skool-gaffer at the skool wi' the yung uns and wuz a good
dawter to her muther as had bin left a widder.'

'As I zed,' continued Willum, 'John Lock an' I had got a bit vrendly
like and wun day I zed to'n "John, good luck wi' Lucy May." Vur I had
watched un in Church on Zundy marnins and having bin drew the
zame process meself I knawed wot thuk look in 'ees eyes myend when
Lucy did kum in. At fust John pretended as he didn't knaw wot I wuz a
referring to, but vurry zoon he tawld I all about it. "But, Willum," he
zes, "I be in a quandayry. Lucy is the only gurl vur I, but when I thenks
o' Bill and Adam and wot a curse thur zeems to be on our vamily I veels
as if I durnt risk brenging truble on Lucy. Wot d'you advise, Willum?"
To tell 'ee the truth I thawt thur wuz a lot in wot he zed, but twuz
nation hard to tell the yung veller zo. "Wot do Lucy zay?" I zed. "I ant
axed her," he zed, "vur I can't myck up me own mind, and I thenks as
tis the mon's place to decide a questyun o' that zart."'

'Well thengs went on vur zum time and nuthin' happened. I spoze it must abin nearly a twelvemuth bevore I zed anytheng to John about it agyen, and then I axed un wot he had done. "Willum," he zed, and I can hyur the shake in 'ees voice now, "Willum, Lucy an' I have decided as the Almighty dwunt intend we to be marrid." "Why, however, did ee kum to that conclusion?" I axed. "I'll tell 'ee," zed John, "Only do 'ee kip it to yerself, Willum. Last New Yur's Day I had a long tawk wi' Lucy and her muther and tawld um all me hopes and fears and how, though I luved Lucy wi' all me heart, I shood hate meself if I brawt her to wot Bill and Adam had brawt thur wives to. We tawked it over atween us and we coodn't make up our minds wun woy or tuther, and twuz then as Missis May zed 'I knaw; we ool leave it to God to decide.' 'How d'you mean?' we both zed. 'We ool get the Bible and each of us ool pray quietly as God will lead us to the right verse. Zo we got the old Family Bible and ater a vyow quiet minutes I shut me eyes and opened the book and placed me vorevenger in the middle o' the page. Then we all dree looked at the verse I had touched; and it wuz 'They neither marry nore are given in marriage, but are as the angels which are in Heaven.' Twuz a shock, Willum, twaz a shock, but we all agreed as twuz a plain direction. Zo Lucy and I went down the garden path and kissed one another vur the last time. And now we be just good vrends zo to speak, and nithing else, but Willum, every day as I lives the more I loves her, and I zumtimes wunders how it'll all end."'

Again the old man paused and we walked in silence for a while. 'Thengs went on about as usual vur zum yurs. I dwun rightly remember how long tood be but I knaw twux about harvest time when the end kum to the story. We had got the karn in safe, and wuz having the Harvest Whum supper in the barn. I remember it vurry well acause twuz the last time as we yeerd old Bobby Tufnell zeng Dorothy Draggletail. We allus got Bobby to zeng thuk zong — do ye knaw it?'

'No,' said I.

'Well the chorus goes zummut like this:

> Twas John kissed Molly,
> And Dick kissed Betty,

And Joe kissed Dolly,
And Jack kissed Katty,
And Dorothy Draggletail,
And Humphrey with his flail,
And Kitty was a charming girl,
To carry the milking pail.'

After this little interlude Willum dropped into a very solemn mood and continued his story.

'We had a couple of strange vellers to help us wi' the ripping (reaping). I didn't like the look on um vrom the fust, and zo I wuzn't vurry much surprised when the news kum as John Lock wuz down wi' the small-pox, vur they had bin lodging at 'ees house. In them days small-pox was a darned sight more common than tis now, thank the Lard!' exclaimed the old man. 'Well, John got it bad, and doctor gid no hopes vrom the beginning. As soon as Lucy heard on't off her went and tended to John all drew. When the end wuz near John called her to'n and zed: "Lucy, praps the Almighty be adoing this out o' kindness to we; we obeyed His command, though twuz turble hard; praps you and I ool kum together sooner than we expected in the home whur we needn't fear vur the consequences." And Lucy, who tawld my missis as her felt as her coodn't shed a tear all the time, zed; "I think you be right, John; I hope so, vur I can't live without ye." And twuz zo.' concluded Willum, with the tears streaming down his face, 'vur wi'in a wik Lucy wur dyead o' the zame complaint, And they burrid um in the zame grave and Mrs May had that stwun putt up as you zid. And tha's the story on't.'

I bade the old man good-night and walked slowly home in the darkness.

CHAPTER 44

BIBLICAL MATTERS

I leaned upon a five barred gate waiting for Willum. In front of me was a field, the Fifteen Acres, I think Willum had called it. As I waited I mused upon the sight before me. And it seemed as if the waving heads of corn bowed a courtly salutation as they bent before the summer breeze. I noted, too, how one could trace the progress of the air currents as they swept across the expanse of green. There was a little whirlwind agitating the growing corn in one corner of the field. I saw it spread, and marked its path across the field by the changing shades of green which it produced in the bowing stalks. In a minute it was gone and the place where it had been was calm and quiet as before. And I thought that here was a parable. In such wise the changing passions and desires of men seize upon the multitudes of lives round about us. For a time there is commotion and movement, and then 'the wind passes and it is gone,' and the old world rolls on to 'that far-off divine event to which the whole creation moves'; just as quietly, just as surely as the green ears of corn ripen into golden grain when the time of harvest comes.

I was so intent on my meditation that I did not hear Willum approaching, and his 'How do?' brought me back with a start to the Cotswold Hills and the odour of the cowshed.

'Good weather for haymaking, Willum,' I said.

'Yuss,' replied the old man, 'we abin wurking like niggurs to get our hay carted, an' thankvull I be as the last load be got in dry.'

'Is it a good crop this year?' I inquired.

'Vairish,' said Willum, 'vairish; might be wuss and agyen might be better, as Sammy Dicks zed about 'ees 'ooden leg. The sangfoy yent much of a crop thaough, the rain kumd a bit too late. I zes too late, but I dwunt knaw wot right I agot to zay so.'

'Sangfoy?' I queried, doubtful of Willum's meaning. Then I remembered that that was how they pronounced 'sanfoin' in Gloucestershire.

'I wonder if you know the story of the Sanfoin, Willum?' I asked.

'No; I dwunt.'

'Well the story goes that when Our Saviour was born at Bethlehem and Blessed Mary laid Him on the hay in the manger, that the hay was so proud and overjoyed at being chosen out of all the world's hay-crop to be that upon which God Incarnate should lie that it broke out into beautiful little flowers all around the baby form of Jesus. And ever after when men saw its pretty bloom they called it "Holy Hay". You see, Willum, "Sanfoin" is French, in English it would be "Holy Hay". And so the old name still clings to the pretty plant, but I expect there are not many who know why a field of "Sanfoin" is a field of "Holy Hay".'

'Well, well, to be zure,' came from the old man. He seemed quite taken with the little fable. 'Just to thenk as I atawked about sangfoy all these yurs and never knawed thuk purtty story. If thur's any kind o' tale as I do like mor'n anuther tis they about Nachur — birds, an' vlowers an' trees.'

We walked on our way for a little while silently. Presently my old friend said:

'I wuz athenking o' your story, and how nearly everytheng about us akot a maning if only we knawed whur to luk to vind it. Pason wuz azaying tuther Zundy zummit about thur being sarmons in stwuns, an' dash it all if he yent right. Now luk at them thur trees.'

I followed the old man's gaze and saw a row of willows by the side of a stream.

'They do zay as no willow tree ool live mor'n about thurty yur, acause twas on willow 'ood as Our Saviour hung, and zo the tree be zart o' cursed, and never grows beyond the age at which He died. Then agyen, acoorse you a' yeerd as on every donkey's back thur is a cross to remind we as twuz on a poor old Neddy as Our Saviour rode into Jerusalem. Thur's a lot o' donkeys on these yur hills and I offen wunders when I zees um being ill-treated and made to pull too heavy loads up steep places whur a hoss oodn't be trusted — I offen wunders, I zes, as that dark cross on thur poor rough backs don't rise up agyenst such treatment.'

'Tawking o' crosses,' went on Willum, after a pause, 'minds I of wot Billy Gardner tawld I yurs ago. Billy used to wurk down in the saw mill and thur wuz a smartish rough lot o' chaps wurking thur then. They used to lade Billy a vine old dance acause he went to Church and tried to zay ees prayers. Thur wuz Willum Hemming or "Cobbler Bill" as we did call'n on account o' ees doing a bit o' cobbling in ees spur time. Cobbler wuz a hawful karakter and like most cobblers as ever I kum across he wuz a atheist. One day Billy wuz being tackled by vawr or vive on um vur whissuling the old tune to "When I survey the wundrous Cross." You knaws the tune I myens?'

'Yes — Rockingham.'

'Well, Cobbler zed, "Tell th' wot tiz, Billy; the bist a darned old fool to believe all the pasons do tell th' about the Cross; I dwunt believe in no Cross; thur never wuz no such theng; I ood as soon believe in thuk thur Cross as thee doost zeng about as I ood believe as thur's a cross in this yur bit o' ood!" And he held up a chunk o' ood as he wuz just againg to put on the zaw. Billy didn't zay nutheng, and the zaw vlashed drew the 'ood like lightening and Cobbler picked up a piece and wuz gwoing to vleng it on the hip (heap). "Wos the matter, Cobbler?" shouts Billy sudden like — "wos the matter, mon?" — for Cobbler was astanding we' ees eyes sturring out o' ees yed luking at the chump o' ood in his hand. Billy went auver to'n and zo did the tuthers. And thur, just az zif 'tad bin drawed by a human hand wus a cross right in the middle o' the bit o' ood. Twuz zum minnits avoor work went on agyen in the shop, and Cobbler vrom thuk day wuz a diffrunt mon.'

We had reached the garden gate as Willum finished his story. I wished him 'Good night' and walked slowly through the gloaming[1] home.

CHAPTER 45

A HIDDEN FORTUNE

'Thurs zum voke as gets drew life wi'out doing much hard wurk,' remarked Willum sagely, 'and on tuther 'and thur's zum as do zeem as zif they wuz barn wurking, and they wurks all thur life and then struggles inta the grave at th' vinish.'

We had been discussing the death of Teddy Burton. I had said that whenever I saw him he was always hard at work.

'Yuss,' continued Willum, 'I dwunt spoze as Teddy cood a zet still doing nuthing if you had paid un vor't. I calls to mind the day as he wuz marrid. In the marnin' Teddy zowd zum eynon zid. Vunny I shud remember zuch a theng as thuk, yen it? But I do, acause I gid un a bit o' my eynon zid vur a bit o' ees parsnip zid an' we both on us got vust prize at the Vlower Show thuk yur. Well, Teddy's gurl kum in while Teddy wuz azowing the zid expecting to vind Teddy in all ees wedding get-up, but thur he wuz, ees shoes not laced up an ees smock as black as the back o' the chimbly. Didn't her let un have it. Teddy tawld I zumtime ater as vur two pins he'd a gone on wi' ees wurk and let the wedding go to Jericho. As twuz, Pason had to ax un twice if he 'ood 'ave thuk 'ooman to be ees wedded wife avoor Teddy 'ood say as he 'ood. But, Lar' bless ye, they wuz as happy as most when they had zettled down. And ees wife wuz just such anuther vur wurk as he wuz. My missis have tawld I as her have knawed Mrs Burton go upstairs and myek all the beds agyen ater her growed up daughters had made um when they wuz whum vur a bit of a holiday thenking to zave the old 'oomun a bit o' trubble.'

'Hullo! Caleb' — Willum nodded to a middle aged man who passed us — 'Doost thenk we be gwoing to 'ave a change?'

Caleb walked six yards without answering; then spat on the ground, stopped in the road, turned round towards us and said: 'We wants rain bad, dwun us. On these yur hills a day's wet every wik dwunt hurt. My garden zids be all burned up. But thur yent no zines o' rain it, as I can zee.'

'Ah! well! tool kum when tis aminded,' said Willum, and we continued our walk.

'Now thur wuz a mon hyur once' — Willum started again in reference to our previous conversation — 'as managed to get all ees hard wurk done var'n. D'you knaw the bit o' ground as they do call "Golden Oaks?"'

'You mean that little cottage with about half an acre of ground round it near the foot of the hill yonder?'

'Aye! thuks it. Well Napper Smith lived thur once. You wunt remember Napper, he abin dyead these ten yur or more. When he bought thuk little place twuz as rough as you cood well imagine an' ood a tuk a long time to abin dug auver and got straight. I spoze Napper made up ees mind as he ood get the wurk dun on the chep. Tennyrate, if you'll believe I, every bit o' thuk vield wuz dug auver wi'in a month ater Napper got thur. And Napper didn't pay a penny vor't neither.'

'However did he manage it?' I asked.

'Ah! tha's the story as I'll tcll ee. Napper wuz wun o' they as get tired quick doing a bit o' wurk, but can kip on a long time awatching other voke at it. When he had got ees bits o' sticks inta the house he goes down to the pub an' has a glass o' beer. Thur wuz Gassy Timbrell thur as uzhul. Acoorse Gassy zes to Napper, "Hast bawt the old house, then, you?" "Oh, ah!" zes Napper. "Wos thenk on't?" zes Gassy. Napper putts on a vurry wise look an' zes, "Ah! thur's no knawing wot's to be vound in them ald housen," and goes on drenking ees beer. Bimeby he turns to go out. Gassy joins un at the door and they walks tards Napper's bit o' ground. "Kum in an' 'ave a luk roun," zes Napper. That wuz just wot Gassy wanted. Zo in they goes. Napper tyeks un all auver the place and tells un a vine old yarn about how he had bawt the consarn acause ees grandveythur had told un as ees grandveythur knawed as ees grandvey-thur had lived in thuk house when twuz vust builded, an' the old man wuz a miser and hided ees money. "An" said Napper, "I ge agwoing to have a shot at vinding on't!" Gassy tuk it all in, and you med be sure he had a vine tale to tell down at the Twelve Bells later on.

'A day or two ater,' Willum continued, 'Gassy sees Napper wurking in the garden. "Hast vound anytheng it?" shouts Gassy. "Zhut thee mouth, you gurt zilly," zes Napper, "I do hope as thee disn't tell nobody wot I tawld thee tuther night." "Acoorse I ant," zes Gassy. "Well, then' atween you an' I an' the gyut-post," zes Napper in a zolum zart of a voice, "I thenks I avound a clue." "Wos that?" says Gassy. "Why a hidea as to whur thuk munny be," zes Napper, "I kum across a old letter as zes the old chap wuz vond o' hiding thengs in the gardon; zo I be just a looking round a bit." "Shall I kum in and help th'?" zes Gassy. "If's the's like – only kip thee mouth shut outside," zes Napper. They both on um wurks hard at degging vur zum time. Then Napper zes, "I ool be back in an hour or zo; I promised Varmer Tucker to go and zi'n at dinner time." When Napper had gone, Gassy stops degging vur a bit and begens thenking how many pints o' beer he could get if he could find the burrid treasure. Then he zets to wurk agyen. Bimeby "Pop" goes zummutt as ees tommy'awk hit the ground. "Wos that," zes Gassy. He carefully pulls away the mould and lo! an' behold! thur's a old ooden box. The lid wuz split and the dirt wuz all inzide. Gassy carefully picks un up and manages to get un upen. Thur wuzn't no munny inside, however, only a bit o' dirty stuff like parchment. Gassy luks at it and zees zum wurds as he coodn't rade acause the writing wuz old vashioned like. He putts down ees tools and walks off to the Twelve Bells. The landlord then wuz Butty Dean. Butty and Gassy putt thur yeds together but coodn't myek yed nor tail on't. So they calls in Richutt Sparra as wuz Clurk on Zunday at Church. He wuz sposed to be a bit of a skollard. Anyhow ater a bit he zes as the writing wuz DIG ME DEEP: SEARCH ME WELL: IN THIS GROUND: GOLD DOTH DWELL.

'Acoorse you must unnerstand I yeerd all this from Gassy aterwards. Nat'ral anuf they dree kep it to thurselves at the time. Next marnin' Gassy runs across Napper. "Hullo!" zes Napper. "Hullo!" zes Gassy, quiut like just to zee which woy the cat wuz gwoing to jump. "Dal it all," zes Napper, "yur 'ave I got a letter vrom me brother in Bristol axing I to go an' stay wi' un vur a wik." "Bist gwoing?" asks Gassy quik like. "No, I dwunt zee as I can," zes Napper, "I wants to get on wi' this yur bit o' ground." "Now luk hyur," zes Gassy, and putts on a hunselfish zart o' air, "tis a pity thee casn't have a bit of a ollyday. Now dwunt let the bit o' ground stop th' acause yur be I as ood only be too glad to do a bit o' degging in me spur time, an' I knaws one or two more as ave tawld I as they zeemed to want a bit o' exercise, if I only axes um I knaws they ood gie I a hand." "Tis vury kind on ee," zes Napper, "but I dwunt thenk I'll go." "I ood," zes Gassy. "Oost?" zed Napper, undecided like. "Aye! thee go an' ave a ollyday mon, th' doosn't knaw when th't get aunuther." "Well, I ool," zes Napper. The next day Napper went vur ees ollyday. He hadn't bin gone a hour avoor Gassy and Butty and Richutt Sparra kum down. An' if you'll believe I, they dug thuk bit o' ground all auver in less nor a wik.'

'Of course they didn't find any gold?' laughed I.

'You bet they didn't,' said Willum, 'the only gold as was vound wuz wot Napper got vur the vegetables as he growed on thuk land aterwards. But as I tawld ee thur's zum voke as knaws how to get hard wurk donc be zumbody else, and Napper wuz wun on um.'

'D'you zee now why they calls the place "Golden Oaks?"' asked Willum as we parted.

'I think I do,' said I.

CHAPTER 46

A TRAGEDY

I saw in a moment that something was the matter with the old man. Usually he carried himself straight and his step was light, notwithstanding his more than seventy years. But to-day there was an unusual pallor over his features, and the rugged lines of his face seemed deeper cut; and his head had that indescribable pose which at once tells of pain, mental or physical.

'You have had some trouble, Willum, since I saw you last week?' I said.

There was a distinct shake in his voice as he replied. 'Yuss, tha't true, and, agyen, in a sense 'tyent. Zo vur as I and mine be consarned we be all on us bout the zame as we wuz, but zence I zid you I abin drew a smartish axperiyunce, I can tell ee.'

The old fellow paused and I felt loth to force his confidence. In a minute, however, he resumed:

''Tool be a relafe to spake on't to zumbody, zo if you'll 'skuze I, I 'ool just tell ee all about it. 'Tis a longish story vur it begun nigh on zixty yur ago an' only vinished — I zes vinished, but I dwunnow as that's the right wurd to use about it — tennyrate the last chapter was only wrote last Tuesday. But thur I'll tell ee me tale straight drew.

'When I vust kum on these yur hills thus wuz a vamily living in thuk old cottage on the brow o' the hill named Martin. Thur wuz the old mon an' ees wife and two bwoys named Thomas and David. The old voke were got on in yurs and the bwoys were about twenty; I dwunt thenk as thur wuz more'n a twelve month atween um. Two well zet up youths they wuz too. But, as praps you have noticed, whur thur's only two in fam'ly they wuz as diffrunt vrom wun anuther as chalk from cheese. Thomas wuz a dark eyed lad and up to all zarts o' mischif. I can remember my sweetheart telling I to be awur o' Thomas Martin as her didn't like the looks on 'im. Thur wuz tales about as he did do a bit o' poaching, but whether 'twuz zo or not I can't zay. Enny'ow Thomas wuz a bit of a harum-scarum. David on tuther hand wuz a hard-wurking industrus lad. You cood zi'n most nights along wi' ees muther aveeding the pegs, and doing odd jobs at whum, vur ees old veythur wuz got beyond doing much. David was vurry fair to look at wi' curly hair and blue eyes, and wuz never happier than when he wuz attending to th' vlower beds or rading to ees muther out o' the Bible on a Zundy aternoon. We all on us wuz vurry fond o' David ——.'

The old man broke down for a moment or two. I could see that the trouble of last week concerned David, and patiently waited for my old friend to go on again.

'When I thenks o' they days,' he began presently, 'it makes I thenk o' me own yung days and how David an' I went acoorting together. Poor David!'

It was some minutes before Willum could calm himself sufficiently to continue his story.

'Bout this time' — and the old man's voice was firmer now — 'old Martin died, and the two bwoys had to kip the whum agwoing vur thur muther. Praps you'll remember as I told ee about me own bit o' sweethearting?' I nodded.

'Well, thur kumd inta the villige just about thuk time me sweet-heart's cousin, an' her name was Pamela Roberts. Wun day my little gurl zes to I, "I do believe as Thomas Martin be agettin' sweet on Pamela." I remember as I felt a bit zorry, vur I had 'oped as David ood ahung ees hat up thur; and Pamela was a nice anuf wench. However, nuthin' happened vur a month or zo, although aterwards I cood remember zeveral little thengs as might a showed I which woy the wind wuz blowing. Then thur kum Cha'vard Veast.[1] I shall never vurgit the night as vollowed as long as I do live. Twuz about midnight an' I wuz just upon gitting inta bed when thur comes a banging on the back door. I luks out o' th' winder an' zes "Who's thur?" 'Twas Mrs

Martin. "O! Willum," her zes, "Do ee come; do ee come," — and her voice wuz all of a shake like. I wuz vurry soon down and we went to her cottage together. The old oomun oodn't spake on the way, but when I gets indoors I zid a zite as I hopes these eyes o' mine ool never look on agyen. Thur wuz David lying on a sack bag wi' ees yed all covered wi' blood, an' thur wuz Thomas drunk in ees old veythur's arm chur. "Wos the matter?" I zes to David, but he coodn't spake. Bimeby we got un to bed and washed the blood off his face and yed. Then I helped Thomas to get between the sheets. Missis Martin and I then set down vur a bit and I yeerd wot had happened. It appears as Thomas had kum on David and Pamela together in Love Lane. He had waited till late at night, and then got vull up wi' beer and vollowed the yung kupple whum, and had zid um parting at Pamela's gyet (gate). I spoze, wot wi' ees disappointment, and the beer, an' ees violent nachur, he just coodn't contain hisself, an' zo he fought ees brother, and tis my belief as he ood abin a murderer if it hadn't bin vur ees old muther who kum in between um.'

'Nex' marnin' — Willum went on — 'we got the doctor to David. He zed at wunce as the zite o' wun eye wuz gone, and vur many a day evrybody thawt as David ood be blind altogether. But he did get as he cood zee a bit wi' wun eye. Thomas waited till the doctor wuz gone. Then he putt a vyow thengs together in a cullerd han'kicher and went off and nobody ever yeerd on im agyen — at least — but you'll zee——.'

'David soon got well agyen, except vur ees eyes. I remembers as zif twuz yesterday how he axed I wot he had better do about Pamela. "I dwunt knaw," zes I. But I axed me sweetheart, and her zed, "You tell David to let Pamela decide." Well, David told Pamela, and Pamela, like the good wench as I knawed her to be, zed as in a sense her wuz the cause o' wot had happened, an' if David ood have her, why thur wuz no rason why they shoodn't get marrid straight awoy. And they wuz marrid and lived wi' old Missis Martin till her died, and then David and Pamela kep' a vyow pegs and zum fowls and got a cow, and in wun woy an' anuther managed to rub along purty cumfurtbl' vur many a yur. They never had no childurn, and acoorse Pamela had to do the biggest part o' the wurk, vur David's eyezite at the best wuzn't much, and when he got about vifty he went blind altogether.'

'And now comes the saddest part of the story,' went on Willum. 'Pamela died ten yurs ago and that broke down poor David. The naburs wuz vurry good and ood a helped un, but ees mind went awandering at times and the doctor zed as in ees own intrest tood be best vor' to go to th' Infirmary. Zo David went to th' Infirmary as quiyut as a lamb. I shall never vurgit the day as he left the old cottage on the hill. Acoorse I went down to say "Good-bye." Thur wuz Prince the dog ajumping round David's legs, and David azaying, "No, Prince; down dog! the casn't kum whur I be gwoing." And the dog slunk awoy and died a wik ater in our wash-house of a broken heart, I virmly believes. David went round ees garden and I yeerd un amuttering to hisself, "Good-bye Pamela; Good-bye, me dear." I saw'n pick a han'full o' penks, and he turned to I and zed, "Twuz her as planted um, Willum." I used to go down an zi'n now and agyen at the Infirmary. He got quite happy thur in time, and the nusses did call'n "Daddy." He wuz a general favrit wi' evrybody.'

'But las' wik' — and Willum's voice became very broken again — 'they zent up to tell I as David wuz zenking. Acoorse I went down at wunce. The old man wuz wanderin' a bit, but he knawed I at times. I noticed as thur wuz a screen round ees bed and also round the next bed to his'n. The nuss whisper'd to I as thur wuz anuther poor old man adying and they didn't even knaw ees name, vur he had bin vound in a railwoy carrige at the station in a fit the day avore. I stayed wi' David all las' Tuesday, and the doctor zed as probably he 'ood die at zunset, zo I med up me mind to stop. Evrytheng wuz as quiyut as the grave as darkness come on. The tuther patients wuz mos'ly aslip. Presently David begins to spake. "I tell ye that Pamela be gwoing to marry I! . . . Don't ee, Tom, now don't ee . . . I wunt vight wi' me own bruther . . . wot ood muther zay? . . . tood brake her heart . . . No, I wun strike back I tell ee, I wunt' . . . and the old man had raised hisself in bed. "Oh! Tom, I didn't thenk it on ee, I didn't . . . My God, I can't see . . . You've blinded I," and he fell back agyen. An' then thur happened a most wundervull theng. I yeerd a voice as even I cood reckernize ater all these yurs zaying, "Is that you, David? Is that you? I be come home to ask ee to vurgive. I didn't know what I wuz doing, David — I didn't knaw. Ool ee vurgive me now?"

'David heard the voice. He opened his eyes and I saw he cood see wot I coodn't. "Is that you, Tom — me own bruther! — how cood ee doo't! But Pamela" — and he turned his eyes wi' a look o' love in um to tuther zide o' the bed — "vurgives ee . . . And zo do I . . . And hee's muther and I knaw as her ool . . . Zo let's shake hands." And David held out ees poor old hand. Then he fell back. And vrom behind the tuther screen thur come a sound as of a strong man in agony. Then all wuz quiet agyen.

'"He's gone," whispered the nurse. And as we went from the bed another nurse came from behind the tuther screen, "He has just died" she zed.'

CHAPTER 47

THE GOLDEN VALLEY

'Willum,' said I, as I met my old friend this week, 'I have come to the conclusion that you do not appreciate half enough the wonderful beauties of your district. Why, in some places I know of the inhabitants spend thousands in advertising the attractions of their neighbourhood, when such attractions cannot be compared with the natural beauties which are showered upon you in this part of Gloucestershire.'

The sun was shining in a cloudless sky; a keen invigorating wind was blowing across the valley, larks were carolling joyfully as they rose higher and higher towards the azure heavens. I had felt something like Shelley must have felt when he burst into that glorious hymn 'To the Skylark':

> 'Hail to thee, blythe spirit!
> Bird thou never art . . .'

It seemed to me that heaven and earth, things seen and unseen, birds and all cattle, mountains and all hills, all the green things upon the earth, were joining in one harmonious chorus and singing 'Bless ye the Lord, praise Him and magnify him for ever.'

'Yuss, tis burry bu'ful,' remarked Willum, 'but lar' bless 'ee voke about hyur dwunt thenk much o'thuk zart o'theng. Davy Buship f'rinstans ood zee more beauty astanding scratting the back o' one o' 'ees pegs an' sniffing on um than he ood if you wuz to putt un avoor

yander 'ood an' tell'n as he wuz to hadmire the beauties o' Nachur. You zee, these yur thengs as you do thenk zo much on we 'ave zid ever zence we wuz childurn; we knaws as the valley down below ool kum up smiling every spreng time, an' thur dwunt zeem anytheng to go into sturrix auver, acause tis bound to happen where or no. An' tis only them thengs as you byent used to zeeing as maakes you shout wi' raptyur. Not, mind you,' — the old fellow continued deprecatingly — 'as I meself dwunt like to zee the 'oods like they be now, acause I do.'

'But, Willum, just look at this beautiful landscape,' I cried, pausing in the road and looking across the valley where the Severn lay like a huge diamond sparkling in the sunlight.

'Oh! ah! tis bu'ful, thur's no zaying as tyent,' agreed Willum, 'maake I thenk o' that as we be tawld on in Revulations. I often thenks as Heaven wunt be Heaven unless thurs green trees and blues skies, an' zenging birds. I knaws tis auld-vashioned to talk o' Heaven as zif twuz a plaace whur the birds do zeng an' evrytheng is bu'ful. But our Saviour talked on't like that an' called it Paradise, an' thur wuz all them bu'ful thengs in Paradise, a clear vlowing river, an' vine green trees. An' He's the only one as rally knaws, zo I vur one blieves wot He do zay. Thurs a place up Zizziter woy in Lard Bathurst's 'oods as they do call Paradise, an' well they might, vur tis one o' the prettiest spots in all the park. 'Ave you ever been there?'

'No,' I said, 'but I hope to go.'

As we walked on Willum pointed out several things to me which had escaped my notice before.

'Doost zee thuk thur Church Spire?' said he, pointing right across the hills.

After some searching I discovered it.

'Well, thas Bizley Steeple; evur been to Bizley?'

'Yes, I drove through it once — a very old-world place.'

'You med well zay thuk,' replied Willum — 'why it do zumtimes go by the nyem of "Bizley-God-help-us". I can't azactly tell 'ee why, but I have yeerd it zed as twuz acause long ago they used to be cut off vrom everybody in the winter and thengs ood get pretty bad wi' um. But tis a nisish place nowadays. Thuk thur steeple you can zee vur miles an' miles round, an' they do tell I as vur dree marnins in the ur, that is the day avoor the zhartest day, the zhartest day, an' the day after, you can zee the shadow o' Bizley Steeple on Ham'ton Common if you do get up early enough.'

'But surely Minchinhampton Common is many miles away,' I said.

'Well, thas wot they do zay, I a'nt a gone up to zee vur meself, but praps, now, you cood just vind out vur yurself in the zummer.'

'Perhaps so,' I said. But I have my doubts, for I share with Dr Arnold and many lesser characters a reluctance to leave my bed in the morning.

'Now, doost zee that Valley?' continued the old man, as he pointed in another direction. 'Thas Cha'ford Valley, or as zum do call't the Golden Valley. I an't bin much o' a gadabout meself, but if thurs a prittyr place wi'in vifty mile I ant zid it nor yeerd ont. Jus' luk at them thur 'oods. Zee 'ow the beech trees be one shade o' green an' the larch trees another, an' the grass in the veelds another. I dwunt thenk as thur's any other colour as agot zo many shades as green, an' just now I should thenk as every shade can be vound on the slopes o' Cha'ford Valley. If you a' got any vrends akumming down you myek um spend a vyow coppers an' go be motor to Cha'ford. They cood get up thur and then along the top to Ham-ton Common bout 'leven in the marnin' and tyek a bit o' gub wi' um. Let um walk up Cowkum Hill whur they cood yet their bit o' tommy and then spend the aternoon on the Common, an' get down to Brimskum avoor dark.'

'I will certainly suggest it to any friends I see,' I remarked.

'Then another day,' Willum went on, 'they cood go to Cha'ford agyen, an' walk up tuther side o' the valley round by Cha'ford Church, up drew the Vrith 'Ood as is alukking vurry vine just now. Zum o' our young voke told I as they cood spend a whole day in thuk 'ood an' not get tired. Then you can walk auver to Bussige, an' although I zes it as shouldn't, if thus wun prittyur view nor another about here tis the one vrom Bussige Churchyard. Then you cood walk down the valley and back agyen to Brimskum.'

We had reached Willum's home. I bade him 'Good-night' and walked down the valley fully persuaded to try the walks the old fellow had suggested to me.

A Natral 'Istory Tale and Roger Plowman's Journey to London

CHAPTER 48

A NATRAL 'ISTORY TALE

Gloucester, March 22nd, 1851.

Mr ——

Knowing what a condesendin good sort o genelman you be un as wat tha calls fell natral istory is a gettin very poplar I tecks the liberty a sendin ya 2 or 3 little hannigotes a hannimals as I ha ad from time ta time in my passesshun un hopes thayl proove uz emusin uz instructiv, uz we sais in our nayberhood, to your club. I kips a public at Kingshome un as my customers princeply drops in ov a evnin bein a hous o call for jurnemen taylors un uther rispectuble treedsmen, in consekence my mornins beent verry much okkypied, un as I hallis ad a turn for observetion I a payd a good deal o tention ta what e calls dimestic hannymals un when you a yeerd my story I thinks youl say as how verry few peaple a livd on such hintimit terms we um, un consekently knauws morr about um, un so without furder preefece I shull enterr on my nurretion. About 12 mos ago I ad 2 pigs brothers un sisters thay was about 2 mos auwld when I had un fust un thay yused to run about o the kitchin un pic up tha crums or watever else tha cud find in tha sheep of grub tul tha got 2 sassy, for my missis got az fond on um az if tha wus er auwn blessed babbies un let um do jest as ad god a minded un atween um bwoth we as a verry nice time on it. If the missis wus a peelin tha teeters ur shellin a few peese tha rind un shells at last wuzent good enuf for um but thay must teek thair chaice afore we cud put by our whack out on um un thayd teek I anothers part so as we dussent saay as the ouse wus our auwn tul as I was obleeged ta shet 1 on um up in tha sty We called one on um Jo un tother Sally. I thinks as Jo wus tha sensyblest o tha 2 but Sally wus tha most mischieviousest un uz wee kep um seppereet why I shul giv you a count on um sepereetly Jo kep a good deal ta do about bein shet up ut fust un yewsted ta cry un whine for all tha wurld like a babby wenever a seed tha missis un I thawt as her ad a pretty ny broke er hart cos I oodn't let her go un let un out but at last a got a kyind a reconciled like un begun ta look out fur other emusement un what dy think a went un dun — why a begun bird ketchin. I ad a dyuse of a lot a robbins in tha garden un tha yusted ta cum un get at tha grains un uther hodments uz I yewsed ta put fur tha pig. I a sin 3 ur 4 ut a time a different parts a tha sty ut a time I a tha trauw, unother a top a tha raylins un tother a jiggin about a feared a tother 2, we a bit uf a fite atwizt um casionully. Wen Jo ad ad anuf ad yused ta lay down of is side jest uz eny uthur genelmen mit do with is cheek jest a restin a tha side a tha trauw fur a piller un watch tha robbins.

Wen thur wus a bit uv a skrimmage among um ud look uz pleezd you can't think un grunt un sort a laff ta isself like tul 1 de a took it inta is yud to ketch 1 on um uz cum reether 2 neer toon, un skrumped un up jest like a nut. Well ater that a wus allis a bird ketchin un was up to all sorts a mooves at that theer geem. Ater a'd cleered out tha trauw pertty well a'd jest skatter about a feeaw grayns athin reach uy is nose, un lay down un pertend ta go ta sleet, un then twaz warrhock ta any sparra or whitefinch or robbin ither uz cum athin is reech. But tha got up toot ut last, un specially tha sparras; un then wot dy think a dun — wy a turnd to upon the Rots.

We ad all at once tha dyuce un all a rots, un wher tha cum from why Ime shure I dwont knauw, but awever tha seemed ta use ta get ther prog princaply from tha pigs vittells.

Well, at fust, a seemed ta use ta like ther cumpney un wen tha did cum 1 or 2 at a time a'd look quite pleesed un stand un watch um un talk to um like jest as a used to do along a tha robbins but when tha birds got shire un tha rots moor numerouser un did cum – a duzn ur a duzn at a time, 1 de quite onexpectedly a piches into um un massy-creewsw 2 on um un ater that wenever a seed a likely chance heed fly at um jest like any uther reglar bred tarrier un a yused ta kip up them ther geems up ta tha de uv is deth wich took pleece soon ater a wus seesed for my rent wich somehow or nother unfortnutly got into rare.

Now as for Sally she wus allis of a weeklier constitution like as we ma say un dident thrive no neer sa well un so we yused for ta let her run in un out a tha taproom un bask afore tha fire along a tha ducks which I shal ave more ta say about them presenly but a got sassier nor ever new there wus 2 or 3 fellas a mendin tha rodes jest bi our ouse un 1 de tha cum in jest ta ave a pint a beer ath ther dinnder wich was bred un chees or summut a that deskrypshun rapped up in ther ankychers. 1 on um appened ta put down isn fur a minnit un I be hanged if Sally dident collar it un finished it (ankycher included) amost afore a cud say Jack Robison. Well ater that none onum cud leave a hankycher about or cum into tha

house ath 1 in his haud but her must knauw all about it un see what a'd got in it but blessy a'd yused ta sarve we wuss nor that. Sumtimes when weed got a bit a beecon un greens or anything a that sort the missis ud teek up the greens out a tha top a tha pot un put um upon the pleet upon the teeble fust (cos we allis likes um biled along a the beecon tha be so much richer) while her wus a getting out the beecon un I wusnt standin sentry like all the time Ime blessed if that ther pig woodnt either jump up on his ind legs on the teble or else upset un un cler tha dish a evry teter or green as wus in in afore a could well look round.

Now tha oversetion as I got to meek about that ther is as this here when a pet dog or amose any other sort a pet a dun anything a roguery he knows on it un'll cut away from e but a pig on't — he'll stand ungrunt un snort un squeak at e like a bear un bully e out on't.

But a got sa mischievious at last as I coodn't kip un no longer ad did offend so many a our customers un so I sowld un to a man at Santers[1] fur amost nothin at all jest ta get rid on in — but I had ard work ta get tha missis ta part with un thauw.

Pon me life tha partin atwixt thay 2 wus quite cuttin un a got out a is sty un cum un see us once or twice ater that. I dwont know what he fed un on ater a left we but a'd a got sa chaice then as a'd ardly yet anthing but bred un butter. The last I yeared the poor cretur wus as a'd died a very pertty pig a about a fourteen score.

Now thems what I considers very interesting hannygotes of a dimestic pig but them ther ducks wus 2 sech ducks as you don't see evry de barring as 1 on um wus a dreek.

Tha wus Mus-covys un wus give ta me by Dr Wells a Nordon[2] I never seed 2 kinder harted creeters in my life Tha meed themselves at home as soon as ever tha cum to us un ater a bit tha got sa fond on us as wenever me or my missis went to tha pump (not having no piece a water for um dy see) thay'd run jabberin up un woodn't let us go away or be at quiet tul weed pumped on um un geed um a good dousin un then thayd go in a dorrs un lay themselves down afore the fire to dry un if we offered for to go away from the pump without doing on it for um thayd run ater us un peck our legs un heels a good un. I a got one on um now — the dreek — but Ime sorry to say as I lost tother about 12 Mos ago un you never see nothin more affectin nor the last moments o that ther duck.

Some time afore — some wicked rascal of a dog — how I wish I'd a ketched him ony praps I shoold a sarved him amost too bad — geed er a tightish nip 1 de un thow with a good deal a nussin un coddlin my missis brought im round again un a was got quite cheerful like a allis walked leem un limped a good deal un didnt seem to injay hisself so well as formyly. Ater a bit a wuzn't so well agyan un seemed us if there was summut az wazn't quite right in her inside. Well now my wife ad bin verry queer fur a wick or 2 with a bad complaint in her chest un one de tha duck seemed wuss nor ushal if anything un my wife was a nussin on her in her lap afore that fire un a seemed very thoughtful un all at once her says say her 'I say Jem if I was to give the poor duck a dose a my medsan' says her 'I shoodn't wonder if it didn't do un good for it have certnly done me a good deal' says her. And so 'Well' says I 'praps 'tood. Ime agreeable' says I an so we geed un two teble spoonfuls a tha chest mixter. Well the poor creeter shook his hed un didn't seem to like it for a bit but at last a got quieter un seemed to beagwain off to sleep un all at once after a'd a layd quiet for about a ten minutes a tried to rouse isself up like un begun ta sheek is yed agean as if to say az twus no go — a give a fayntish queevering kind of a quack un the a looked up in my missises feece un died in a minnit. Now thats I considers a very interestin annygote of a Muscovy duck an its my firm belief as theres very few peeple as knows what affection dimestic animals may be brought to for um for want a treetin on um properly but all as Ive got to say about it is this here which is as if its of any use to you or the Cotsuld club[3] as its verry much at your service un I remain Sir

Your humble servant to command

JEEMS NICKS.

CHAPTER 49

ROGER
PLOWMAN'S
JOURNEY TO
LONDON

Monday marnin' I wur to start early. Aal the village know'd I wur a-gwain an' sum sed as how I shood be murther'd avoor I cum back. On Sunday I called at the manur 'ouse an' asked cook if she hed any message vor Sairy Jane. She sed:

'Tell Sairy Jane to look well arter 'e, Roger, vor you'll get lost, tuck in, an' done vor.'

'Rest easy in yer mind, cook,' I zed; 'Roger is toughish, an' he'll see thet the honour o' the old county is well show'd out and kep' up.'

Cook wished me a pleasant holiday.

I started early on Monday marnin', 'tarmined to see as much as possible. I wur to walk into Cizzeter, an' vram thur goo by train to Lunnon.

I wur delighted wi' Cizzeter. The shops an' buildins round the market-place wur vine; an' the church wur grand; didn't look as how he wur built by the same sort of peeple as put the shops up.

When the Roomans an 'anshunt Britons went to Church arm-in-arm it wur always Whitsuntide, an' arter church vetched their banners out wi' brass eagles on, an' hed a morris dance in the market-place. The anshunt Britons never hed any tailory done, but thay wur all artists wi' the paint pot. The Consarvatives painted thurselves bloo, an the Radicals yaller, an' thay as danced the longest, the Roomans sent to Parlyment to rool the roost.

I wur show'd the pleace wur the peeple started vor Lunnon. I walked in, an' thur wur a hold in the purtition, an' I seed the peeple a-payin' thur money vor bits o' pasteboard. I axed the mon if he could take I to Lunnon.

He sed, 'Fust, second, or thurd?'

I sed, 'Fust o' course, not arter; vor Sairy Jane ull be waitin'.'

He sed 'twer moor ner a pound to pay.

I sed the paason sed 'twer about eight shillin'.

'That's thurd class,' he sed; an' that thay ud aal be in Lunnon at the same time.

So I paid thurd class, an' he shuved out sum pasteboord, an' I put it in my pocket, an' walked out; an' thur wur a row o' carridges waitin' vor Lunnon; an' off we went as fast as a racehoss.

I heerd sum say thay wur off to Cheltenham, Gloucester, Tewkesbury, North Wales; an' I sed to meself, 'I be on the rong road. Dang the buttons o' that little pasteboord seller! he warn't a "safe mon" to hev to do wi'.'

I enquired if the peeple hed much washin' to do for the railway about here, an' thay wanted to know what I required to know vor.

I sed because thur wur such a long clothesline put up aal the way along. An' thay bust out a-larfin,' an' sed 'twur the tallergraph; an' one sed as how if the Girt Western thought as how 'twood pay better, thay ud soon shet up shop, an' take in washin'.

Never in aal me life did I go at such a rate under and awver bridges an droo holds in the 'ills. We wur soon at Swindon, wur a lot wur at work as black as tinkers. We aal hed to get out, an' a chap in green clothes sed we shood hev to wait ten minits.

Thur wur a lot gwain into a room, an' I seed they wur eatin' and drinkin'; so I ses to meself, 'I be rayther peckish, I'll go in an' see if I can get summat ' So in I goes; an' 'twer a vine pleace, wi' sum nation good-looking gurls a-waitin'.

'I'll hev a half-quartern loaf,' I sed.

'We doan't kip a baker's shop,' she sed. 'Thur's cakes, an' biskits, an' sponge cakes.'

'Hev 'e got sum good bacon, raythur vattish?' I sed.

'No, sur; but thur's sum good poork sausingers at sixpence.'

'Hand awver the pleat, young 'ooman,' I sed, 'an I'll trubble you vor the mustard, an' salt, an' that pleat o' bread an' butter, an' I'll set down an' hev a bit of a snack.'

The sausingers wur very good, an' teasted moorish all the time; but the bread an' butter wur so nation thin that I had to clap dree or vour pieces together to get a mouthful. I didn't seem to want a knife or vork, but the young 'ooman put a white-handled knife an' silver vork avoor me.

The pleat o' bread an' butter didn't hold out vor the sausingers, so I hed another pleat o' bread an' butter, an' wur getting on vine. I seem's to want summut to wet me whistle, an' wur gwain to order a quart o' ale, when I heers a whistle an' a grunt vram a steamer, an' out I goos; an', begum! he wur off.

I beckumed to the chap to stop the train, wi' me vork as I hed jest stuck into the last sausinger. I hed clapt a good mouthful in, or I could hev hollur'd loud enough vor him to heer. The train didn't stop, an' the vellers in green laughed to see I wur left in the lurch, as I tell'd them that Sairy Jane would be sure to meet the Lunnon train. Thay sed I could go in an' vinish the sausingers now, an' that wur what I intended to do.

I asked the young 'ooman for a bottle o' ale, when she put a tallish bottle down wi' a beg head; an' as I wur dry I knocked the neck off, an' the ale kum a-fizzing out like ginger pop, — an' 'twer no use to try to stop the fizzle. I had all I could get in a glass, an' it zeemed goodish. She soon run back wi' another bottle in her hand, an' I tell'd her 'twer pop she hed put down.

'What hev you bin an' dun, sur?' she sed; 'that wur a bottle o' Moses's shampane, at seven shillin's an' sixpence a bottle.'

I tell'd her I know'd 'twer nothin' but pop, as it fizzled so. Thur wur two or dree gentlemen in, an' thay larfed at the fizzle an' I. It seemed to meak me veel merryish, an; I zed, 'What's to pay, young 'ooman?'

She sed, 'Thirteen shillin's, sur.'

'Thirteen scaramouches!' I sed. 'What vor?'

'Seven sausingers, dree and sixpence; twenty-vour slices o' bread an' butter, two shillins; an' a bottle of shampane, seven and sixpence; — kums to thirteen shillins,' she sed.

'Yer tell'd me as how the sausingers wur sixpence,' I sed; 'an' the slices o' bread ud cut of a tuppency loaf.'

She sed the sausingers wur sixpence each, an' twenty-four slices o' bread an butter wur a penny each — two shillins.

I sed, 'Do 'e call that reysonable, young 'ooman? 'cause I bain't a-gwain to pay thirteen shillins vor't, an' lose me train, an' disappoint Sairy-Jane. Thirteen shillins vor two or dree sausingers, a few slices o' bread an' butter, an' a bottle o' pop — not vor Roger, if he know it.'

Up kums a chap an' ses, 'Be you gwain to pay vor wat you hev hed?'

'To be sure I be. Thur's sixpence vor the sausingers, tuppence vor bread an' butter, an' dreppence the pop, — that meaks 'levenpence'; an' I drows down a shillin', and ses, 'Thur's the odd penny vor the young 'ooman as waited upon me.'

'You hed thirteen shillins worth o' grub an' shampane, an' you'll hev to pay twelve shillins moor or I shall take 'e away an' lock 'e up vor the night.' he sed.

'Do 'e thenk as how you could do aal that, young man?' I sed. 'No disrespect to 'e though, vor that don't argify; but I could ketch hold on 'e by the scroff o' yer neck an' the seat o' yer breeches, an' pitch 'e slick into the roadway among the iron.'

'Look heer, Meyster Turmot, you'll hev to pay twelve shillin' moor avoor you gwoes out o' here, or Lunnon won't hold 'e to-night.'

I know'd Sairy Jane ud be a-waiting', an' as he sed the train were moast ready, I drows down a suverin', an' hed the change, an' as I wur a-gwain out I hollurs out as how I shood remember Swindleum stashun. I heer'd the lot a-larfin, an' hed moat a mind to go in an' twirl me ground ash among um vor thur edification.

I wur soon on the road agen, a-gwain like a house a-vire, an' thur wur more clotheslines aal the way along on pwosts.

W'en we got nearish to Lunnon I seed sum girt beg round barrels painted black. I axed a chap what thay wur, an' he sed that thay wur beg barrels o' stingo, an' thur wur pipes laid on the peeple's housen vor thay to draw vram.

I sed that wur very good accommodashun to hev XXX laid on vor use.

We soon druv into the beggest pleace I wur ever in since I wur born'd. They sed 'twer Paddington, an' that I wur to get out, vor they wurn't a-gwain to drive no furder. I hed paid to go to Lunnon, an' thay shood drive all the way when thay wur paid avoor and I wur tell'd Paddington wur the Lunnon stashun by a porter, an' I look'd round vor Sairy Jane, as she sed as how her ud be heer at one o'clock; and porter sed 'twer then dree o'clock, an' likely Sairy Jane had gone away. Drat thay sausingers as mead I too late vor the train!

I set down to wait for Sairy Jane, as I didn't know her directions, an' had left the letter she sent at whoam. Arter waitin' for a long while I started out, an' 'oped to see her in sum part o' Lunnon.

NOTES AND GLOSSARY

With notes it is difficult to know where to start and where to end. Most of the dialect is reasonably understandable, although it would have been more so to the readers of one hundred years ago than today. This is not just because of the language, but through the variety of the topical events referred to, which would have been known to the contemporary audience but are history to the modern reader. So much has changed this last century that if an editor became over-enthusiastic, this book could be turned into a social history instead of a pleasant read. Suffice it to say that it is not just coinage and weights and measures that have changed. In the 1890s public houses remained open all day serving beer and cider by the jug, compulsory education had only been in place for a score or more years and more than a quarter of all children born died before the age of one year!

The notes and glossary are intended to assist in the understanding of some of the more obscure dialect, and to identify events, but they are not intended to be anywhere near exhaustive. Most place-names in the text are reasonably obvious, but where the dialect spelling is vague they have been noted.

CHAPTER 2 THE FARMER
1. The expression ''er' or ''ers' does not necessarily have a gender connotation. On the Cotswolds this was used instead of 'he' or 'she'. The expression was very widely used, and appears throughout these tales. The *Oxford English*

Dictionary (*OED*) describes this form of usage as Welsh or Gaelic, highlighting the fact that the local language is not so purely derived from Saxon as might otherwise be assumed, although it is fair to say that the nineteenth-century Cotswolder did use archaic expressions which can be traced back to medieval and Anglo-Saxon times.

2. The expression ''nation' was also widely used locally, as an adverbial equivalent of 'very'. For instance, 'Peter, yer know, arter arl, is a 'nation sad feller for the drink. . . .' The *OED* says that the expression is a euphemistic abbreviation of 'damnation'.

CHAPTER 7 THE WOOD SALE

1. 'I'll teak my sollum Davy on't.' A corruption of affidavit.

CHAPTER 8 THE HARVEST HOME

1. Hayricks were commonly thatched for weatherproofing, although by this time it was becoming more common to use tarpaulins or other forms of sheeting for protection against rain.

2. A 'strapper' was a journeyman labourer hired just for harvest time, as against a labourer hired for the year.

3. 'Caving', or 'to cave', is a corruption or dialect version of 'chave', meaning to separate chaff from grain. The form that Buckman has here is unclear as he is using it in connection with mangolds. There has to be a suspicion that he heard the term used, but was unaware of its true meaning as even in his time it was an archaic expression.

4. 'Hot coppers' was the expression for having the mouth and throat parched through excessive drinking.

5. 'The biter bit' was a traditional expression. A 'biter' was a deceiver, one who amused himself at another's expense. 'The biter bit' was when the deceiver became unstuck.

CHAPTER 15 THE ELECTION

1. 'Brummagem Joe' was Joseph Chamberlain, a radical politician and a member of Gladstone's cabinet who did much to improve social and sanitary conditions in his native Birmingham.

2. Chamberlain fought energetically for the agricultural labourers and was one of the prime movers in gaining them the vote in 1884. In addition he was a champion of landowning reform and of Irish Home

Rule. His land reforms are alluded to, and it is not surprising that among illiterate and unworldly agricultural labourers his attempts and well-meaning electoral offers should have been misunderstood. The Irish question was extremely topical at the time that Buckman wrote, and the reference reflects this topicality among all classes.

3. 'Quine' – an obsolete term for coin, payment etc.

CHAPTER 17 IN A PUBLIC-HOUSE KITCHEN

1. Bank holidays were still a relatively new experience to the British public. They were introduced by Sir John Lubbock in his Bank Holiday Act, passed by parliament in 1871.

2. A 'varden' is a corruption of a farthing, a quarter of an old penny.

CHAPTER 18 A DEAD CHILD

1. A 'carboy' is a bottle, usually green and globular and partially surrounded by wickerwork for protection, used to store acids.

2. 'Quilt', or sometimes 'quilty', is an archaic local word for 'to swallow'.

CHAPTER 19 WHERE THE MISSUS IS MASTER

1. 'Drabbut' would seem to be a corruption of 'drub', or more likely a hybrid of 'drub' and 'beat'. The word 'drub', according to the *OED*, means to beat with a stick, and was first recorded after 1600, with probable origins in the Orient.

CHAPTER 22 AUTUMN

1. The use of 'stooks' and 'cocks' together is interesting. Both words were generally obsolete by 1890 and it seems that Buckman was not totally sure of the usage, although it does seem time and time again that he picked up labourers' jargon without understanding the historic meaning of the words. A 'stook' was a bundle of straw; a 'cock' was a measure of hay.

2. 'Schoppek-stael'. For this term, I had to admit defeat in the first edition of this book in 1991. However, thanks to Mr Richard Medley and Mr Peter Wright who kindly contacted me with information, I now know that this is, in fact, a pitchfork handle.

3. 'Whimbling' – miserable or insignificant, usually associated with people or creatures. An obsolete word before the nineteenth century, it was used by Ben Jonson in the play *Masques, Love Restored* in 1616.

4. 'Hoggerymaw' is presumably the words 'hoggery' and 'maul' linked for

emphasis. The *OED* gives 'hoggery' as a rare word for 'hoggishness', 'swinishness' or 'brutishness'. 'Maw' is another spelling of 'maul', a word of many meanings, including 'to damage seriously', 'to handle roughly', but also 'to toil', or 'to work hard'.

5. 'Z—' is undoubtedly Cirencester. The old local name was 'Ciceter', 'Cizzeter', 'Cisseter' or even 'Zisseter'. The evidence is given two paragraphs later when Bill mentions 'a young feller in them parts as had a-cum to larn the varming . . .'. This must refer to the Agricultural College, where Buckman's father was Professor of Geology.

CHAPTER 24 THESIGER CROWNE, THE MASON

1. 'Ciceter Mop' was Cirencester Mop Fair, held twice during October in the last century as a 'hiring' fair. It was the usual practice for servants and labourers to be hired for the year at the fair, with the changes taking place at Michaelmas. A maid-servant would carry a mop as a sign of her office; a carter would tie a piece of whipcord to his jacket; and a shepherd would adorn his hat with a piece of wool, or otherwise carry a crook.

2. This event occurred not 'forty years since' but about twenty-five years previously. The Pest House in Water Lane, Oakridge, was destroyed by fire in 1895.

CHAPTER 29 WILLUM INTRODUCES HIMSELF

1. The colour for political parties varied from region to region. With Willum taking his father too literally, he was doing exactly what his father did not want him to do.

CHAPTER 31 ELECTION STORIES

1. Superphosphate.

CHAPTER 34 THE CHRISTMAS GHOST

1. Old Age Pensions first came into being on 1 January 1909, following an Act of Parliament passed in 1908 under the Liberal government. This must date this particular story to 1908, and the old men must have been looking forward with some anticipation to the following week when they would receive their pensions for the first time.

CHAPTER 38 THE EARL O' SIPLAS

1. Erysipelas, an inflammation of the skin producing a deep red colour.

CHAPTER 44 BIBLICAL MATTERS
1. 'Gloaming' is an archaic term for 'twilight'.

CHAPTER 46 A TRAGEDY
1. Chalford Feast.

CHAPTER 48 A NATRAL 'ISTORY TALE
1. Sandhurst, near Gloucester.
2. Norton, between Gloucester and Tewkesbury.
3. The Cotteswold Naturalists Field Club.

A-GWINE A-going, going
ABIDE To endure
ADRY Thirsty
AFEARED Frightened
AFORE Before
AGEN Opposite to, against
AGWAIN A-going, going
ANNEAL To shape by softening
ANNEARST Near
ANUNST Over against
ATER After
ATHERT Across
ATTERMATH Grass after mowing
AYERD Heard
AWAY WITH To bear with
AX, AXE To ask
AXEN Ashes

BACK-SIDE The back of a house
BAD To beat husks
BAG The udder of a cow
BALD-RIB Spare-rib
BAN-NUT The walnut
BARKEN The homestead
BARM Yeast
BARROW-PIG A gelt pig

BASTE To beat
BAULK A bank or ridge
BEASTS Horned cattle
BEHOLDEN Indebted to
BELLY To swell out
BELLUCK Bellow
BENNET, BENT Dry standing grass
BESOM A word of reproach
BETEEM To indulge with
BIDE To stay, to dwell
BIN Because
BISN'T Be you not, are you not
BITTLE Beetle, a heavy mallet
BLATHER To talk indistinctly
BLOWTHE Blossom
BODY An individual
BOOT Help, defence
BOTTOM A valley
BRAKE A small coppice
BRASH Light stony soil
BRAVE Healthy
BRAY Hay, spread to dry
BRIT SHED Over-ripe corn
BRIZZ The gad-fly
BROOK To endure
BROW The abrupt ridge of a hill

BUDGE To move a short distance

BUFF To stammer

BURDEN As much hay or straw as a man can carry

BURR Calf sweetbread

BURROW Any shelter

BUTTY A comrade in labour

CADDLE To busy with trifles

CANDER Yonder

CANDER-LUCKS Look yonder

CANDLE-TINNING Candle-lighting

CANT To toss lightly

CARK Care

CASALTY, CASULTY Casualty, in context of 'failing to be right'

CASN'T, COUSSENT Can't, Can you not

CHAM To chew

CHAR A job (charwoman)

CHARM A noise, clamour

CHATS The chips of wood when a tree is felled

CHAUDRON Entrails of a calf

CHAW To chew

CHAWN To gape

CHILVER A ewe-lamb

CHISSOM To bud forth

CHITLINGS Chitterlings, pig's small intestine

CHOCK-FULL Full to choking

CLAMMY Sticky

CLAVEY Chimney-piece

CLEATS A small wedge

CLEAVE To burst hard bodies asunder

CLOUT A heavy blow

COLLY The blackbird

COLT A landslip

COMB A valley with only one inset

COMICAL Strange

COO-TER The wood pigeon's note

COUNT To consider, to suppose

CRAB A stick from a crab-apple tree

CRANK A dead branch of a tree

CRINCH A morsel

DAAK To dig up weeds

DAP To sink and rebound

DARZE Damn

DAY-WOMAN A Dairymaid

DEADLY A word meaning intenseness in a bad sense, as 'deadly stupid'

DESIGHT A blemish

DESPERD Beyond measure, extremely

DISANNUL To annul

DISMAL An evil in excess

DISSENT, DIS'NT Didn't you

DO'EE, DO YOU Will you, 'Do 'ee please come', 'will you please come'

DOFF To take off clothing

DOLLOP A lump, a mass of anything

DON To clothe, to put on

DOUT To extinguish a light

DRAT, DRATTED Expression of vexation

DRINK Used as a term for beer

DROXY Decayed wood

DRUNGE To embarrass

DUDDLE To stun with noise

DUDGEON Ill temper

DULKIN, DELKIN A small dell or dale

DUMMLE Dull, slow, stupid

DUNCH, DUNNY Deaf, an imperfection

DWUN Don't

ENTENNY The main doorway of a house

ER Her, but sometimes used also for he 'he did this', 'er did this'

ETTLES Nettles

EYAS A young hawk

EYE A brood of pheasants

FAGGOT Derogatory term for old woman

FAGGOT Cut wood

FALL Autumn, to grow yellow

FEND To forbid

FILLS Shaft of a cart

FILTHY, VILTRY Filth of any kind

FLAKES A wattled hurdle

FLICK The fat between the bowels of a slaughtered animal

FLOWSE Flowing, flaunting

FLUMP Applied to a heavy fall

FOGGER An agricultural labourer, involved in livestock feeding

FOR-WHY Because

FORE-RIGHT Opposite to

FRITH Young white thorn

FROM-WARD Opposite to 'toward'

FRORE Frozen

FRUM, FROOM, FREM, FRIM Full, abundant

GAITLE To wander idly

GAITLING An idler

GALLOW To alarm, frighten

GALORE An exclamation of abundance

GAMUT Sport

GEAR Harness, apparel

GIMMALS Hinges

GLOWR To stare moodily

GLOUT To look surly

GLUM, GLUMP Gloomy

GODE Past tense of 'to go'

GRIP A drain

GRIT Sandy, stony land

GROUNDS Fields, grass-lands

GROUTS, GRITS Oatmeal

GULCH A fat glutton

GULLY A deep ravine

GUMPTION Spirit, sense, quick observation

GURGINS The coarse meal of wheat

GURT Great

GYET Gate

HAINE To shut up a meadow for hay

HALE To draw with violence, or a team

HANDY Near, convenient

HANK A skein of any thread

HARBOUR To abide

HASSENT Hadn't

HATCH A door which only half fills the doorway

HAULM Dead stalks

HAUNCHED To be gored by cattle

HAY-SUCK Hedge-sparrow

HAYWARD An officer appointed at the court leet

HAZEN To chide

HEATHER The top-binding of a hedge

HEFT Weight, burden

HELE To cover

HELIAR A thatcher

HIGHST To uplift

HILLARD, HILLWARD Towards the hill

HILT *see* Yelt

HINGE The liver, lungs, and heart of a sheep

HISSEN His

HIVE To cherish

HOG A sheep of either sex, one year old

HOLT A high wood

HOOP The bulfinch

HOPE A hill

HOUSEN Plural of houses

HUT or HOT Past tense of 'to hit'

INGLE Fondling, favourite

ININ, INNION The onion

INNARDS The intestines

JARL The title 'Earl'

JETTY To thrust out

JIGGER To put out of joint

JOGGET A small load of hay

JOMETTRY Geometry, considered almost as magic

JOWL The jaw bone
JUNKETS Sweetmeats, dainties

KALLENGE Challenge, as pronounced
KECK To heave at the stomach
KEECH A lump of congealed fat
KEER LUCKS Look here
KERFE A cutting from a hayrick
KITTLE Anything requiring nice
management

LAGGER A long strip of land
LAIKING Idling, playing truant
LAMB To beat (lambast)
LANDAM To abuse with rancour
LARROP To beat, to flog
LATTERMATH Grass after mowing
LEE, LEW Shelter from wind or rain
LEECH A cow doctor
LEER Empty, hungry
LEESE To glean corn
LICKER Drink, alcoholic
LIFF, LIEVER Rather, more inclined to
LIKE A frequent pleonasm, as 'dead-like',
'pretty-like'
LIMBER Weak, pliant, flagging
LIMP Flabby, flexible
LINCH A small precipice, usually grass
covered
LISSOME Active, nimble
LITHER Light, active, sinewy
LOATH Unwilling
LOP To cut growing wood
LUG A measure of land, a perch
LUSH Abundant, flourishing
LUSTY Strong, in full health

MAIN Expression of emphasis, 'Main
dull', 'awfully dull'
MAKE Mate, companion, lover
MATE Meat
MAUNDER To ramble in mind

MERE A strip of grass as a boundary in
open fields
MICHE, MYCHE, MOOCHE To idle, play
truant
MIDDLIN, MIDDLING Of indeterminent or
poor health
MIND To remember
MINE Depending on context, husband or
wife
'MIRE To wonder, to admire
MIRKSHET Twilight
MOIL, MYLE To labour, to toil
MORT A vast quantity
MORTAL Excessively, extremely
MOSSEL Morsel
MOUND A fence, a boundary
MUN An affirmative interjection,
probably 'Man'
MUSSIFUL Merciful, mindful
MUST The crushed apples or pears
pressed for cider or perry
MYEN Mean, meaning of

NAGGLE, NIGGLE To tease, to fret
NALE An alehouse
NARON None, never, ne'er a one
NATION Very
NATRAL Naturally
NESH Weak, tender
NOT, NOTTED Applied to cattle without
horns
NUNCHEON Luncheon

ODDS A difference between two specimens
or statements
ON Of, 'One on 'em', 'One of them'
OODLE, HOODLE, WOOD-WAH The
nightingale
OONT or WOONT The mole
OR Before, 'ere
ORTS Chaff, any worthless matter

PACE To raise with a lever

PARGITER A plasterer

PEASEN Plural of peas

PELT To throw stones, etc.

PICK A hay fork

PIDDLE To trifle

PILL The pool caused at the junction of two streams

PIRGY Quarrelsome

PITCH To fall down heavily

PLASH A small pool

PLEACH To intertwine the branches of pollards for hedging

PLIM To swell with moisture

PLY To bend

PRIZE To weigh

PRONG A large hay-fork

PUCK A quantity of sheaves stacked together

PURE In good health

QUAR A stone quarry

QUICKSET Young whitethorn for hedges

QUIST A woodpigeon

QUITCH Couch-grass

QUOB, QUOP To tremble

QUOMP To subdue

RAG To chide, to abuse

RAMES Dead stalks

RAMSHACKLE To move noisily, in a loose, disjointed manner

RATH Early, quick, rash

RAUGHT The past tense of reach

RAVELMENT Entanglement

RAVES The rails which surround the bed of a wagon

REED Counsel

REEN A small stream

RETCH To strain before sickness

RIME Hoar-frost

RIVE To split asunder

RONGS Rungs of a ladder

ROVE The past tense of Rive

RUCK A crease in a garment

RUMPLE To discompose linen, bedding, wearing apparel

RUSTY Spoken of rancid bacon

SCORT The hoof-marks of horses, cattle, deer

SCREECH A bird, the swift

SCRUB Shrubs

SEG Stale human urine used in the manufacture of woollen cloth

SHARD A breach in a fence

SHATTERS Fragments of broken pottery, glass

SHOT OF Got rid of

SIGHT A vast number

SLAMMERKIN A slut

SLANS Sloes

SLICK Slippery

SLINGE Stolen wool from a clothier

SLIVER A slice

SNEAD The handle of a scythe

SNITE To blow the nose

SPIT A spade

SPRACK Lively, brisk, vigorous

SPREATHE To have the hands or face roughened by frost

SPURTLE To sprinkle with any fluid

STANK A pool caused by a dam on a stream

STRAIGHTWAYS Immediately

SWICH Such

TACK Drink, alcoholic

TALLUT The hayloft

TATERS Potatoes

TED To spread abroad new-mown grass for hay

TEEM To empty; spoken of a tub

TEG A lamb

TESTER Sixpence

THEAVE A ewe in the second year

THIC, THACH This, that

TICE To entice

TICKLE Uncertain in temper

TINE To kindle

TRIG Neat, quick, ready

TUD An apple dumpling

TUMP Earth thrown up

TUSSOCK A thick tuft of grass

TWINK The chaffinch

TWISSLE To turn about rapidly

TWITCH To touch

TYNING An enclosure from a common field

TYUK Take

UNKARD, UNKET Unknown, uncouth, lonely

UPSHOT The amount of reckoning, the outcome

VALUE, VALLY Used with much the same meaning as Upshot

VENTERSOME Heedless, daring

VINNEY Mildewed, mouldy

VITTALS Victuals, food

VOLK Folk, people

VORRUD Forward

VOSSLE, FOSSLE To entangle, to confuse business

WAIN-COCK A wagon-load of hay

WALLOP To beat

WAPPERED Fatigued; beaten

WARN, WARND To assure, to make certain, warrant

WEETHY Soft, pliant, flexible

WET Used as a substantive for rain, 'Come in, out of the wet'

WHEEDLE To coax, to deceive by flattery

WHELM To overthrow

WHOAM Home

WILL-GILL An effeminate person

WIMMIN Women

WINDER Window

WIT-WALL The large black and white woodpecker

WOMEN-VOLK Women

WONDERMENT, 'OONDERMENT Anything not understood

WORSEN To make worse

YAPPERN An apron

YARBS Herbs

YEAWS Ewes

YELT A young sow

YOPPING, YOPPETING Dogs barking

ZENNERS Sinews

ZOG To soak

ZUVRIN Sovereign, a gold £1 coin

ZWATHE (SWATHE) Grass when first mowed

ACKNOWLEDGEMENTS

I would like to thank Jill Voyce and Stanley Gardiner for the help and advice they have given in finding information on S.S. Buckman, G. Edmund Hall and John Drinkwater. The illustrations are mainly from the Cotswold Countryside. Collection in Northleach, supplemented from other collections. In the following list, illustrations are listed as *SG* for Stanley Gardiner, *AS* for author collection, *GRO* for Gloucestershire Records Office, *OCL* for Oxfordshire County Library, *OCM* for Oxfordshire County Museum Services and *MERL* for the Museum of English Rural Life in Reading. All other photographs are from the Cotswold Countryside Collection. The line illustrations are taken from the first edition of *John Darke*.

Dust jacket photograph Lower Guiting, *OCL*; page i posters at Hatherop, 1894; page ii haymaking in the Hatherop Estate, *c.* 1890; page iii ploughing near Snowshill; page 1 fair at Lechlade, 1921; page 2 Ebrington Club Day procession, *c.* 1900; page 4 work in progress restoring Old Farm Chedworth; page 10 wagons at Notgrove, 1910, *MERL*; page 15 outside the Puesdown Inn, Hampnett; page 21 station staff at Moreton-in-Marsh; page 38 villagers at Icomb, *OCM*; page 41 rick thatching, *MERL*; page 64 a wedding in Chedworth; page 68 railway workmen at Mickleton; page 77 cottages at Dean Row, Coln St Aldwyns; page 79 an ox-drawn cart at Fyfield, Eastleach, *OCM*; page 83 cottage garden and Barnsley church, 1914; page 86 Cotswold sheep on the Batsford Park Estate; page 89 farm buildings at Great Barrington, *c.* 1893, *OCL*; page 108 bacon curing in the farmhouse kitchen; page 117 High Street, Northleach; page 124 detail from dust jacket photograph,

Lower Guiting, *OCL*; page 125 Chedworth Football Club, 1908–9; page 126 the burnt pest house at Oakridge, *SG*; football supporters at the cup final at Upper Slaughter, 1921; page 133 the river Coln at Fairford, *OCL*; page 137 Upper Puck's Mill Lock on the Thames and Severn Canal near Sapperton, 1905, *SG*; page 145 Hawling Lodge, Guiting Power; page 147 elderly couple at Bourne's Green, near Stroud, *SG*; page 148 Shadrach Hayden at Bampton, Oxfordshire, *c.* 1909; page 158 Mr Perry at Chedworth, *c.* 1908 courtesy of Mr W. Harvey; page 177 horse and cart at Shortwood, Nailsworth; page 184 among the goats; page 186 a traditional Cotswold sheep with owner; page 191 Mr Charles Blackwell outside Church Farm, Northleach; page 197 Mrs Mary Hall, University Farm Cottage, Bledington; page 209 the Oak Inn near Chalford, *SG*; page 214 Bussage village, *SG*; page 218 misty view from Minchinhampton Common, *AS*; page 219 street scene at Chipping Campden, *GRO*; page 220 John Hall, Bledington; page 223 St Catherine Street, Gloucester, *AS*; page 230 a GWR express, *c.* 1880, *AS*.